The Fashioned Body

This book is dedicated to the memory of my
grandmother, Winnie Cowhig.

The Fashioned Body

Fashion, Dress and Modern Social Theory

Joanne Entwistle

polity

Copyright © Joanne Entwistle 2000

The right of Joanne Entwistle to be identified as author of this work has been
asserted in accordance with the Copyright, Designs and Patents Act 1988.

First published in 2000 by Polity Press in association with Blackwell Publishers Ltd.
Reprinted 2002, 2003, 2004

Editorial and production office:
Polity Press
65 Bridge Street
Cambridge CB2 1UR, UK

Published in the USA by
Blackwell Publishers Inc.
350 Main Street
Malden MA 02148, USA

Marketing:
Blackwell Publishers Ltd
108 Cowley Road
Oxford OX4 1JF, UK

ISBN 0–7456–2006–X
ISBN 0–7456–2007–8 (pbk)

A catalogue record for this book is available from the British Library.

Library of Congress Cataloguing-in–Publication Data
Entwistle, Joanne.
    The fashioned body : fashion, dress, and modern social theory / Joanne Entwistle.
        p. cm.
    Includes bibliographical references and index.
    ISBN 0–7456–2006–X – ISBN 0–7456–2007–8
    1. Fashion—Social aspects. 2. Costume—Social Aspects.
    3. Body, Human—Social aspects. I. Title.
    GT525 .E57 2000
    391--dc21   99-049559
Typeset in 10.5 on 12pt Plantin
by Kolam Information Services Pvt. Ltd, Pondicherry, India
Printed in Great Britain by T. J. International, Padstow, Cornwall

This book is printed on acid-free paper.

Contents

Acknowledgements

This book could not have been completed without the help and support of a number of people who played a significant part in my life during the time it took to write it. I am grateful to the University of North London for supporting the research from the beginning and for giving me study leave in spring/summer 1999 to complete the manuscript. I am grateful also to my colleagues at UNL for their support during this time: in particular, Elizabeth Wilson, who kindly read early versions of this book and supported the research throughout; and also Milly Williamson and Des Freedman for picking up the pieces I left behind. I would also like to thank the students at UNL for their lively engagement with the material in seminars. Further thanks must go to Reina Lewis and Sean Nixon for their support, advice and intellectual companionship, especially in the early days of research at the British Library. Since some of the ideas in this book stem from my Ph.D. thesis, I wish to thank the staff at Goldsmiths' College for their encouragement. I am especially grateful to Helen Thomas for supervising the research and for her intellectual guidance and constant support. I am also grateful to Paul Filmer, Ros Gill, Chris Jenks, Celia Lury, Angela McRobbie and Mica Nava for their helpful comments and to Ruth Thackeray for her careful editorial advice. The staff at the picture library at the Victoria and Albert Museum kindly helped me locate some of the illustrations. Finally, I am indebted to Don Slater for his guidance, intellectual companionship and editorial advice from beginning to end as well as for cooking so many excellent good dinners throughout. His support and encouragement can never be repaid but will never be forgotten.

Introduction

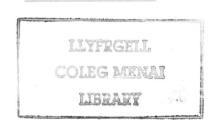

Fashion is about bodies: it is produced, promoted and worn by bodies. It is the body that fashion speaks to and it is the body that must be dressed in almost all social encounters. Within the west, and increasingly beyond as well, fashion structures much of our experience of dress, although, as I argue in this book, it is not the only factor influencing dress in everyday life since other factors, such as sex, class, income and tradition, play their part. Fashionable dress is dress that embodies the latest aesthetic; it is dress defined at a given moment as desirable, beautiful, popular. In articulating the latest aesthetic, and in making available certain kinds of clothes, fashion provides the 'raw material' of daily dress, produced by a multitude of bodies operating across a variety of sites. Understanding fashion requires understanding the relationship between these different bodies operating within the fashion system: fashion colleges and students, designers and design houses, tailors and seamstresses, models and photographers, as well as fashion editors, distributors, retailers, fashion buyers, shops and consumers. In other words, studying fashion involves moving from production to distribution and consumption: without the countless seamstresses and tailors there would be no clothes to consume; without the promotion of fashion by cultural intermediaries, such as fashion journalists, 'fashion' as the latest style would not be transmitted very far; and without the acceptance of consumers, fashionable dress would lie unworn in factories, shops, wardrobes. Thus, when we speak of fashion we speak simultaneously of a number of overlapping and interconnecting bodies involved in the production and promotion of dress as well as the actions of individuals acting on their bodies when 'getting dressed'.

In their account of fashion, Fine and Leopold (1993; also Leopold 1992) argue that fashion is a 'hybrid subject': the study of fashion requires understanding the 'interrelationship between highly fragmented forms of production and equally diverse and often volatile patterns of demand (Fine and Leopold 1993. 93). Thus, the study of fashion covers the 'dual concept' of fashion as a 'cultural phenomenon and as an aspect of manufacturing with the accent on production technology' (Leopold 1992: 101). However this hybridity is not generally acknowledged by the literature which tends towards one or other aspect of fashion without acknowledging the relationships between the different elements of production and consumption. According to Leopold (1992: 101), this duality has resulted in a separation 'in which the histories of consumption and production plough largely separate and parallel furrows'. The histories of consumption trace the rise and fall of demand of a product and link this to social developments. It tends to focus attention on individual psychology and/or the fashionable object itself, exploring it as 'the embodiment of cultural and social values prevailing at a specified time and place' (Fine and Leopold 1993: 93). Within this literature, production becomes passive, explained not only as a reflection of consumer or individual demands, but more often than not, as reflecting the fluctuating (and irrational) desires of women. The second study of fashion on the production side grapples with industrial history and deals also with the history of supply. This literature charts the innovations in technology, as well as the growth and organization of labour within the fashion industry. It makes general assumptions about the reasons for growth in demand but does not look at the specifics of it, nor the specific characteristics of demand in particular clothing markets. Thus, as Leopold argues (1992: 101), the history of clothing production has made little contribution to an understanding of the 'fashion system'. Moreover, these different bodies of literature do not connect with each other to provide an integrated approach.

Both Fine and Leopold put forward a case for a materialist analysis of fashion. They point to the need for historical specificity in the analysis of the fashion system, arguing that *within* the fashion system itself there are differences in the provision of clothes. There is no one 'fashion system' but a number of systems producing clothes for different markets. Alongside mass production, small systems of 'made to measure' clothing persist in *haute couture* and bespoke tailoring which operate with rather different modes of production, marketing, distribution and consumption than does factory production for the high street. A full account of fashion needs to acknowledge the different practices within the fashion industry and also bring together the crucially linked and overlapping practices of production and consumption. However, so far little attempt has been made by social theory to bridge the gulf between production and consumption. Sociology, cultural studies and psychology have tended to focus on the consumption side, while economic theory, marketing and industrial history have tended to examine the development of production. This book provides a summary of this literature and, in doing so, explores both the literature on consumption and production, although it considers the former in rather more detail. The reason for this lies in the contemporary significance of this work, which has grown exponentially since the 1980s in comparison to literature on production. This means that this book replicates to some extent the division between literature on consumption and production: only chapter 7 deals specifically with the literature on production, while the other chapters focus more on the consumption and meanings of fashion. However, I agree with Fine and Leopold that this division is an artificial one and that new studies on fashion and dress need to address the interconnections between production and consumption. I therefore argue in this book that a sociological account of fashion and dress must acknowledge the connections between production and consumption, considering the relationship between different agencies, institutions, individuals and practices.

I also argue that such a study needs to connect *fashion* to everyday *dress*, since the two are also crucially linked to one another. Fashion is an important determinant on everyday dress but fashion becomes widely recognized only when it is translated into dress on the part of individuals. However, here again, a division exists within the literature between studies of fashion (as a system, idea or aesthetic) and studies of dress (as in the meanings given to particular practices of clothing and adornment). The literature on fashion produced by sociology, cultural studies, costume history and psychology tends to be theoretical in scope and does not examine the mechanisms by which fashion translates into dress in everyday life. In much of this literature 'fashion' tends to be studied as an abstract system, and theoretical explanations are sought to explain its mysterious movements. Studies of dress, on the other hand, produced mainly by anthropologists, tend to be empirical in scope, examining dress in everyday life within particular communities and by particular individuals, and since they focus mainly on non-western and traditional communities have little to say about fashion as it exists in the west. Accounts of dress by psychologists are also limited as they tend to be individualistic rather than social in their analysis of dress practices. I argue in this book that this division between fashion and dress is as problematic as the division between production and consumption and suggest that a sociology of fashion/dress is needed which bridges the gap between these various bodies of literature and which looks at the way in which fashion determines dress and dress interprets fashion. Such an account would overcome the tendency to reify fashion and treat it as an abstract system which, as I argue in chapter 2, leads to over-generalization and simplification that ignores the complexity of fashion. This overly theoretical literature neglects to examine the way in which fashion is situated in culture and the way in which it is interpreted, accepted or rejected by people in their everyday experiences of dress. In other words, these explanations have little relevance to the experience of fashion in people's everyday lives.

Chapter 1 introduces and develops the concept of 'situated bodily practice' as a framework for bridging the gap between fashion and dress. This framework insists on understanding fashion as a structuring determinant on dress but examines the way in which fashion is translated into everyday dress. In doing so, it focuses attention on the body as the link between the two: fashion articulates the body, producing discourses on the body which are translated into dress through the bodily practices of dressing on the part of individuals. In other words, in everyday life, fashion becomes embodied. This positioning of the body at the centre of the analysis of fashion/dress allows us to examine practices and strategies from the micro-level of the individual experience of dress, through to the macro-level of the fashion industry, corporate strategies and marketing, which must keep the body in mind when designing, promoting and selling fashion.

This book is primarily concerned with detailing the way in which fashion has been thought of and written about. It therefore focuses on the attitude of intellectuals to fashion, examining how social theorists have tended to ignore the body (and by implication fashion); when they have looked at fashion/dress, they tend to disembody it. Intellectuals who have written about fashion have tended to leave the body out and to concentrate on other aspects such as fashion writing (Barthes 1985), fashion photographs (Ewen 1976, Evans and Thornton 1989, Lewis and Rolley 1997) or general theory, for instance, 'emulation' and status competition (Simmel 1971, Veblen 1953) or the 'shifting erogenous zone' (Laver 1950, 1995). There are some exceptions to this: Tseëlon (1997), Wilson (1985, 1992), and Wright (1992), for example, explore the way in which fashion operates on the body. But, on the whole, the specific ways in which fashion speaks of the body have been ignored. So, too, has the relationship between discourses on the body and embodiment. Even the literature which takes account of the body tends to focus on the textual or discursive body and not the lived, experiential body that is articulated through practices of dress. Dress in everyday life is about the experience of living in and acting on the body, but this embodied aspect of dress has been little discussed in the literature, as I argue in chapters 1 and 2.

This book offers a summary of the existing literature on fashion and dress, concerning itself with the (largely inadequate) ways in which they have been conceived. However, in proposing a study of fashion/dress as situated bodily practice, it also aims to set out a framework for future sociological analysis, as discussed in chapters 1 and 2. Chapter 1 also sets out the theoretical resources for such a study of fashion/dress from the point of view of the body and embodiment. The remaining chapters outline some of the major preoccupations and themes with which theorists working across a range of disciplines have been concerned. Most of the literature in these chapters, as noted above, focuses on consumption rather than production. In particular, it often seeks to explain fashion as a specific modern form of dress; the emergence of this tendency is detailed in chapter 3. Much of the literature draws attention to the way in which fashion articulates identity in modernity and postmodernity, and this theme is examined in chapter 4. Two related issues to do with identity – and, indeed, the body – namely gender and sexuality, are discussed in detail in chapters 5 and 6. In critiquing the literature from the perspective of situated bodily practice, the book aims not only to show some of the ways in which the body and the idea of situated practice can be brought into account in this literature, but to point the direction for a future sociology of fashion/dress.

1

Addressing the Body

Dress and the Body

'There is an obvious and prominent fact about human beings', notes
Turner (1985: 1) at the start of *The Body and Society*, 'they have
bodies and they are bodies'. In other words, the body constitutes the
environment of the self, to be inseparable from the self. However,
what Turner omits in his analysis is another obvious and prominent
fact: that human bodies are *dressed* bodies. The social world is a world
of dressed bodies. Nakedness is wholly inappropriate in almost all
social situations and, even in situations where much naked flesh is
exposed (on the beach, at the swimming-pool, even in the bedroom),
the bodies that meet there are likely to be adorned, if only by
jewellery, or indeed, even perfume: when asked what she wore to
bed, Marilyn Monroe claimed that she wore only Chanel No. 5,
illustrating how the body, even without garments, can still be
adorned or embellished in some way. Dress is a basic fact of social
life and this, according to anthropologists, is true of all known human
cultures: all people 'dress' the body in some way, be it through
clothing, tattooing, cosmetics or other forms of body painting. To
put it another way, no culture leaves the body unadorned but adds to,
embellishes, enhances or decorates the body. In almost all social
situations we are required to appear dressed, although what constitutes 'dress' varies from culture to culture and also within a culture,
since what is considered appropriate dress will depend on the
situation or occasion. A bathing-suit, for example, would be inappropriate and shocking if worn to do the shopping, while swimming

in one's coat and shoes would be absurd for the purpose of swimming, but perhaps apt as a fund-raising stunt. The cultural significance of dress extends to all situations, even those in which we can go naked: there are strict rules and codes governing when and with whom we can appear undressed. While bodies may go undressed in certain spaces, particularly in the private sphere of the home, the public arena almost always requires that a body be dressed appropriately, to the extent that the flaunting of flesh, or the inadvertent exposure of it in public, is disturbing, disruptive and potentially subversive. Bodies which do not conform, bodies which flout the conventions of their culture and go without the appropriate clothes are subversive of the most basic social codes and risk exclusion, scorn or ridicule. The 'streaker' who strips off and runs across a cricket pitch or soccer stadium draws attention to these conventions in the act of breaking them: indeed, female streaking is defined as a 'public order offence' while the 'flasher', by comparison, can be punished for 'indecent exposure' (Young, 1995: 7).

The ubiquitous nature of dress would seem to point to the fact that dress or adornment is one of the means by which bodies are made social and given meaning and identity. The individual and very personal act of getting dressed is an act of preparing the body for the social world, making it appropriate, acceptable, indeed respectable and possibly even desirable also. Getting dressed is an ongoing practice, requiring knowledge, techniques and skills, from learning how to tie our shoelaces and do up our buttons as children, to understanding about colours, textures and fabrics and how to weave them together to suit our bodies and our lives. Dress is the way in which individuals learn to live in their bodies and feel at home in them. Wearing the right clothes and looking our best, we feel at ease with our bodies, and the opposite is equally true: turning up for a situation inappropriately dressed, we feel awkward, out of place and vulnerable. In this respect, dress is both an intimate experience of the body and a public presentation of it. Operating on the boundary between self and other is the interface between the individual and the social world, the meeting place of the private and the public. This meeting between the intimate experience of the body and the public realm, through the experience of fashion and dress, is the subject of this chapter.

So potent is the naked body that when it is allowed to be seen, as in the case of art, it is governed by social conventions. Berger (1972) argues that within art and media representations there is a distinction between naked and nude, the latter referring to the way in which bodies, even without garments, are 'dressed' by social conventions

and systems of representation. Perniola (1990) has also considered
the way in which different cultures, in particular the classical Greek
and Judaic, articulate and represent nakedness. According to
Ann Hollander (1993) dress is crucial to our understanding of the
body to the extent that our ways of seeing and representing the naked
body are dominated by conventions of dress. As she argues, 'art
proves that nakedness is not universally experienced and perceived
any more than clothes are. At any time, the unadorned self has more
kinship with its own usual *dressed* aspect than it has with any
undressed human selves in other times and other places' (1993:
xiii). Hollander points to the ways in which depictions of the nude
in art and sculpture correspond to the dominant fashions of the day.
Thus the nude is never naked but 'clothed' by contemporary conventions of dress.

Naked or semi-naked bodies that break with cultural conventions,
especially conventions of gender, are potentially subversive and treated with horror or derision. Competitive female body builders, such as
those documented in the semi-documentary film *Pumping Iron II: The
Women* (1984), are frequently seen as 'monstrous', as their muscles
challenge deeply held cultural assumptions and beg the questions:
'What is a woman's body? Is there a point at which a woman's body
becomes something else? What is the relationship between a certain
type of body and "femininity"?' (Kuhn 1988: 16; see also Schulze
1990, St Martin and Gavey 1996). In body building, muscles are like
clothes, but unlike clothes they are supposedly 'natural'. However,
according to Annette Kuhn,

> 'muscles are rather like drag, for female body builders especially:
> while muscles can be assumed, like clothing, women's assumption of
> muscles implies a transgression of the proper boundaries of sexual
> difference'. (1988: 17)

It is apparent from these illustrations that bodies are potentially
disruptive. Conventions of dress attempt to transform flesh into
something recognizable and meaningful to a culture; a body that
does not conform, that transgresses such cultural codes, is likely to
cause offence and outrage and be met with scorn or incredulity. This
is one of the reasons why dress is a matter of morality: dressed
inappropriately we are uncomfortable; we feel ourselves open to
social condemnation. According to Bell (1976), wearing the right
clothes is so very important that even people not interested in their
appearance will dress well enough to avoid social censure. In this
sense, he argues, we enter into the realm of feelings 'prudential,

ethical and aesthetic, and the workings of what one might call sartorial conscience' (1976: 18–19). He gives the example of a five-day-old
beard which could not be worn to the theatre without censure and
disapproval 'exactly comparable to that occasioned by dishonourable
conduct'. Indeed, clothes are often spoken of in moral terms, using
words like 'faultless, 'good', 'correct' (1976: 19). Few are immune to
this social pressure and most people are embarrassed by certain
mistakes of dress, such as finding one's flies undone or discovering
a stain on a jacket. Thus, as Quentin Bell puts it, 'our clothes are too
much a part of us for most of us to be entirely indifferent to their
condition: it is as though the fabric were indeed a natural extension of
the body, or even of the soul' (1976: 19).

This basic fact of the body – that it must, in general, appear
appropriately dressed – points to an important aspect of dress,
namely its relation to social order, albeit micro-social order. This
centrality of dress to social order would seem to make it a prime
topic of sociological investigation. However, the classical tradition
within sociology failed to acknowledge the significance of dress,
largely because it neglected the body and the things that bodies do.
More recently, sociology has begun to acknowledge dress, but this
literature is still on the margins and is relatively small compared with
other sociological areas. A sociology of the body has now emerged
which would seem germane to a literature on dress and fashion.
However, this literature, as with mainstream sociology, has also
tended not to examine dress. While sociology has failed to acknowledge the significance of dress, the literature from history, cultural
studies, psychology and so on, where it is often examined, does so
almost entirely without acknowledging the significance of the body.
Studies of fashion and dress tend to separate dress from the body: art
history celebrates the garment as an object, analysing the development of clothing over history and considering the construction and
detail of dress (Gorsline 1991, Laver 1969); cultural studies tend to
understand dress semiotically, as a 'sign system' (Hebdige 1979
Wright 1992); or to analyse texts and not bodies (Barthes 1985
Brooks 1992 Nixon 1992 Triggs 1992); social psychology looks at
the meanings and intentions of dress in social interaction (Cash
1985, Ericksen and Joseph 1985, Tseëlon 1992a, 1992b, 1997). All
these studies tend to neglect the body and the meanings the body
brings to dress. And yet, dress in everyday life cannot be separated
from the living, breathing, moving body it adorns. The importance of
the body to dress is such that encounters with dress divorced from the
body are strangely alienating. Elizabeth Wilson (1985) grasps the
importance of the body in terms of understanding dress and describes

the unease one feels in the presence of mannequins in the costume museum. The eeriness of the encounter comes from the 'dusty silence' and stillness of the costumes and from a sense that the museum is 'haunted' by the spirits of the living, breathing humans whose bodies these gowns once adorned:

> The living observer moves with a sense of mounting panic, through a world of the dead...We experience a sense of the uncanny when we gaze at garments that had an intimate relationship with human beings long since gone to their graves. For clothes are so much part of our living, moving selves that, frozen on display in the mausoleums of culture, they hint at something only half understood, sinister, threat-ening, the atrophy of the body, and the evanescence of life. (Wilson 1985: 1)

Just as the discarded shell of any creature appears dead and empty, the gown or suit once cast off seems lifeless, inanimate and alienated from the wearer. The sense of alienation from the body is all the more profound when the garment or the shoes still bear the marks of the body, when the shape of the arms or the form of the feet are clearly visible. However, dress in everyday life is always more than a shell, it is an intimate aspect of the experience and presentation of the self and is so closely linked to the identity that these three – dress, the body and the self – are not perceived separately but simultaneously, as a totality. When dress is pulled apart from the body/self, as it is in the costume museum, we grasp only a fragment, a partial snapshot of dress, and our understanding of it is thus limited. The costume museum makes the garment into a fetish, it tells of how the garment was made, the techniques of stitching, embroidery and decoration used as well as the historical era in which it was once worn. What it cannot tell us is how the garment was worn, how the garment moved when on a body, what it sounded like when it moved and how it felt to the wearer. Without a body, dress lacks fullness and movement; it is incomplete (Entwistle and Wilson 1998).

A sociological perspective on dress requires moving away from the consideration of dress as object to looking instead at the way in which dress is an embodied activity and one that is embedded within social relations. Wright's analysis of clothing (1992) acknowledges the way in which dress operates on the body and how clothing worn deliber-ately small (such as leggings or trousers that do not meet the ankles) works to emphasize particular body parts. However, in general, stud-ies of dress neglect the way in which it operates on the body and there remains a need to consider dress in everyday life as embodied practice: how dress operates on a phenomenal, moving body and how it is a practice that involves individual actions of attending *to* the body *with* the body. This chapter considers the theoretical resources for a sociology of dress that acknowledges the significance of the body. I propose the idea of dress as situated bodily practice as a theoretical and methodological framework for understanding the complex dynamic relationship between the body, dress and culture. Such a framework recognizes that bodies are socially constituted, always situated in culture and the outcome of individual practices directed towards the body: in other words, 'dress' is the result of 'dressing' or 'getting dressed'. Examining the structuring influences on the dressed body requires taking account of the historical and social constraints on the body, constraints which impact upon the act of 'dressing' at a given time. In addition, it requires that the physical body is constrained by the social situation and is thus the product of the social context as Douglas (1973, 1984) has argued.

Becoming a competent member involves acquiring knowledge of the cultural norms and expectations demanded of the body, something Mauss (1973) has examined in terms of 'techniques of the body'. Goffman (1971) has described forcefully the ways in which cultural norms and expectations impose upon the 'presentation of self in everyday life' to the extent that individuals perform 'face work' and seek to be defined by others as 'normal'. Dressing requires one to attend unconsciously or consciously to these norms and expectations when preparing the body for presentation in any particular social setting. The phrase 'getting dressed' captures this idea of dress as an activity. Dress is therefore the outcome of *practices* which are socially constituted but put into effect by the individual: individuals must attend to their bodies when they 'get dressed' and it is an experience that is as intimate as it is social. When we get dressed, we do so within the bounds of a culture and its particular norms, expectations about the body and about what constitutes a 'dressed' body.

Most of the theorists I discuss do not specifically relate their account of the body to dress, but I have aimed to draw out the implications of each theoretical perspective for the study of the dressed body. The main discussion focuses on the uses and limitations both of structuralist and post-structuralist approaches, since these have been influential in the sociological study of the body: in particular, the work of Mauss (1973), Douglas (1973, 1984) and the post-structuralist approach of Foucault (1977, 1980) are pertinent to any discussion of the body in culture. However, another tradition, that of phenomenology, particularly that of Merleau-Ponty (1976, 1981) has also become increasingly influential in terms of producing an account of embodiment. These two theoretical traditions have, according to Crossley (1996), been considered by some to be incommensurable but, as he argues, they can offer different and complementary insights into the body in society. Following both Csordas (1993, 1996) and Crossley (1995a, 1995b, 1996), I argue that an account of dress as situated practice requires drawing on the insights of these two different traditions, structuralism and phenomenology. Structuralism offers the potential to understand the body as a *socially constituted and situated object*, while phenomenology offers the potential to understand dress as an *embodied experience*. In terms of providing an account of the dressed body as a practical accomplishment, two further theorists are of particular importance, Bourdieu (1984, 1994) and Goffman (1971, 1979). Their insights are discussed at the end of this chapter to illustrate the ways in which a sociology of the dressed body might bridge the gap between the traditions of structuralism, post-structuralism and phenomenology.

Theoretical Resources

The body as cultural object

All the theorists discussed in this chapter can broadly be described as 'social constructivists', in that they take the body to be a thing of culture and not merely a biological entity. This is in contrast to approaches that assume what Chris Shilling (1993) refers to as the 'naturalistic body'. These approaches, for example, sociobiology, consider the body 'as a pre-social, biological basis on which the superstructures of the self and society are founded' (1993: 41). Since the body has an 'obvious' presence as a 'natural' phenomenon, such a 'naturalistic' approach is appealing and indeed it may seem odd to suggest that the body is a 'socially constructed' object. However, while it is the case that the body has a material presence, it is also true that the material of the body is always and everywhere culturally interpreted: biology does not stand outside culture but is located within it. That said, the 'taken-for-granted' assumption that biology stands outside culture was, for a long time, one of the reasons why the body was neglected as an object of study by social theorists. While this is now an object of investigation within anthropology, cultural studies, literary studies, film theory and feminist theory, it is worthwhile pointing out the ways in which classical social theory previously ignored or repressed the body, since this may account, at least in part, for why it has largely neglected dress.

Turner (1985) gives two reasons for this academic neglect of the body. First, social theory, particularly sociology, inherited the Cartesian dualism which prioritized mind and its properties of consciousness and reason over the body and its properties of emotion and passion. Further, as part of its critiques of both behaviourism and essentialism, the classical sociological tradition tended to avoid explanations of the social world which took into account the human body, focusing instead on the human actor as a sign-maker and a maker of meaning. Similarly, sociology's concern with historicity and with social order in modern societies, as opposed to ontological questions, did not appear to involve the body. As Turner argues, instead of nature/culture, sociology has concerned itself with self/society or agency/structure. A further reason for the neglect of the body is that it treated the body as a natural and not a social phenomenon, and therefore not a legitimate object for sociological investigation.

However, there has been growing recognition that the body has a history and this has been influential in establishing the body as a prime object of social theory (Bakhtin 1984, Elias 1978, Feher et al. 1989, Laquer and Gallagher 1987, Laquer and Bourgois 1992, Sennett 1994). Norbert Elias (1978) points to the ways in which our modern understandings and experiences of the body are historically specific, arising out of processes, both social and psychological, which date back to the sixteenth century. He examines how historical developments such as the increasing centralization of power to fewer households with the emergence of aristocratic and royal courts served to reduce violence between individuals and groups and induce greater social control over the emotions. The medieval courts demanded increasingly elaborate codes of behaviour and instilled in individuals the need to monitor their bodies to produce themselves as 'well mannered' and 'civil'. As relatively social mobile arenas, the medieval courts promoted the idea that one's success or failure depended upon the demonstration of good manners, civility and wit and in this respect the body was the bearer of social status, a theme later explored in contemporary culture by Bourdieu (1984, 1994) in his account of 'cultural capital' and the 'habitus'. The impact of these developments was the promotion of new psychological structures which served to induce greater consciousness of oneself as an 'individual' in a self-contained body.

Along with histories of the body, anthropology has been particularly influential in terms of establishing the legitimacy of the body as an object of social study (Benthall 1976, Berthelot 1991, Featherstone 1991a, Featherstone and Turner 1995, Frank 1990, Polhemus 1988, Polhemus and Proctor 1978, Shilling 1993, Synnott 1993,

Turner 1985, 1991). Turner (1991) gives four reasons for this. First, anthropology was initially concerned with questions of ontology and the nature/culture dichotomy; this led it to consider how the body, as an object of nature, is mediated by culture. A second feature of anthropology was its preoccupation with needs and how needs are met by culture, an interest which focuses in part on the body. Two further sets of concerns focus on the body as a symbolic entity: for example, the body in the work of Mary Douglas (1973, 1979b, 1984) is considered as a primary classification system for cultures, the means by which notions of order and disorder are represented and managed; in the work of people like Blacking (1977) and Bourdieu (1984) the body is taken to be an important bearer of social status.

For the anthropologist Marcel Mauss the body is shaped by culture and he describes in detail what he calls the 'techniques of the body' which are 'the ways in which from society to society men [sic] know how to use their bodies' (1973: 70). These techniques of the body are an important means for the socialization of individuals into culture: indeed, the body is the means by which an individual comes to know and live in a culture. According to Mauss, the ways in which men and women come to use their bodies differ since techniques of the body are gendered. Men and women learn to walk, talk, run, fight differently. Furthermore, although he says little about dress, he does comment on the fact that women learn to walk in high heels, a feat which requires training to do successfully, and which, as a consequence of socialization, is not acquired by the majority of men.

Douglas (1973, 1979b, 1984) has also acknowledged the body as a natural object shaped by social forces. She therefore suggests that there are 'two bodies': the physical body and the social body. She summarizes the relationship between them in *Natural Symbols*:

> the social body constrains the way the physical body is perceived. The physical experience of the body, always modified by the social categories through which it is known, sustains a particular view of society. There is a continual exchange of meanings between the two kinds of bodily experience so that each reinforces the categories of the other. (1973: 93)

According to Douglas, the physiological properties of the body are thus the starting-point for culture, which mediates and translates them into meaningful symbols. Indeed, she argues that there is a natural tendency for all societies to symbolize the body, for the body and its physiological properties, such as its waste products, furnish culture with a rich resource for symbolic work: 'the body is capable of furnishing a natural system of symbols' (1973: 12). This means that the body is a highly restricted medium of expression since it is heavily mediated by culture and expresses the social pressure brought to bear on it. The social situation thus imposes itself upon the body and constrains it to act in particular ways. Indeed, the body becomes a symbol of the situation. Douglas (1979b) gives the example of laughing to illustrate this. Laughter is a physiological function: it starts in the face but can infuse the entire body. She asks, 'what is being communicated? The answer is: information from the social system' (1979b: 87). The social situation determines the degree to which the body can laugh: the looser the constraints, the more free the body is to laugh out loud. In this way, the body and its functions and boundaries symbolically articulate the concerns of the particular group in which it is found and, indeed, become a symbol of the situation. Groups that are worried about threats to their cultural or national boundaries might articulate this fear through rituals around the body, particularly pollution rituals and ideas about purity (1984). Douglas's analysis (1973) of shaggy and smooth hair also illustrates this relationship between the body and the situation. Shaggy hair, once a symbol of rebellion, can be found among those professionals who are in a position to critique society, in particular, academics and artists. Smooth hair, however, is likely to be found among those who conform, such as lawyers and bankers. This focus on the body as a symbol has led Turner (1985) and Shilling (1993) to agree that Douglas's work is less an anthropology of the body and more 'an anthropology of the symbolism of risk and, we might add, of social location and stratification' (Shilling 1993: 73).

This analysis can of course be extended to dress and adornment. Dress in everyday life is the outcome of social pressures and the image the dressed body makes can be symbolic of the situation in which it is found. Formal situations such as weddings and funerals have more elaborate rules of dress than informal situations and tend to involve more 'rules', such as the black tie and evening dress stipulation. This dress in turn conveys information about that situation. In such formal situations one also finds conventional codes of gender more rigidly enforced than in informal settings. Formal situations, such as job interviews, business meetings and formal evening events tend to demand clear gender boundaries in dress. A situation demanding 'evening dress' will not only tend to be formal but the interpretation of evening dress will be gendered: generally this will be read as a gown for a woman and black tie and dinner jacket for a man. Men and women choosing to reverse this code and cross-dress risk being excluded from the situation. Other specific situations which demand clear codes of dress for men and women can be found within the professions, particularly the older professions such as law, insurance and City finance. Here again, the gender boundary is normally clearly marked by the enforcement, sometimes explicit, sometimes implicit, of a skirt for women. Colour is also gendered more clearly at work: the suit worn by men in the City is still likely to be black, blue or grey but women in the traditional professions are allowed to wear bright reds, oranges, turquoises and so on. Men's ties add a decorative element to the suits and can be bright, even garish, but this is generally offset by a dark and formal backdrop. The professional workplace, with its norms and expectations, reproduces conventional ideas of 'feminine' and 'masculine' through the imposition of particular codes of dress. In this way, codes of dress form part of the management of bodies in space, operating to discipline bodies to perform in particular ways. To follow Douglas's idea of the body as a symbol of the situation, the image of the body conveys information about that situation. Even within the professions there is some degree of variation as to the formality of bodily presentation: the more traditional the workplace, the more formal it will be and the greater the pressures on the body to dress according to particular codes which are rigidly gendered. I return to this theme in more detail below, when I examine the applications of Foucault's work to the analysis of power-dressing, which is a gendered discourse on dress operating in the professional workplace.

While anthropology has been influential in suggesting how the body has been shaped by culture, Turner (1985) suggests that it is the work of the historian and philosopher Michel Foucault that has effectively demonstrated the importance of the body to social theory, helping to inaugurate a sociology of the body. In contrast to classic social theorists who ignore or repress the body, Foucault's history of modernity (1976, 1977, 1979, 1980) puts the human body centre stage, considering the way in which the emergent disciplines of modernity were centrally concerned with the management of individual bodies and populations of bodies. His account of the body as an object shaped by culture has never been applied specifically to dress but is of considerable relevance for understanding fashion and dress as important sites for discourses on the body.

The influence of Foucault

Foucault's account of modernity focuses on the way in which power/ knowledge are interdependent: there is no power without knowledge and no knowledge that is not implicated in the exercise of power.

According to Foucault, the body is the object that modern know-ledge/power seizes upon and invests with power since 'nothing is more material, physical, corporeal than the exercise of power' (1980: 57–8). Foucault's ideas about the relations between power/knowledge are embedded in his notion of a discourse. Discourses for Foucault are regimes of knowledge that lay down the conditions of possibility for thinking and speaking: at any particular time, only some statements come to be recognized as 'true'. These discourses have implications for the way in which people operate since dis-courses are not merely textual but put into practice at the micro-level of the body. Power invests in bodies, and in the eighteenth and nineteenth centuries this investment replaces rituals around the body of the monarch: 'in place of the rituals that served to restore the corporal integrity of the monarch, remedies and therapeutic devices are employed such as the segregation of the sick, the monitoring of contagions, the exclusion of delinquents' (Foucault, 1980: 55).

Turner (1985) suggests that Foucault's work enables us to see both how individual bodies are managed by the development of specific regimes, for example in diet and exercise, which call upon the indi-vidual to take responsibility for their own health and fitness (the discipline of the body), and how the bodies of populations are man-aged and co-ordinated (bio-politics). These two are intimately related, particularly with respect to the way in which control is achieved, namely through a system of surveillance or panopticism. This is forcefully illustrated in *Discipline and Punish*, in which Fou-cault describes how new discourses on criminality from the late eighteenth century onwards resulted in new ways of managing the 'criminal', namely the prison system. From the early nineteenth century new ways of thinking about criminality emerged: 'criminals' were said to be capable of 'reform' (rather than being inherently 'evil' or possessed by the devil) and new systems for stimulating this reform were imposed. In particular, the mechanism of surveillance encourages individual prisoners to relate to themselves and to their bodies and conduct in particular ways. This is reinforced by the organization of space in modern buildings around the principle of an 'all-seeing eye': an invisible but omnipresent observer such as that described in the 1780s by Jeremy Bentham (1843) in his design for the perfect prison, the 'Panopticon'. This structure allowed for max-imum observation: cells bathed in light are arranged around a central watch tower which always remains dark, making the prisoners un-aware of when they were watched and by whom. This structure is used by Foucault as a metaphor for modern society which he saw as 'carceral' since it was a society built upon institutional observation, in schools, hospitals, army barracks etc., with the ultimate aim to 'nor-malize' bodies and behaviour. Discipline, rather than being imposed on the 'fleshy' body through torture and physical punishment, oper-ates through the establishment of the 'mindful' body which calls upon individuals to monitor their own behaviour. However, while from the eighteenth to the early twentieth century 'it was believed that the investment in the body by power had to be heavy, ponderous, meticulous and constant', Foucault suggests that by the mid-twen-tieth century this had given way to a 'looser' form of power over the body and new investments in sexuality (1980: 58). Power for Fou-cault is 'force relations'; it is not the property of anyone or any group of individuals but is invested everywhere and in everyone. Those whose bodies are invested in by power can therefore subvert that same power by resisting or subverting it. He therefore argues that where there is power there is resistance to power. Once power has invested in bodies, there 'inevitably emerge the responding claims and affirmations, those of one's own body against power, of health against the economic system, of pleasure against the moral norms of sexuality, marriage, decency ... power, after investing itself in the body, finds itself exposed to a counter attack in the same' (1980: 56). This idea of 'reverse discourse' is a powerful one and can help to explain why discourses on sexuality from the nineteenth century onwards, used at first to label and pathologize bodies and desires, subsequently produced sexual types such as the 'homosexual'; such labels were adopted to name individual desires and produce an alternative identity.

Foucault's insights can be applied to contemporary society, which encourages individuals to take responsibility for themselves. As Shilling (1993) notes, potential dangers to health have reached global proportions, yet individuals in the west are told by govern-ments that as good citizens they have a responsibility to take care of their own bodies. Contemporary discourses on health, appearance and the like tie the body and identity together and serve to promote particular practices of body care that are peculiar to modern society. The body in contemporary western societies is subject to social forces of a rather different nature to the ways in which the body is experi-enced in more traditional communities. Unlike traditional commun-ities, the body is less bound up with inherited models of socially acceptable bodies which were central to the ritual life, the communal ceremonies of a traditional community, and tied more to modern notions of the 'individual' and personal identity. It has become, according to Shilling (1993) and others (Giddens 1991, Featherstone

1991b) 'a more reflexive process'. Our bodies are experienced as the 'envelope' of the self, conceived of as singular and unique.

Mike Featherstone (1991a) investigates the way in which the body is experienced in contemporary 'consumer culture'. He argues that since the early twentieth century there has been a dramatic increase in self-care regimes of the body. The body has become the focus for increasing 'work' (exercise, diet, make-up, cosmetic surgery etc.) and there is a general tendency to see the body as part of one's self that is open to revision, change, transformation. The growth of healthy lifestyle regimes is testament to this idea that our bodies are unfinished, open to change. Exercise manuals and videos promise transformation of our stomachs, our hips and thighs and so on. We are no longer content to see the body as finished, but actively intervene to change its shape, alter its weight and contours. The body has become part of a project to be worked at, a project increasingly linked to a person's identity of self. The care of the body is not simply about health, but about feeling good: increasingly, our happiness and personal fulfilment is pinned on the degree to which our bodies conform to contemporary standards of health and beauty. Health books and fitness videos compete with one another, offering a chance to feel better, happier as well as healthier. Giddens (1991) notes how self-help manuals have become something of a growth industry in late modernity, encouraging us to think about and act upon our selves and our bodies in particular ways. Dress fits into this overall 'reflexive project' as something we are increasingly called upon to think about: manuals on how to 'dress for success' (such as Molloy's classic *Women: Dress for Success, 1980*) image consultancy services (the US-based 'Color Me Beautiful' being the obvious example) and television programmes (such as the *Clothes Show* and *Style Challenge* in the UK) are increasingly popular, all encouraging the view that one can be 'transformed' through dress.

Featherstone (1991a) argues that the rise in products associated with dieting, health and fitness points not only to the increasing significance of our appearance but to the importance attached to bodily preservation within late capitalist society. Although dieting, exercising and other forms of body discipline are not entirely new to consumer culture, they operate to discipline the body in new ways. Throughout the centuries and in all traditions, different forms of bodily discipline have been recommended: Christianity, for example, has long advocated the disciplining of the body through diet, fasting, penance and so on. However, whereas discipline was employed to mortify the flesh, as a *defence* against pleasure which was considered sinful by Christianity, in contemporary culture such techniques as dieting are employed in order to *increase* pleasure. Asceticism has been replaced by hedonism, pleasure-seeking and gratification of the body's needs and desires. The discipline of the body and the pleasure of the flesh are no longer in opposition to one another: instead, discipline of the body through dieting and exercise has become one of the keys to *achieve* a sexy, desirable body which in turn will bring you pleasure.

Discourses of dress   Since Foucault said nothing about fashion or dress, his ideas about power/knowledge initially seem to have little application to the study of the dressed body. However, his approach to thinking about power and its grip on the body can be utilized to discuss the way in which discourses and practices of dress operate to discipline the body. As I argued at the beginning of this chapter, the dressed body is a product of culture, the outcome of social forces pressing upon the body. Foucault's account therefore offers one way of thinking about the structuring influence of social forces on the body as well as offering a way of questioning commonsense under-standings about modern dress. It is common to think about dress in the twentieth century as more 'liberated' than previous centuries, particularly the nineteenth. The style of clothes worn in the nine-teenth century now seem rigid and constraining of the body. The corset seems a perfect example of nineteenth-century discipline of the body: it was obligatory for women, and an uncorseted woman was considered to be morally deplorable (or 'loose' which metaphorically refers to lax stays). As such it can be seen as something more than a garment of clothing, something linked to morality and the social oppression of women. In contrast, styles of dress today are said to be more relaxed, less rigid and physically constraining: casual clothes are commonly worn and gender codes seem less rigidly imposed. However, this conventional story of increasing bodily 'liberation' can be told differently if we apply a Foucauldian approach to fashion history: such a simple contrast between nineteenth- and twentieth-century styles is shown to be problematic. As Wilson argues (1992), in place of the whalebone corset of the nineteenth century we have the modern corset of muscle required by contemporary standards of beauty. Beauty now requires a new form of discipline rather than no discipline at all: in order to achieve the firm tummy required today, one must exercise and watch what one eats. While the stomach of the nineteenth-century corseted woman was disciplined from the out-side, the twentieth-century exercising and dieting woman has a stomach disciplined by exercise and diet imposed by self-discipline (a transformation of discipline regimes something like Foucault's move from the 'fleshy' to the 'mindful' body). What has taken place has been a *qualitative* shift in the discipline rather than a quantitative one, although one could argue that the self-discipline required by the modern body is *more* powerful and more demanding than before, requiring great effort and commitment on the part of the individual which was not required by the corset wearer.

Foucault's notion of power can be applied to the study of dress in order to consider the ways in which the body acquires meaning and is acted upon by social and discursive forces and how these forces are implicated in the operation of power. Feminists such as McNay (1992) and Diamond and Quinby (1988) argue that Foucault ignores the issue of gender, a crucial feature of the social construction of the body. However, while he may have been 'gender blind', his theoretical concepts and his insights into the way the body is acted on by power can be applied to take account of gender. In this respect, one can use his ideas about power and discourse to examine how dress plays a crucial part in marking out the gender boundary which the fashion system constantly redefines each season. Gaines (1990: 1) argues that dress delivers 'gender as self-evident or natural' when in fact gender is a cultural construction that dress helps to reproduce. Dress codes reproduce gender: the association of women with long evening dresses or, in the case of the professional workplace, skirts, and men with dinner jackets and trousers is an arbitrary one but nonetheless comes to be regarded as 'natural' so that femininity is connoted in the gown, masculinity in the black tie and dinner jacket. Butler's work on performativity (1990, 1993), influenced by Foucault, looks at the way in which gender is the product of styles and techniques such as dress rather than any essential qualities of the body. She argues that the arbitrary nature of gender is most obviously revealed by drag when the techniques of one gender are exaggerated and made unnatural. Similarly Haug (1987), drawing heavily on Foucault, denaturalizes the common techniques and strategies employed to make oneself 'feminine': the 'feminine' body is an effect of styles of body posture, demeanour and dress. Despite the fact that Foucault ignores gender in his account of the body, his ideas about the way in which the body is constructed by discursive practices provides a theoretical framework within which to examine the reproduction of gender through particular technologies of the body.

A further illustration of how dress is closely linked to gender and indeed power is the way in which discourses on dress construct it as a 'feminine' thing. Tseëlon (1997) gives a number of examples of how women have historically been associated with the 'trivialities' of dress in contrast to men who have been seen to rise above such mundane concerns having renounced decorative dress (Flügel 1930). As Tseëlon (1997) suggests, women have historically been defined as trivial, superficial, vain, even evil because of their association with the vanities of dress by discourses ranging from theology to fashion. Furthermore, discourses on or about fashion have therefore constructed women as the object of fashion, even its victim (Veblen 1953, Roberts 1977). Dress was not considered a matter of equal male and female concern and, moreover, a woman's supposed 'natural' disposition to decorate and adorn herself served to construct her as 'weak' or 'silly' and open her to moral condemnation. A Foucauldian analysis could provide insight into the ways in which women are constructed as closer to fashion and 'vain', perhaps by examining, as Efrat Tseëlon (1997) does, particular treatises on women and dress such as those found in the Bible or the letters of St Paul.

These associations of women with dress and appearance continue even today and are demonstrated by the fact that what a woman wears is still a matter of greater moral concern than what a man wears. Evidence of this can be found in cases of sexual harassment at work as well as sexual assault and rape cases. Discourses on female sexuality and feminine appearance within institutions such as the law associate women more closely with the body and dress than men. Wolf (1991) notes that lawyers in rape cases in all American states except Florida can legally cite what a woman wore at the time of attack and whether or not the clothing was 'sexually provocative'. This is true in other countries as well. Lees (1999) demonstrates how judges in the UK often base their judgements in rape cases on what a woman was wearing at the time of her attack. A woman can be cross-examined and her dress shown in court as evidence of her culpability in the attack or as evidence of her consent to sex. In one case a woman's shoes (not leather but 'from the cheaper end of the market') were used to imply that she too was 'cheap' (1999: 6). In this way, dress is used discursively to construct the woman as 'asking for it'. Although neither Wolf nor Lees draws on Foucault, it is possible to imagine a discourse analysis of legal cases such as these which construct a notion of a culpable female 'victim' through a discourse on sexuality, morality and dress. In addition, greater demands are made upon a woman's appearance than a man's and the emphasis on women's appearance serves to add what Wolf (1991) calls a 'third shift' to the work and housework women do. Hence, the female body is a potential liability for women in the workplace. Women are more closely identified with the body, as Ortner (1974) and others have suggested; anthropological evidence would seem to confirm this (Moore 1994). Cultural association with the body results in women having to monitor their bodies and appearance more closely than men. Finally, codes of dress in particular situations impose more strenuous regimes upon the bodies of women than they do upon men. In these ways, discourses and regimes of dress are linked to power in various and complex ways and subject the bodies of the women to greater scrutiny than men.

Returning to the issue of dress at work, we can apply Foucault's insights to show how institutional and discursive practices of dress act upon the body and are employed in the workplace as part of institutional and corporate strategies of management. Carla Freeman (1993) draws on Foucault's notion of power, particularly his idea about the Panopticon, to consider how dress is used in one data-processing corporation, *Data Air*, as a strategy of corporate discipline and control over the female workforce. In this corporation a strict dress code insisted that the predominantly female workers dress 'smartly' in order to project a 'modern' and 'professional' image of the corporation. If their dress did not meet this standard they were subject to disciplinary techniques by their managers and could even be sent home to change their clothes. The enforcement of this dress code was facilitated by the open-plan office, which subjects the women to constant surveillance from the gaze of managers. Such practices are familiar to many offices, although the mechanisms for enforcing dress codes vary enormously. Particular discourses of dress, categorizing 'smart' or 'professional' dress, for example, and particular strategies of dress, such as the imposition of uniforms and dress codes at work, are utilized by corporations to exercise control over the bodies of the workers within.

As I have demonstrated, Foucault's framework is quite useful for analysing the situated practice of dress. In particular, his notion of discourse is a good starting-point for analysing the relations between ideas on dress and gender and forms of discipline of the body. However, there are problems with Foucault's notion of discourse as well as problems stemming from his conceptualization of the body and of power, in particular his failure to acknowledge embodiment and agency. These problems stem from Foucault's post-structuralist philosophy and these I now want to summarize in order to suggest how his theoretical perspective, while useful in many respects, is also problematic for a study of dress as situated practice.

Problems with Foucault's theory and method   As a post-structuralist, Foucault does not tell us very much about how discourses are adopted by individuals and how they are translated by them. In other words, his is an account of the socially processed body and tells us how the body is talked about and acted on but it does not provide an account of practice. In terms of understanding fashion/ dress, his framework cannot describe dress as it is lived and experienced by individuals. For example, the existence of the corset and its connection to moral discourses about female sexuality tell us little or nothing about how Victorian women experienced the corset, how they chose to lace it and how tightly, and what bodily sensations it produced. Ramazanoglu (1993) argues that the notion of reverse discourse is potentially very useful to feminists, but it is not developed fully in his analysis. It would seem that by investing importance in the body, dress opens up the potential for women to use it for their own purposes. So while the corset is seen by some feminists (Roberts 1977) as a garment setting out to discipline the female body and make her 'docile' and subservient, an 'exquisite slave', Kunzle (1982) has argued in relation to female tight-lacers that these women (and some men) were not passive or masochistic victims of patriarchy, but socially and sexually assertive. Kunzle's suggestion is that women more than men have used their sexuality to climb the social ladder and, if his analysis is accepted, could perhaps be seen as one example of the 'reverse discourse'. He illustrates (unwittingly since he does not discuss Foucault) that once power is invested in the female body as a sexual body, there is a potential for women to utilize this for their own advancement.

Foucault's particular form of post-structuralism is thus not sensitive to the issue of practice. Instead it *presumes* effects, at the level of individual practice, from the existence of discourse alone. He thus 'reads' texts *as if* they were practice rather than a possible structuring influence on practice that might or might not be implemented. In assuming that discourse automatically has social effects, Foucault's method 'reduce[s] the individual agent to a socialised parrot which must speak/perform in a determinate manner in accordance with the rules of language' (Turner 1985: 175). In failing to produce any account of how discourses get taken up in practices, Foucault also fails to give an adequate explanation of how resistance to discourse is possible. Rather, he produces an account of bodies as the surveilled objects of power/knowledge. This, as McNay (1992) argues, results in an account of 'passive bodies': bodies are assumed to be entirely without agency or power. This conception undermines Foucault's explicit contention that power, once invested in bodies, is enabling and productive of its own resistance.

Turner (1985) commends the work of Volosinov as an alternative to this version of structuralism. In Volosinov's work, language is a system of possibilities rather than invariant rules; it does not have uniform effects but is adapted and amended in the course of action by individuals. Bourdieu (1989) also provides a critique of structuralism that claims to know in advance, from the mere existence of rules, how human action will occur. He attempts a 'theory of practice' which considers how individuals orient themselves and their actions to structures but are not entirely pre-determined by them. His notion of practice is sensitive to the tempo of action; to how, in the course of action, individuals improvise rather than simply reproduce rules. (Bourdieu's critique of structuralism is examined in more detail at the end of this chapter.)

This focus on structures (as opposed to practices) in Foucault's work is closely related to the second major problem with structuralism and post-structuralism, namely the lack of any account of agency. For Foucault, the body replaces both the liberal-humanist conception of the individual and the Marxist notion of human agency in history. However, the focus on 'passive bodies' does not explain how individuals may act in an autonomous fashion. If bodies are produced and manipulated by power, then this would seem to contradict Foucault's concern to see power as force relations which are never simply oppressive. The extreme anti-humanism of Foucault's work, most notably in *Discipline and Punish*, is questioned by Lois McNay (1992) because it does not allow for notions of subjectivity and experience. With this problem in mind, McNay is critical of the attention feminists have paid to this aspect of his work and turns instead to Foucault's later work on the 'ethics of the self'. She argues that in his later work Foucault develops an approach to questions of the self and how selves act upon themselves, thus counteracting some of the problems of his earlier work. He acknowledged the problems with his earlier work and addressed some of these criticisms by arguing that

> if one wants to analyse the genealogy of the subject in Western civilisation, one has to take into account not only technologies of domination but also technologies of self... When I was studying asylums, prisons and so on, I perhaps insisted too much on the technologies of domination... it is only one aspect of the art of governing people in our societies. (Foucault in McNay 1992: 49)

Hence, Foucault's later work began to examine techniques of subjectification – how humans relate to and construct the self – and he considered how, for example, sexuality emerges in the modern period as an important arena for the constitution of the self. In the second volume of *The History of Sexuality* Foucault (1985; also 1986, 1988) goes on to consider how the self comes to act upon itself in a conscious desire for improvement. These 'technologies of the self' do go some way to counteract the problems of Foucault's earlier work and are potentially useful for understanding the way in which individuals 'fashion' themselves. For example, discourses on dress at work operate less by imposing dress on the bodies of workers, and more by stimulating ways of thinking and acting on the self. Power-dressing can be analysed as a 'technology' of the self: in dress manuals and magazine articles the 'rules' of power-dressing were laid out in terms of techniques and strategies for acting on the self in order to 'dress for success'. Thus the discourse on power-dressing, which emerged in the 1980s to address the issue of how professional women should present themselves at work, invoked notions of the self as 'enterprising'. As I have argued elsewhere (Entwistle 1997b, 2000) the woman who identified with power-dressing was someone who came to think of herself as an 'enterprising' subject, someone who was ambitious, self-managing, individualistic. The techniques for dressing laid out in these manuals implicated the self and stimulated one to act towards one's body in particular ways. However, the problem with Foucault's 'technologies of the self' is that they are peculiarly disembodied and this point highlights a problem endemic to Foucault's work, namely his account of the body.

The body versus embodiment

While Foucault's approach to the body is useful since it enables the analysis of the body without resorting to biological determinism, his body is peculiarly lacking in features which would seem crucial. As noted above, Foucault's account of the body and its relationship to power is problematic for feminists such as McNay (1992) and Ramazanoglu (1993) because it is not sensitive to the question of gender which, they insist, is crucial to any account of the body and how bodies are operated on by power. As McNay (1992) argues, not only is gender the most crucial division between bodies but power does not act on male and female bodies in the same way.

Furthermore, Foucault's analysis is internally inconsistent at times and his conception of the body confused. Turner notes that Foucault vacillates between some idea of a 'real' material body and a body constructed by discourse:

> at times he treats the body as a real entity – as, for example, in the effects of population growth on scientific thought or in his analysis of the effect of penology on the body. Foucault appears to treat the body as a unified, concrete aspect of human history which is continuous across epochs. Such a position is, however, clearly at odds with his

views on the discontinuities of history and with his argument that the
body is constructed by discourse. (1985: 48)

Thus, on the one hand, Foucault's bio-politics would appear to
construct the body as a concrete, material entity, manipulated by
institutions and practices; on the other, his focus on discourse
seems to produce a notion of the body which has no materiality
outside the representation. Such a vacillation is problematic since
the question of what constitutes a body is one that cannot be avoided
– does the body have a materiality outside language and representation? The body cannot be at one and the same time both a material
object outside language and a solely linguistic construction. Terrance
Turner suggests that Foucault's body is contradictory and problematic in terms of his own claim to critique essences: it is 'a featureless
tabula rasa awaiting the animating disciplines of discourse ... an a
priori individual unity disarmingly reminiscent of its arch-rival, the
transcendental subject' (1996: 37). Further, the dominance of the
discursive body in Foucault's work would seem to undermine his aim
to produce a 'history of bodies' and the investments and operations of
power on them. What is most material and most vital about a body if
not its flesh and bones? What is power doing if not operating on,
controlling or dominating the material body? Turner makes this point
emphatically, arguing that Foucault's notion of the body as the most
material thing is 'transparently spurious. Foucault's body has no
flesh; it is begotten out of discourse by power (itself an immaterial,
manna-like force)' (1996: 36).

Foucault's approach denies the fact that, however difficult it might
be to access the body as an independent realm, we are nonetheless
embodied and contained within the parameters of a biological entity
and that this experience, however culturally mediated, is fundamental to our very existence. Bodies are not simply representations; they
have a concrete, material reality, a biology that is in part determined
by nature. Bodies are the product of a dialectic between nature and
culture. Such an acknowledgement of the body as a natural object
does not automatically result in biologism and indeed, a number of
social constructivist accounts recognize the body as a biological entity
but consider how it is subject to social construction (Douglas 1973,
1979a, 1979b, 1984; Elias 1978, Mauss 1973). However, if the body
has its own physical reality outside or beyond discourse, how can we
theorize this experience?

With these issues in mind, Thomas Csordas (1993, 1996) details
the way forward for what he calls a 'paradigm of embodiment', posed
as an alternative to the 'paradigm of the body' that characterizes the

structuralist approach. His express aim is to counter-balance the 'strong representational bias' of the semiotic/textual paradigm found in works such as that of Douglas (1979a), Foucault (1977) and Derrida (1976). Csordas calls for a shift away from a semiotic/ textualist framework to a notion of embodiment and 'being in the world' drawn from phenomenology. A similar distinction is drawn by Nick Crossley, who argues that the 'sociology of the body' is concerned with 'what is done to the body', while 'carnal sociology' examines 'what the body does' (1995b: 43). The methodological shift for which both argue 'requires that the body be understood as the existential ground of culture – not an object that is "good to think with" but as a subject that is "necessary to be"' (Csordas 1993: 135). Csordas argues for a study of embodiment that draws on the phenomenology of Maurice Merleau-Ponty (1976, 1981) as well as Pierre Bourdieu's 'theory of practice' (1989). His paradigm of embodiment thus marks a shift away from a concern with texts to a concern with *bodily experience* and *social practice*. Crossley also identifies the concern with bodily experience with both Merleau-Ponty and Erving Goffman. I now go on to detail the theoretical and methodological assumptions underlying a 'paradigm of embodiment', looking first at phenomenology and focusing on the work of Merleau-Ponty (1976, 1981), then at Goffman (1971 1972, 1976) and finally at Bourdieu (1989), whose concepts are especially useful for developing a *sociological* account of embodiment.

Merleau-Ponty and embodiment

Merleau-Ponty (1976, 1981) places the body at the centre of his analysis of perception. He argues that the world comes to us via perceptive awareness, that is from the place of our body in the world. Merleau-Ponty stresses the simple fact that the mind is situated in the body and comes to know the world through what he calls 'corporeal or postural schema': in other words we grasp external space, relationships between objects and our relationship to them through our position in, and movement through, the world. Thus the aim of his work on perception, as he points out in *The Primacy of Perception*, is to 're-establish the roots of the mind in its body and in its world, going against doctrines which treat perception as a simple result of the action of external things on our body as well as against those which insist on the autonomy of consciousness' (1976: 3–4).

As a result of Merleau-Ponty's emphasis on perception and experience, subjects are reinstated as temporal and spatial beings. Rather than being 'an object in the world' the body forms our 'point of view on the world' (1976: 5). The tendency in Foucault to see the body as a passive object is thus counteracted. According to Merleau-Ponty, we come to understand our relation in the world via the positioning of our bodies physically and historically in space. 'Far from being merely an instrument or object in the world our bodies are what give us our expression in the world, the *visible form of our intentions*' (1976: 5, emphasis added). In other words, our bodies are not just the place from which we come to experience the world, but it is through our bodies that we come to be seen in the world. The body forms the envelope of our being in the world; selfhood comes from this location in the body. Therefore, for Merleau-Ponty, subjectivity is not essential and transcendental: the self is located in a body, which in turn is located in time and space.

The notion of space is for Merleau-Ponty crucial to lived experience, since the movement of bodies through space is an important feature of people's perception of the world and their relationship to others and objects in the world. This concern with space is also apparent in Foucault's work, as discussed above. Foucault brings to his account of space an acknowledgement of its social and political dimensions, the way in which space is infused with power relations, something Merleau-Ponty overlooks. However, Foucault's work lacks any sense of how people experience space, how they use it and move through it; this can be found in phenomenology. For Merleau-Ponty, we are always subjects in space but our experience of it comes from our movement around the world and our grasping of objects in that space through perceptual awareness.

It may seem difficult at first to apply these phenomenological concepts, as a philosophical method, to the analysis of the dressed body. However, in bringing embodiment to the fore and emphasizing that all human experience comes out of our bodily position, Merleau-Ponty offers some very useful insights for the analysis of dress as situated bodily practice. Dress in everyday life is always located spatially and temporally: when getting dressed one orientates oneself to the situation, acting in particular ways upon the body. However, one does not act upon the body as if it were an inert object but as the envelope of the self. Instead, our bodies are, in Merleau-Ponty's words quoted above, 'the visible form of our intentions', indivisible from a sense of self. What, therefore, could be more visible an aspect of the body/self than dress? In unifying body/self and in focusing on the experiential dimensions of being located in a body, Merleau-Ponty's analysis demonstrates how the body is not merely a textual entity produced by discursive practices but is the active and perceptive vehicle of being.

There are, however, a number of problems with Merleau-Ponty's phenomenology. First, he neglects gender. The body moves through time and space with a sense of itself as gendered and this is the reason why the spaces of the public realm of work are experienced differently by women and men and why the presentation of the body through dress is also experientially different. Furthermore, as argued earlier, women are more likely to be identified with the body than men and this may generate differential experiences of embodiment: it could be argued that women are more likely to develop greater body consciousness and greater awareness of themselves as embodied than men whose identity is less situated in the body. Second, Merleau-Ponty's approach remains philosophical: as a method, it cannot be easily applied to the analysis of the social world.

Despite these problems, however, both Crossley (1995a) and Csordas (1993) see much potential in Merleau-Ponty's approach and look to the works of Goffman and Bourdieu respectively; the latter two draw some inspiration from phenomenology but develop approaches to embodiment which are sociological rather than philosophical in that they are grounded in empirical evidence of practice. The following discussion applies phenomenological concepts to the study of dress and draws not only on Merleau-Ponty but the work of these two sociologists in order to suggest some of the ways in which the study of dress might approach it as an embodied practice.

Dress and embodiment   The phenomenology of Merleau-Ponty provides one way of understanding the operations of dress as it is constituted and practised in everyday life. The experience of dress is a subjective act of attending *to* one's body and making the body an object of consciousness and is also an act of attention *with* the body. Understanding dress then means understanding this constant dialectic between body and self: it requires, as Merleau-Ponty suggests, recognizing that 'The body is the vehicle of being in the world, and having a body is, for a living creature to be involved in a definite environment, to identify oneself with certain projects and to be continually committed to them' (1981: 82).

By adopting Merleau-Ponty's notion of the dialectical nature of body/self, it is possible to examine the *unity* of the body and the self and to explore how these constitute each other. Getting dressed involves different levels of consciousness in terms of how one thinks about the body and how to present it. We are sometimes aware of our bodies as objects to be looked at, if entering particular social spaces, while at other times and in other spaces, such as at home, we do not tune into our bodies as objects to be looked at. This tuning into the body and awareness of the body as an object when in public spaces is similar to Goffman's notion of 'front stage' (1971): in public spaces we may feel ourselves to be on view, while when alone at home we are 'back stage'. In certain circumstances one might also be made self-conscious of appearance and dress if, say, dressed inappropriately. If dress is varied and always 'situated' (i.e. directed towards very different situations), then it might be that there are some moments when the act of getting dressed constitutes an unreflective act – analogous with grocery shopping or picking up children from school – and others when the act of dressing is brought to consciousness and reflected upon – such as dressing for a job interview or important meeting. The different practices of dress therefore raise phenomenological questions about the nature of consciousness of self, for example about how one makes oneself an object of attention. Tseëlon's (1997) study seems to confirm that there are different states of attending to dress and appearance. Asked to describe their dress for different occasions, the women she interviewed identified a range of situations which varied according to the degree to which they attend to and are aware of their dress: the highest degree of self-consciousness of appearance was manifest in very formal occasions such as weddings or job interviews, while moving around the home, or doing the weekly shopping, had rather lower levels of attention. Although she does not draw on phenomenology to articulate an analysis of body consciousness, her findings can be used to demonstrate how appearance and thus dress are subject to varying degrees of consciousness according to the situation. Consciousness of bodily appearance is gendered: Berger (1972) has suggested that women more than men view their bodies as objects 'to be looked at' and this may indeed inform the choices women make when getting dressed for some situations. Tseëlon's (1997) analysis of women's relationships to their appearance would also seem to illustrate the different levels of body consciousness that inform women's dress choices. The women she interviewed indicate that they are conscious of self and appearance in complex ways: tuning in and out of consciousness, they are at times lost in the temporality of the action and at other times acutely aware of the action.

These patterns of body consciousness and dress practice are not individualistic, although they may be experienced acutely by individuals. However, as Tseëlon (1997) identifies, there are practices of dressing that operate above the level of the individual and must be seen as social and cultural. As I argued at the beginning of this chapter, dress is a technical and practical accomplishment which draws on accumulated social and cultural knowledge. In my analysis of power-dressing (Entwistle 1997b, 2000) I argue that it is a practice of dress that has to be learnt, sometimes from experiences of the workplace, sometimes explicitly through courses offered by image consultants. Many professions and careers are still male dominated and, for some women attempting to climb the ladder in particular institutions, it is important to attend to the body and dress very carefully so as to 'manage' or limit the potential sexuality of their bodies.

Understanding dress in everyday life requires a consideration of the socially constructed categories of experience, namely time and space. Both time and space order our sense of self in the world, our relationships and encounters with others, and indeed our mode of attending to our bodies and the bodies of others through dress. When getting dressed, whether unreflective or not, one constitutes self as a series of continuous 'nows'. The everyday practice of getting dressed involves conscious awareness of time because to engage with the experience of dress (in the west at least) one cannot usually avoid the temporal constraints of fashion. The experience of fashion imposes an external sense of time: fashion changes, indeed fashion is by definition temporal. Time is socially constructed by the fashion system through the circle of collections, shows and seasons which serve to halt the flow of 'now' by means of projections into the future. Fashion orders the experience of self and the body in time, and this ordering of time must be accounted for in the consideration of subjective modes of attending to one's body through clothing and style. The fashion system, particularly fashion journalism, constantly freezes the flow of everyday practices of dress and orders it into distinct entities of past, present and future ('this winter, brown is the new black', or 'forget last year's lime-green, cool beige is the colour to wear this summer'). The self, while experiencing an undifferentiated internal time, is also forever being 'caught', frozen, temporally fixed by fashion. One only has to think of the discomfort which is commonly felt when looking at old photographs of oneself in clothes which are no longer fashionable to see how fashion imposes a sense of time onto the experience of the adorned self. This moment of reflection on the presentation of self is a moment when the internal *durée*, the internal flow of time, is halted or disrupted and the self as experienced in the 'now' has to reflect upon the 'old' presented self. In this way, then, a sociology of dress and the practices of the fashion industry could use these phenomenological terms to look at how the experience of attending to and expressing the body is socially and temporally constituted.

Space is the other crucial dimension of our experience of our bodies and identity. While Foucault's analysis looks at space in relation to social order and, ultimately, power, a phenomenological analysis of space such as that offered by Merleau-Ponty considers how we grasp external space via our bodily situation or 'corporeal or postural schema'; thus, 'our body is not in space like things; it inhabits or haunts space' (1976: 5). The concern with space in the work of both Foucault and Merleau-Ponty, albeit different in methodological viewpoint, is one of the points of contact Crossley (1996) identifies between the two theorists. One could argue that in terms of dress both conceptions of space – how it is ordered and how it is experienced – need to be acknowledged and here Goffman's work is particularly useful. Space is both external to individuals, in that it imposes particular rules and norms upon them, and internal to individuals, in that it is experienced and indeed transformed by them. There is a moral order to the social world that imposes itself upon individuals who generally come to recognize that there are 'right' and 'wrong' ways of being in a space, 'correct' and 'incorrect' ways of appearing (and dressing). In this respect, Goffman's work owes much to the ideas of Emile Durkheim, who argued that social life is not only functionally ordered but morally regulated too. To be a 'good' person requires conformity to this moral order: when dressing, we have to orientate ourselves to different spaces which impose particular sorts of rules on how to present ourselves. When we fail to conform we risk censure or disapproval: the female guest at a wedding so daring as to wear white is often met with the disapproving eye of relatives who regard this as rude or blatantly disregarding to the bride. In his acknowledgement of the moral and experiential dimensions of space, Crossley (1995a) argues that Goffman takes the analysis of bodily demeanour in social situations further than either Mauss or Merleau-Ponty. He notes that Goffman develops Mauss's idea of techniques of the body, not only recognizing that such things as walking are socially structured, but considering the situation in which an activity such as walking takes place and how walking is not only a part of the interaction order, but serves also to reproduce it. Thus, for Goffman, the spaces of the street, the office, the shopping mall, operate with different rules and determine how we present ourselves and how we interact with others. Space is also experientially different according to the time of day: at night the street is threatening and our perceptual awareness is sharper than in the daytime and the zone around our bodies is widened and monitored more closely. Goffman reminds us of the territorial nature of space and describes how we have to negotiate crowds, dark quiet spaces and so on. Another important point to bear in mind is that action transforms space: encountering objects and others is about the negotiation of space. Because his sense of space is both social and perceptual, Goffman (1972) provides a link between the structuralist/post-structuralist analysis of space delineated by Douglas (1979a) and Foucault (1977) in terms of social order and regulation and the phenomenological analysis of space as experiential. Crossley (1995b) suggests that while Merleau-Ponty is good at articulating spatiality and the perception of it, Goffman provides concrete accounts of how this occurs in the social world.

This account of space as structuring movement and presentation of self and as something that individuals have to grasp and interpret is valuable to an account of dress as a situated bodily practice. Dress forms part of the micro-social order of most social spaces and when we dress we have to orientate ourselves to the implicit norms of these spaces: is there a code of dress we have to abide by? who are we likely to meet? what activities are we likely to perform? how visible do we want to be? (do we want to stand out in the crowd or blend in?) and so on. We may not always be aware of all these issues consciously; indeed only some circumstances, such as formal situations, demand a high degree of body/dress consciousness. However, even when not attending to these issues consciously, we internalize particular rules or norms of dress which we routinely employ unconsciously. Spaces are also gendered: women may have to think more carefully about how they appear in public than men, at least in some situations; and how women experience public spaces such as offices, boardrooms, quiet streets at night, is likely to be different to how men experience them. I have argued elsewhere (Entwistle 1997a) that the professional woman is more likely to be conscious of her body and dress in public spaces of work than at home or even in her private office. Space is experienced territorially by professional women who routinely talk of putting on their jacket to go to meetings and when walking around their workplace, but taking it off when in the privacy of their office (the reason being to cover the breasts so as to avoid sexual glances from men). As this example illustrates, spaces at work carry different meanings for women and they have developed particular strategies of dress for managing the gaze of others, especially men, in public spaces at work. In a similar way, women dressing up for a night out might wear a coat to cover up an outfit that might otherwise make them feel vulnerable on the street. In a night-club, short skirts and skimpy tops might be perfectly appropriate (depending on the wearer's confidence and/or intentions), but on a quiet street late at night, the same clothing might be experienced differently and make one feel vulnerable. The space imposes its own structures onto the individual who, in her turn, may come up with strategies of dress aimed at managing this space.

Crossley (1995a) suggests that there are many other fruitful connections to be made between Goffman and Merleau-Ponty. He suggests that both depart from the Cartesian dualism central to much classical sociological thought. Goffman's analysis (1971) examines the crucial role the body plays in social interaction. His work (1971, 1972, 1979) highlights how 'presentation of self in everyday life' is embodied. The body as the vehicle of the self has to be 'managed' in daily interaction and failure to manage one's body appropriately can result in embarrassment, ridicule and/or stigma. This performative aspect of self is particularly useful for understanding and interpreting dress practice. Davis argues that dress frames the embodied self, serving as 'a kind of visual metaphor for identity and, as pertains in particular to the open society of the west, for registering the culturally anchored ambivalence that resonates within and among identities' (1992: 25). In other words, not only is our dress the visible form of our intentions, but in everyday life dress is the insignia by which we are read and come to read others. Dress is part of the presentation of self; ideas of embarrassment and stigma play an important part in the experience of dress in everyday life and can be applied to discuss the ways in which dress has to 'manage' these as well as the way dress may sometimes be the source of our shame. However, the ridicule is not simply that of personal *faux pas*, but the shame of failing to meet the standards required of one by the moral order of the social space. A commonly cited dream for many people is the experience of suddenly finding oneself naked in a public place: dress, or the lack of it in this case, serves as a metaphor for feelings of shame, embarrassment and vulnerability in our culture as well as indicating the way in which the moral order demands that the body be covered in some way. Dressed inappropriately, we feel vulnerable and embarrassed, as is the case when our dress 'fails' us on finding that in a public place we've lost a button, stained our clothes or that our flies are undone. These examples illustrate the way in which dress is part of the micro-order of social interaction and intimately connected to a (rather fragile) sense of self. Dress is therefore a crucial dimension in the articulation of personal identity (a theme explored in more detail in chapter 4). Understanding dress in everyday life requires, therefore, looking not only at how individuals turn to their bodies but how dress operates between individuals as an inter-subjective experience as well as a subjective one. This returns me to the theme with which I opened this chapter, namely that dress is both a social and an intimate activity.

***Dress, embodiment and* habitus**   Bourdieu's work (1984, 1989, 1994) offers another potentially useful sociological analysis of embodiment, which not only builds a bridge between approaches that prioritize either objective structures or subjective meanings, but provides a way of thinking through dress as a situated practice. Bourdieu is critical of approaches that do not acknowledge the dialectic relationship between social structures on the one hand and agency on the other. Objectivists, he argues, impose upon the world reified structures and rules which are seen to be independent from agency and practice, but breaking from these structures should not result in subjectivism 'which is quite incapable of giving an account of the necessity of the social world' (1994: 96). His 'theory of practice' is an attempt to develop a dialectic between these two.

His notion of the *habitus* marks an attempt to overcome the either/ or of objectivism and subjectivism. The *habitus* is 'a system of durable, transposable dispositions' that are produced by the particular conditions of a class grouping (1994: 95). These dispositions are embodied: they relate to the way in which bodies operate in the social world. All class groupings have their own *habitus*, their own dispositions which are acquired through education, both formal and informal (through family, schooling and the like). The *habitus* is therefore a concept that links the individual to social structures: the way we come to live in our bodies is structured by our social position in the world, in particular for Bourdieu, our class position. Taste is one obvious manifestation of the *habitus* and, as the word taste itself would seem to indicate, it is a highly embodied experience. Taste forms part of the bodily dispositions of a class grouping: tastes for particular foods, for example caviar, are said to be 'acquired' (i.e. they are learnt, developed or nurtured) and are indicative of class position. In this way, the *habitus* is the objective outcome of particular social conditions, 'structured structures', but these structures cannot be known in advance of their lived practice. Thus, the notion of lived practice is not individualistic, it is more than 'simply the aggregate of individual behaviour' (Jenkins 1992). According to McNay (1999), in foregrounding embodiment in his notion of the *habitus* and in arguing that power is actively reproduced through it, Bourdieu provides for a more complex and nuanced analysis of the body than Foucault, whose 'passive body' is inscribed with power and an effect of it. The potential of the *habitus* as a concept for thinking through embodiment is that it provides a link between the individual and the social: the way we come to live in our bodies is structured by our social position in the world but these structures are reproduced only through the embodied actions of individuals. Once acquired, the *habitus* enables the generation of practices that are constantly adaptable to the conditions it meets.

Bourdieu's theoretical and methodological perspective is useful for overcoming the bias towards texts but not practices which, as I argue in chapter 2, runs through much of the literature on fashion. His work also sets out concepts useful for a study of dress as situated bodily practice: dress in everyday life cannot be known in advance of practice by examination of the fashion industry or fashion texts alone. Choices over dress are always defined within a particular context: the fashion system provides the 'raw material' of our choices but these are adapted within the context of the lived experience of the woman, her class, race, age, occupation and so on. Dress in everyday life is a practical negotiation between the fashion system as a structured system, the social conditions of everyday life such as class, gender and the like as well as the 'rules' or norms governing particular social situations. The outcome of this complex interaction cannot be known in advance precisely because the *habitus* will improvise and adapt to these conditions. The notion of the *habitus* as a durable and transposable set of dispositions allows some sense of agency: it enables us to talk about dress as a personal attempt to orientate ourselves to particular circumstances and thus recognizes the structuring influences of the social world on the one hand, and the agency of individuals who make choices as to what to wear on the other.

The *habitus* is useful for understanding how dress styles are gendered and how gender is actively reproduced through dress. However much gendered identity has been problematized and however much gender roles may have changed, gender remains entrenched within the body styles of men and women or, as McNay puts it, 'embedded in inculcated, bodily dispositions' which are 'relatively involuntary, pre-reflexive' (1999: 98). To return to the issue of dress at work, it is apparent that there are gendered styles of dress within the workplace, especially the white collar and professional workplace. Here we find that the suit is the standard 'masculine' dress and, while women have adopted suits in recent years, theirs differ in many respects from men's. Women have more choices of dress in that they can, in most workplaces, wear various skirts or trousers with their jackets; there is also a wider range of colour than the usual black, grey, navy of most male suits for the conventional office and a wider range still of jewellery and other decorative accessories (Molloy 1980; Entwistle 1997a, 1997b, 2000).

Significantly, women's adoption of tailored clothes has to do with the orientation of women's bodies to the context of the male workplace and its *habitus* which designates the suit as the standard 'uniform'. In this environment, the suit works to obscure the male body, hiding its sexed features, as Collier (1998) has argued. Women's movement into this sphere, as secretaries and later as professionals, required them to adopt a similar need for a uniform to designate them as workers and thus as public as opposed to private figures. However, as discussed in chapter 6, the feminine body is always, potentially at least, a sexual body and women have not been able to escape this association entirely, despite their challenge to tradition and the acquisition, in part, of sexual equality. In other words, women are still seen as located in the body, whereas men are seen as transcending it. Thus, while a woman can wear a tailored suit much the same as a man's, her identity will always be that of a 'female professional', her body, her gender being outside the norm 'masculine' (Sheppard 1989, 1993, Entwistle 2000). This is not to say that women are embodied and men are not, but that cultural associations do not see men embodied in the way that women are. Therefore, understanding women's dress for the professional workplace, how they come to wear the clothes they do, requires situating their bodies within a very particular social space and acknowledging the workings of a particular *habitus*.

As a theoretical and methodological perspective Bourdieu's *habitus* is useful for understanding the dressed body as the outcome of situated bodily practices. The strength of Bourdieu's account is that it does not see dress as the outcome of either oppressive social forces on the one hand, or agency on the other: instead it drives a steady course between determinism and voluntarism: as McNay argues, 'it yields a more dynamic theory of embodiment than Foucault's work which fails to think through the materiality of the body and thus vacillates between determinism and voluntarism' (1999: 95). Bourdieu provides an account of subjectivity which is both embodied, unlike Foucault's passive body and his 'technologies of the self', and which is active in its adaptation to the *habitus*. As such, it enables an account of dress which does not fall into voluntarism and assume that one is free to fashion oneself autonomously. Polhemus's analysis of 'streetstyle' (1994) is illustrative of such an approach to fashion and dress which has tended to define recent work in this area. In his idea of the 'supermarket of style', Polhemus argues that the mixing of youth culture 'tribes' in recent years has meant less clearly differentiated boundaries between groups, while his image of the supermarket suggests that young people are now free to choose from a range of styles as if they were displayed on supermarket shelves. However, such emphasis on free and creative expression glosses over the structural constraints of class, gender, location and income that set material boundaries around young people, as well as the constraints at work in a variety of situations that serve to set parameters around dress choice.

This chapter has set out the theoretical framework for a sociology of dress as situated bodily practice. Such an approach requires acknowledging the body as a social entity and dress as the outcome both of social factors and individual actions. Foucault's work may contribute to a sociology of the body but is limited by its inattention to the lived body and its practices, and to the body as the site of the 'self'. Understanding dress in everyday life requires understanding not just how the body is represented within the fashion system and its discourses on dress, but also how the body is experienced and lived and the role dress plays in the presentation of the body/self. Abandoning Foucault's discursive model of the body does not, however, mean abandoning his entire thesis. This framework, as shown above, is useful for understanding the structuring influences on the body and the way in which bodies acquire meaning in particular contexts.

Dress involves practical actions directed by the body upon the body, resulting in ways of being and ways of dressing, for example ways of walking to accommodate high heels, ways of breathing to accommodate a corset, ways of bending in a short skirt and so on. In this way, the analysis of dress as embodied and situated practice enables us to see the operations of power in social spaces (and in particular how this power is gendered) and how power impacts upon the lived body and results in particular strategies on the part of individuals. I have attempted to provide such an account in my own research (Entwistle 1997a, 1997b, 2000), which examines the way in which power-dressing operates as a discourse on how the career woman should dress for the professional workplace and how such a discourse, with its array of 'rules', becomes translated into actual dress practice in the everyday life of a number of career women. In sum, the study of dress as situated practice requires moving between, on the one hand, the discursive and representational aspects of dress and the way the body/dress is caught up in relations of power, and on the other, the embodied experience of dress and the use of dress as a means by which individuals orientate themselves to the social world.

2

Theorizing Fashion and Dress

The previous chapter argues for a study of fashion/dress that acknowledges the way in which it operates on the body, producing discourses about the body as well as practices of dress which work on the living, phenomenal body. While literature on the body has so far almost entirely ignored fashion, literature on fashion has generally ignored the body. What is needed is an account of fashion and dress which looks at the ways in which they are interrelated. The idea of fashion/dress as situated bodily practice acknowledges a very basic sociological tension between structure and agency: structures such as the fashion system impose parameters around dress; however, within these constraints, individuals can be creative in their interpretations of fashion and their practices of dress.

Various terms are employed in the literature: 'fashion' and 'dress', 'clothing', 'costume', 'adornment' and 'decoration', 'style' are among the most obvious; establishing the distinctions between them is an essential starting-point for this chapter. Different disciplines tend towards one or other term and therefore one way to make sense of the terminology is to locate these words within disciplinary traditions. For example, the terms 'dress' and 'adornment' are associated with anthropological literature, a major strand of which involves the search for universals and therefore an all-inclusive term that denotes all the things people do to their bodies in order to modify them. These words can be said to describe a more general kind of activity than either 'fashion' or 'costume'. The term 'fashion' carries with it the more specific meaning of a system of dress that is found in western modernity and as such is generally used within sociology or cultural studies as well as by social or cultural historians of fashion, while the term 'costume' tends to be found in historical texts. However, while it is possible to discern a body of anthropological literature on 'dress' distinct from a sociological, historical and cultural body of literature on 'fashion', in practice the picture is more complex than this. Far from clearly employing one or other term and defining it precisely, there is a considerable degree of confusion in the various bodies of literature with many authors employing a number of different terms, often using them interchangeably. A review of the literature illustrates the fact that there is no consensus on the definition and use of these words and no agreement on precisely what phenomena they describe.

The aims of this chapter are therefore two-fold: the first is to address the relative lack of sociological research on fashion and dress; the second is to summarize the literature that has emerged from anthropology, art history, cultural studies and social psychology in relation to fashion and dress. However, before embarking on such a discussion, the terms 'dress' and 'fashion' need defining and the way in which they are interrelated needs clarification. This involves considering their definitions within various bodies of literature and the debates that have emerged around them.

Defining the Terms

Sociology and anthropology: defining the difference

Anthropology and the disciplines of modernity (sociology, cultural studies, psychology) adopt different approaches to the body and matters of its adornment. Turner (1985) gives a clear summary of the important distinctions between anthropology and sociology and his book can be drawn on to explain the different approaches taken by both disciplines to bodily adornment as well as account for the differences in terminology. He notes that, at its inception in the nineteenth century, anthropology focused attention on ontological questions about the nature of humanity, in particlar through the distinction between nature and culture. The result of this interest was the emergence of a major strand concerned with the search for universals, the things that pertain to all peoples and cultures. He goes on to note that classical sociology, on the other hand, is not concerned with ontological distinctions and universals but with historicity and the forms of social life that emerge with modernity.

This distinction between anthropology and sociology is a historical one which has changed in recent years: anthropology now studies modern western societies and not just traditional communities, while, as argued in chapter 1, since the 1970s or so a sociology of the body has emerged to address questions of the body. The historical difference between the two disciplines, however, has made for discernibly different traditions of writing: an anthropological body of literature concerned with accounts of 'dress' or 'adornment', evident in the work of Barnes and Eicher (1992), Cordwell and Schwarz (1979) and Polhemus and Proctor (1978); and another body of literature on 'fashion' in modern societies, produced by theorists from sociology, cultural studies and psychology (Ash and Wilson 1992, Bell 1976, Flügel 1930, Lurie 1981, Simmel 1971, Veblen 1953, Wilson 1985). This distinction still holds, although there is also considerable cross-fertilization between the various disciplines. Contemporary anthropological literature tends to focus on the meanings and practices of adornment or dress in non-western cultures, or, in the case of some anthropological collections such as Barnes and Eicher (1992), Cordwell and Schwarz (1979) and Polhemus and Proctor (1978), there is an interest in cross-cultural variations which might involve considering dress in the western fashion system as well. Another feature of this anthropology is an ethnographic concern with practices surrounding dress, clothing and fabric. The authors of the fashion literature, however, unlike anthropologists, are less interested in ethnographic accounts of the practices surrounding dress than in the fashion system, which they treat in a historical or theoretical rather than ethnographic or empirical way.

Defining dress

The early anthropological concern with universals led anthropologists such as Benthall (1976) and Polhemus and Proctor (1978) to argue that there was a universal human propensity to adorn. This argument is now widely accepted by writers on dress and fashion, and anthropological evidence that all cultures 'dress' the body and that no culture leaves the body 'unadorned' is cited by most of the key texts in the area. Indeed, it is taken for granted in contemporary anthropological texts on dress. The nineteenth-century concern to demonstrate the universality of adornment has therefore been displaced by concern with the actual practices and meanings of human adornment and the meanings and practices of particular garments (Barnes and Eicher 1992).

However, there still remains a concern within recent anthropological works to define an appropriately universal and all-inclusive term to describe 'all the things people do to or put on to their bodies in order to make the human form, in their eyes, more attractive' (Polhemus and Proctor 1978: 9), although the notion of being 'attractive' is only one explanation for the many body modifications performed by various cultures, as I discuss below. Anthropological works such as Roach and Eicher (1965), Polhemus and Proctor (1978) and Barnes and Eicher (1992) often open their introductions by asserting the need for, as Roach and Eicher put it, 'the most descriptive and inclusive' phrase to describe the human act of adorning. The terms 'adornment' and 'dress' are most commonly used by anthropologists such as Roach and Eicher. 'Dress', they suggest, signals 'an act' that emphasizes 'the process of covering', while 'adornment stresses the aesthetic aspects of altering the body' (1965: 1). Given that the form of activity that constitutes most adornment in the west involves covering the body with garments, as opposed to scarification or tattooing, 'dress' is perhaps the most suitable term to use for this process in this book, since it captures the idea of the act (or series of acts) involved. Indeed, this activity is neatly summed up in the everyday words we use to describe our practices of preparing the body, such as 'getting dressed' or 'dressing up'. However, 'dress' does not exclude the possibility of encompassing the aesthetic concept of 'adornment': the choices made in getting dressed can be aesthetic as much as 'functional'. Moreover, as demonstrated below, in the west the practice of 'getting dressed' is framed by the fashion system, one dimension of which is aesthetics. The fashion system not only provides garments for wear, it endows garments with beauty and desirability, sometimes making direct contact with art. In doing so, it weaves aesthetics into the daily practice of dressing. However, before any discussion of fashion can take place, a more precise definition is needed.

Defining fashion

Barnes and Eicher (1992) and Polhemus and Proctor (1978) disagree on the meaning of the term 'fashion'. Polhemus and Proctor argue that 'fashion' refers to a special system of dress, one that is historically and geographically specific to western modernity. In contrast, Barnes and Eicher do not recognize fashion as a special instance of dress, and indeed make no reference to it except to argue that it is a mistake for researchers to consider fashion as 'a characteristic only of societies

with complex technology' (1992: 23). On the other hand, the literature produced by the disciplines of modernity – sociology, history,
cultural studies, psychoanalysis and social psychology – have persuas-
ively argued that fashion must be considered as a distinctive system
for the provision of clothes. Fashion is understood as a historically
and geographically specific system for the production and organization of dress, emerging over the course of the fourteenth century in
the European courts, particularly the French court of Louis XIV, and
developing with the rise of mercantile capitalism (Bell 1976, Finkelstein 1991, Flügel 1930, Laver 1969, 1995, McDowell 1992, Polhemus and Proctor 1978, Rouse 1989, Veblen 1953, Wilson 1985).
Wilson's account, for example, situates fashion as a feature in the
emergence and development of western modernity.

    These authors all agree that fashion emerges within a particular
kind of society, one where social mobility is possible. One recurring
theme, proposed by Bell (1976), Simmel (1971) and Veblen (1953),
and more recently McDowell (1992) and Tseëlon (1992a), is that
during the movement towards a capitalist society and the emergence
of a bourgeois class, fashion developed as a tool in the battle for social
status. Fashion, they argue, was one of the means adopted by the new
capitalist class to challenge aristocratic power and status, first by
openly flouting the sumptuary laws imposed by royalty and aristocracy, and second, by adopting and aggressively keeping pace with
fashion in an attempt to maintain status and distinction (Simmel
1971, Veblen 1953). These authors support the idea that 'emulation'
is a motivating factor in fashion (this theory is discussed more fully
both below and in chapter 3). Thus, as Bell (1976) and Braudel
(1981) argue, fashion is not found in feudal Europe, which provided
little opportunity for social movement. It is also not found in contemporary cultures where social hierarchies are rigid, although it has
increasingly developed a global reach through the spread of consumer capitalism. Fashion, then, is a particular system of dress
found under particular social circumstances. Tseëlon (1992a) argues
that the history of fashion can be divided into three major stages:
classical, modernist and postmodernist. The classical period of
fashion, from the fourteenth to the eighteenth century, saw the feudal
status order challenged by the expansion of trade and the rise of
'urban patricians'. However, dress still marked 'the courtly from
common' more clearly than during the modern and postmodern
period, in which the relationship between clothes and social hierarchy
has been progressively challenged. In his influential analysis, J. C.
Flügel (1930) made the distinction between 'fixed' and 'modish'
dress: the latter type predominates in the west, 'a fact that must be

regarded as one of the most characteristic features of modern European civilisation' (Flügel, quoted in Rouse 1989: 73). In contrast to 'modish' dress, 'fixed' dress is another term for traditional dress, such as the kimono or sari, which is characterized by its continuity with the past rather than the logic of 'change for change's sake'. As Rouse (1989) notes, this kind of dress can also be found in traditional communities within the west such as the Hasidic Jewish community in Britain. In a similar vein, Polhemus and Proctor (1978) point out that the official dress of Queen Elizabeth II is likewise largely immune to fashion, her coronation clothing in 1953, for example, implying continuity rather than change.

There is, therefore, consensus among a number of theorists regarding the definition of fashion as a system of dress characterized by an internal logic of regular and systematic change: as Wilson puts it, 'fashion is dress in which the key feature is rapid and continual changing of styles: fashion in a sense *is* change' (1985: 3). Similarly, Davis argues that 'clearly any definition of *fashion* seeking to grasp what distinguishes it from style, custom, conventional or acceptable dress, or prevalent modes must place its emphasis on the element of *change* we often associate with the term' (1992: 14).

Not only can fashion be said to have emerged under specific social and historical circumstances and developed its own momentum, quite unlike that of dress associated either with feudal society in Europe or traditional communities in existence today, but the actual economic, industrial and technological dynamics of clothing provision under fashion also need to be considered when defining it. 'Fashion' is a general term which can be used to refer to any kind of systemic changes in social life, in architecture or even academia; the 'fashion system' as it pertains to dress refers to a particular set of arrangements for the production and distribution of clothing. Most historians of fashion such as Bell (1976) and cultural theorists such as Wilson (1985) agree that the fashion system refers to a particular industry, a special and unique system for the production and consumption of dress that was born out of historical and technological developments in Europe. Indeed, given the momentum of systemic change inherent in the notion of fashion, very particular relations of production have to develop. The phrase 'fashion system' as used in this book refers to the relationship between the manufacturing, marketing and distribution of clothing into retail outlets. In her account of the fashion system, Leopold (1992) argues that fashion is 'a hybrid subject' requiring the study of the interconnectedness between production and consumption. Fine's and Leopold's materialist analysis (1993) points to the need for historical specificity in the analysis of the fashion system and argues that the fashion system under capitalism comprises very particular relations of production and distribution. Indeed, as discussed in chapter 7, there are different modes *within* the fashion system, as women's fashion is organized rather differently from men's and children's. Leopold (1992) states that fashion should be considered a complex system, so that it can be understood not just as a cultural phenomenon, but as an aspect of manufacturing and technology as well as marketing and retail. The same acknowledgement of fashion as 'hybrid' comes from Ash and Wright (1988) and also from Willis and Midgley (1973), who suggest that the study of fashion requires an integrated approach combining the study of technology, politics, economics, social context, communities and individuals. However, as Leopold (1992) suggests, such an approach has yet to emerge, with most fashion literature focusing attention on either supply or consumption.

This consensus on the nature of fashion as an aspect of western modernity has been explicitly challenged by Craik (1993) and Barnes and Eicher (1992). The latter do not give a precise definition of what they mean by the term but argue that there is no reason to differentiate fashion as a special system of dress found only in some cultures. Indeed, they go so far as to talk about fashions in scarification, suggesting that 'old fashions in the design and texture of scarification give way to new ones' (1992: 22–3). This use of the word 'fashion' is entirely at odds with the authors discussed above, who argue for a structural and historically specific definition of fashion. There are two problems with Barnes's and Eicher's argument: they fail to define what they mean by fashion (although they would seem to use the term to refer to any dress that changes); and they criticize those authors who identify it with changing style on the basis that they assume that traditional dress is unchanging. However, this is a misrepresentation of the idea of fashion as used by many authors such as Polhemus and Proctor (1978) and Bell (1976) who do not argue that *no* change in traditional dress takes place. Here the use of the word 'fixed' by Flügel (1930) is misleading, since it does imply that no change takes place in traditional dress when it is more likely that modifications to dress do occur, but not at the speed and with the regularity of fashion in modern societies. With this in mind, Polhemus and Proctor (1978) more usefully distinguish 'fashion' and 'anti-fashion' instead of 'modish' and 'fixed' dress. They therefore argue that 'anti-fashion' (for example folk dress) is not fixed and unchanging. Rather, folk dress changes slowly, often so slowly that the changes are imperceptible to the people themselves (Polhemus and Proctor 1978). Bell (1976) similarly contrasts modern and traditional dress when he compares European dress since the fourteenth century with traditional dress in China. He argues that there must have been variations in dress from dynasty to dynasty but these would be not of the dramatic kind found in Europe where fashionable dress is characterized by the logic of 'change for change's sake'. To return to the argument about scarification (Barnes and Eicher 1992): while certain styles may be open to change, these are not driven by the logic of regular and systemic change characteristic of fashion in the west; their application of the term 'fashion' in this context is therefore inappropriate.

Craik (1993) has also attacked what she considers the ethnocentrism of authors who apply the term 'fashion' only to western communities. Like Barnes and Eicher (1992), she fails to define what she means by fashion, and this is the most serious flaw in her argument. The closest she comes to a definition is to suggest that 'in short, the western fashion system goes hand in hand with the exercise of power' which she goes on to argue is also true of other fashion systems found in non-western cultures: 'the exercise of power cannot simply be associated with the unfolding development of modern consumer capitalism' (Craik 1993: x). In this way, she employs a rather idiosyncratic and narrow conception of fashion which focuses on power and neglects the other features of fashion defined by a large number of historians and cultural theorists. She goes on to reject the accepted view of fashion as a western system of dress on the grounds that it is based upon a privileging of the elite fashions of *haute couture* which bear little or no relation to the everyday dress of most people in the west. However, she fails to see that much of the contemporary literature on fashion no longer restricts itself to *haute couture* and now includes everyday dress or 'streetstyle' (Polhemus 1994, Ash and Wilson 1992). In short, Craik's assertion that 'fashion systems should not be confined to particular economic or cultural sets of arrangements' (1993: x) goes unqualified and ungrounded, while her own conception of fashion is vague. Furthermore, it could also be argued that in failing to take account of specific social and historical conditions – including conditions for the production and consumption of fashion – that underpin the fashion system, it is Craik who is guilty of ethnocentrism, universalizing fashion as a system of dress found in all cultures.

In sum, the evidence for treating fashion as a historically and geographically specific system of dress is overwhelming and convincing. There are several features which make-up the commonly accepted definition of fashion, as argued earlier: it is a system of dress found in societies where social mobility is possible; it has its own particular relations of production and consumption, again found in a particular sort of society; it is characterized by a logic of regular and systemic change.

Everyday Dress and Fashion

Having outlined the main terms to be used – 'dress' as an activity of clothing the body with an aesthetic element (as in 'adornment') and 'fashion' as a specific system of dress – it is now possible to discuss the relationship between these two. A number of authors, such as Wilson (1985), have argued that the fashion system provides the raw material for most everyday dress, not only producing the garments themselves, but also discourses and aesthetic ideas around the garments. These discourses of fashion serve to present clothes as meaningful, indeed beautiful and desirable for, as Rouse (1989) puts it, fashion is more than a commodity, it is 'an attribute with which some styles are endowed. For a particular style of clothing to become fashion it actually has to be worn by some people and recognized and acknowledged to be fashion' (1989: 69).

Fashion therefore refers not just to the production of some styles as popular or elite, but also to the production of aesthetic ideas which serve to structure the reception and consumption of styles. The 'fashion system', as defined by Leopold (1992), comprises not only manufacturing and the provision of certain styles of clothing, but also marketing, retail and cultural processes; all of these serve to produce 'fashion' and in doing so structure almost all experiences of everyday dress, excepting some forms of dress practice found in traditional and sometimes religious communities in the west. This structuring influence is so strong that, as Wilson (1985) argues, even dress which is labelled 'old-fashioned' and dress which is consciously oppositional to fashion is meaningful only because of its relationship to the dominant aesthetic propagated by fashion. Alternative dress is 'alternative' in relation to prevailing styles and also, in some cases, in relation to lifestyle. Indeed, devising an alternative 'uniform' was an important feature in many nineteenth-century Utopian movements which aimed, according to Luck, to give members a 'family likeness' which 'marked their difference from outsiders, thus acting as a powerful indicator of shared values and community boundaries' (1992: 202). The various dress reform movements of the nineteenth century adopted styles of dress which were oppositional to the prevailing fashionable aesthetic: campaigns against the corset posed an alternative, 'natural' waist for women, while bifurcated dress was proposed by some Utopian thinkers and feminists of the nineteenth century as an alternative to the crinoline skirts of their time (Luck 1992, Newton 1974, Ribeiro 1992, Steele 1985).

However, fashion is not the only determinant on everyday dress. One tendency in fashion literature is to place too great an emphasis on fashion as the central determining force of dress at any given moment. While fashion is important for defining styles at a given moment, these styles are always mediated by other social factors, such as class, gender, ethnicity, age, occupation, income and body shape, to name but a few. Not all fashions are adopted by all individuals: at any one time some aspects of fashion may be taken on board while others are rejected. Other important social factors that influence clothing decisions include historical bonds to now traditional national costume (for example, kilts and the use of tartan in Scotland) and, in everyday life, the social situation or context one is to enter. Different situations impose different ways of dressing, sometimes by imposing 'rules' or codes of dress or sometimes simply through conventions that most people adhere to most of the time. Weddings, funerals, job interviews, shopping, hiking, sports, clubbing and so on all impose particular ways of dressing and serve to constrain dress choices. Even when individuals choose to ignore such codes of dress, they are likely at least to be aware of the pressure to conform and that their decision not to do so might be read as rebellious. The factors listed here are not meant to be exhaustive, but are intended to suggest some of the kinds of social factors influencing everyday dress within the fashion system. I now discuss these factors in more detail to demonstrate how fashion is only one determining factor on dress.

Polhemus and Proctor (1978) have considered the social influences impinging on dress in both western and non-western cultures. They suggest, for instance, that class is effectively marked out by dress and that these class associations do not necessarily come from fashion. They note that members of the upper class use clothes to mark out their identity, adopting their 'own traditional anti-fashion costume' the symbolism of which is *lasting quality* and aggressive 'anti-fashion' (1978: 68). They give the example that opera dress at Glyndebourne cannot always be accurately dated. The symbolism of quality and classic style adopted by the upper class contradicts the view that 'fashion is the prerogative of the upper class' (1978: 68). They also cite the Burberry, a light raincoat, usually of gabardine, the style of which has changed little over the years, as an example of this class's predilection for 'anti-fashion'. It is sometimes argued that the middle classes once used fashion as a weapon for social climbing and that they now have their own styles of dress which are resistant to fashion: for example, while changing slowly over time, the general style of the business man has remained quite consistent; similarly, the middle-class style of Laura Ashley changes very little with each season and does not respond particularly to the swings of fashion. It would therefore seem that class is one feature of dress and plays a role in predisposing individuals to particular styles, not all of which exhibit the fashion impulse of change, but sometimes the anti-fashion impulse of continuity. However, the notion of anti-fashion proposed by Polhemus and Proctor and its adoption by a class grouping has meaning only in relation to fashion. Given the arbitrary swings fashion takes, it is always possible that an anti-fashion item like the Burberry can temporarily lose some of its class association, becoming just another fashion.

Obviously class has a material bearing on clothing choices. In particular, class tends to determine income and this needs to be considered as a factor in choices of purchase. So, for example, only a minority of the world's women have the income required to purchase *haute couture* (Colderidge 1989) and even 'off-the-peg' designer clothes, offered by many *couture* houses, remain beyond the reach of most people. However, class also structures dress decisions through taste. A taste for high-quality clothing will have a bearing on how much money is spent: the upper-class notion of 'quality and not quantity' will be reflected not only in decisions about the amount spent on individual items, but on the fabrics chosen (for example, silk, linen and cashmere as opposed to their synthetic substitutes). The predisposition to certain kinds of fabric and the notion of 'quality' may be explained in the notion of 'cultural capital' (Bourdieu 1984). Knowing what counts as quality and recognizing it in the dress of others requires knowledge in the form of 'cultural capital'. Indeed, in an age when jeans and casual clothes are worn by all, making class less obviously discernible in dress, it could be argued that finer gradations of difference require an ever greater degree of cultural capital. Those 'in the know' are likely to spot the distinction between a Savile Row suit and a high-street one, a designer dress and its cheap high-street imitations. Taste is closely linked to the body, indeed it is a bodily experience, since to talk of having a taste for a particular food or item of clothing is to refer to the sensual qualities of the thing itself. The taste orientations of classes are therefore, in part, bodily orientations. These bodily orientations are captured by Bourdieu's concept of the *habitus* which refers to the bodily dispositions of classes. This concept, discussed in more detail in chapters 1 and 4, is used by Bourdieu to convey the idea that class position is reproduced through bodily dispositions. All classes have their own ways of inhabiting the body – walking, talking, body postures, gestures and the like, which convey subtle information about class. Although he does not say so, this applies equally to dress: a taste for fine linen, silk or cashmere carries subtle indications of one's class that can be used to mark out oneself as 'distinctive' or a person of 'good taste'.

Peer groups, and in particular youth subcultures, also play a part in predisposing their members to particular styles of dress and involve the deployment of 'subcultural capital' in the interpretation and understanding of style (Thornton 1995). As Brake (1985) notes, style is important in marking out the subcultural group identity not only to those within the subculture, but to those outside. In his now classic study of youth subcultures, Hebdige (1979) considers the important role played by style in the subculture. He notes that the subculture plunders consumer culture, adopting certain commodities as its own, often to the extent that the commodity becomes shorthand for the group itself: the moped for the mods, the safety pin or ripped clothes for punks. This plundering or 'appropriation' sees the subculture 'inflect' these commodities with its own meanings, often subverting the original meaning of the commodity in mainstream culture. The teddy boys' adoption of the Savile Row gentleman's suit is one example of a style of dress 'inflected' with a rather different meaning from its original association as upper-class dress. On the body of the teddy boy, the 'zoot suit' became inflected with a menacing, working-class aggression (Cosgrove 1989).

A further aspect framing the clothing choices of individuals comes from occupation. While this might not affect all the decisions made about dress, only ones that pertain to daily working life, this experience of dressing can take up a significant amount of time, energy and expense. Many occupations within the working or lower middle classes prescribe a uniform or lay down clear rules of dress, restricting the types of garments and colours suitable for work. The professions, on the other hand, generally operate with looser codes of dress that are left up to the individual to interpret. As shown in my analysis of the dress choices of female professionals (Entwistle 2000), different occupational settings exhibit different codes of dress: law and banking will tend to be less fashion conscious than the media and creative professions. Within these constraints, individual professional women interpret what is and what is not appropriate to wear to work.

Finally, while the social factors thus far discussed mediate everyday dress, they do not in themselves produce a singular and uniform method of dressing for a particular class or peer or occupational group. Most individuals do not wear the same clothes to all occasions, but rather adapt their dress for the particular social context they are to enter. This is true in the case of some youth subcultures, such as the mods, who, as Hebdige (1979) suggests, adapted their dress to the demands of work (usually clerical work) and the demands of the 'weekend' when they could devote greater attention to subcultural activities such as dress. The social situation therefore plays an important part in structuring dress choices.

I now move on to gender, perhaps the single most important factor in practices of dress in almost all social situations where dressed bodies meet. Fashion is 'obsessed with gender... constantly working and reworking the gender boundary' (Wilson 1985: 117) and thus any consideration of dress cannot leave out recognition of gender. This is discussed in more detail in chapter 5 but it is important to note here that it is difficult to consider gender as a category separate from class, peer group and occupation, since the concept of gender is constituted differently by each, and is constituted differently according to the social context. Codes of gender vary enormously, depending on all sorts of factors operating in a given context. The skirt, for example, is the most heavily gender-coded garment, worn almost exclusively by women in the west, often explicitly enforced in certain dress codes, for example those of exclusive restaurants and nightclubs where women are supposed to look 'feminine', or more subtly enforced by social convention as in the case of certain professional occupations such as business, politics or law where a skirt is 'preferred'. However, it is also possible for some women never to wear a skirt if their occupation and lifestyle do not demand it, while in a number of different contexts skirts are worn by men (at an official ceremony in Scotland, at a 'drag night' in a club, at an avant-garde fashion event and so on). If fashion is 'obsessed with gender' and constantly plays with the gender boundary, precisely *how* it does so and precisely how gender gets codified in dress is highly variable and dependent upon factors operating within the social context. Gender is refracted through these many factors and is produced differently within different situations.

The discussion above points to the complexity of fashion and the necessity of employing an analysis of it which examines the interactions between fashion and a host of other social factors. To understand dress in everyday life requires acknowledging a wide range of social factors that frame individual clothing decisions, of which fashion is important, but by no means the only factor.

Approaches to Fashion and Dress

Sociology and fashion

The sociological neglect of fashion reflects the historical location of fashion within the arts rather than within the social sciences, although the most cursory consideration of fashion demonstrates its sociological importance as an individual yet social, active yet structured, creative yet controlled phenomenon: in short, a perfect example of structure and action. (Edwards 1997: 1)

As the above quotation from Edwards notes, fashion has been largely neglected by sociology, a fact which he explains in terms of its historical location in the arts. This neglect is surprising when one considers that fashion has been important to the development and character of western modernity and remains an industry of considerable economic and cultural significance today. Further, when one considers how important fashion is in framing our everyday choices about dress, how it is a major structuring influence in the social presentation of the body in everyday life, it seems quite remarkable that sociology should have largely ignored it.

The reasons why sociology has not tackled fashion and the forms of everyday dress found in the west are not clear. However, one possible explanation is that from its inception in the nineteenth century sociology tended to focus on action and rationality, a fact that meant the subsequent repression of the body as an object of sociological investigation and thus the neglect of practices, such as dress, which surround it (Benthall 1976, Berthelot 1991, Turner 1985). Furthermore, as Polhemus (1988) suggests, western society has largely dismissed body decoration and adornment as unimportant, ephemeral nonsense, unworthy of serious analysis. Fashion has also been subject to prejudices which prevent it from being taken seriously; it has been viewed as trivial, frivolous, irrational, wasteful and ugly. Bell argues that 'the seeming triviality of such questions, the virtual impossibility of linking our sartorial decisions with the grand spiritual passions of mankind, make clothes not less but more important to those who seek to understand their fellow men' (1976: 16–17).

Even several of the few classic studies which have attempted to treat fashion in a serious manner have fallen prey to some of these prejudices (Baudrillard 1981, Flügel 1930, Veblen 1953; see also Wilson 1985 for an account of these). An additional ingredient which makes fashion even more prone to condemnation is its connection to 'vanity'. This is one example of how fashion is often the subject of moral discussion and censure. However, as Bell (1976) and McDowell (1992) in particular point out, this moral component is itself testimony to the power and significance of dress in the social world: 'that dress is burdened with so many moral provisos is a proof of its power and significance within society'. And yet 'in clear contradiction of the fact, many writers have persisted in denigrating an interest in fashion as proof of vanity, or worse, and are critical of those who take more than a fleeting interest in appearance' (1992: 15). Despite the influence of postmodernism, which has served to re-evaluate old hierarchies of cultural value, these prejudices still linger and fashion is still the subject of moral and aesthetic condemnation (Baudrillard 1981, Veblen 1953).

A further explanation for the low status of fashion *vis-à-vis* sociological analysis, according to Polhemus (1988) and Tseëlon (1997), is its association with the 'feminine'. The subject (or object?) of fashion is commonly thought to be the woman who falls prey to the 'dreadful' delights of fashion. Moreover, Polhemus (1988) argues that pursuits labelled 'frivolous' and 'foolish' tend to be those associated with women. Until around the 1980s consumption practices associated with women were neglected or treated with derision. A number of feminists, in particular those associated with cultural studies, have pointed out that, within the Academy, feminine consumer behaviour such as the reading of romance novels or the enjoyment of soap operas has traditionally been downgraded as silly and trivial (e.g. Ang 1985, Radway 1987). By implication, condemning fashion as trivial, silly and vain has meant an implicit condemnation of women and women's culture (Tseëlon 1997). Some of this condemnation of fashion has come from feminists who have not meant to criticize the women who wear fashion but characterize women's relationship to fashion as one of exploitation. This kind of critique has been directed at certain garments, such as the corset, which some feminists regard as oppressive (Roberts 1977). In addition to medical and aesthetic criticisms of the corset enunciated by the Dress Reform Movement, feminist voices have been raised against it (see Kunzle 1982, Newton 1974, Steele 1985 for a summary of these arguments). Feminist theory has become rather more confused on the matter of women's relationship to fashion but has at least begun to recognize the pleasure it affords women (Evans and Thornton 1989, Wilson 1985).

Fashion, as Edwards (1997) argues, is about the individual and the social, a creative force on the one hand, and a structured (and structuring) phenomenon on the other, and he is right to point out that these facts alone make it an obvious candidate for sociology which has typically concerned itself with the questions of structure and agency. However, these questions have not been the prime focus of studies of fashion in those disciplines which have studied it since fashion writing, from art history, psychoanalysis, social psychology to cultural studies which tend to address other issues. Research on fashion and dress in these areas has concerned itself with various questions, for example: how and why does fashion change as it does? (a common concern of costume history); or what does fashion mean and what form of communication is it? (a frequent concern of social psychology and also cultural studies). There is, therefore, a tendency in the literature on fashion to find a general theory or overarching explanation for its presence in western society. This all too often leads to explanations which are reductive and deny the complexity of fashion. I argue that the study of fashion needs to analyse the way in which social forces framing dress – such as the fashion system, social location, class, income, gender, ethnicity, region and occupation – structure dress in everyday life. In other words, I advocate a study of fashion *and* dress which would analyse how they relate to each other: how fashion structures dress and how dress always involves the creative interpretation of fashion by individuals. Such a study takes for granted Edwards's contention that fashion is a phenomenon involving both agency and structure and would counteract the tendency towards generalization and simplification characteristic of the current literature.

Addressing the literature on fashion

Addressing the literature on fashion requires crossing many disciplinary boundaries. The diversity of disciplines and approaches within the literature is further testimony to Leopold's claim that fashion is a 'hybrid subject' (1992: 101). Fashion is treated as an aspect of industry, manufacturing, marketing, design and aesthetics, consumption and lifestyle. It has attracted the attention of theorists working in different fields and operating from very different viewpoints. The degree of interest fashion has attracted among many disciplines makes sociology's relative silence all the more intriguing. As argued above, anthropology has treated dress with some seriousness as a universal feature of human culture, although it focuses more attention on non-western dress. The analysis of western dress, specifically the development of fashion, has been explored by a range of disciplines, some closely related to sociology. One major strand is costume history, which developed out of art history as a means of dating paintings. This body of literature explores the development of styles and techniques of dress, usually *haute couture* and elite fashions, and is largely descriptive (e.g. Gorsline 1991, Kohler 1963, Ribeiro 1983, Tarrant 1994). Out of this literature has sprung cultural and social histories such as Breward (1994), de la Haye (1988) and Hollander (1993, 1994), which attempt some analysis of the cultural context of fashion, and Taylor and Wilson (1989), who examine styles of dress from the Victorian era to the present day, focusing on what 'ordinary' people have worn. A further branch of fashion literature includes histories and contemporary accounts of the economic and technological aspects of the fashion system (e.g. Leopold 1992, Fine and Leopold 1993) and those accounts (e.g. Chapkis and Enloe 1984, Coyle 1982, Elson 1984, Phizacklea 1990, Ross 1997) which examine the exploitation of sweated workers within the fashion system. Cultural studies now also explore the contemporary fashion system (Ash and Wright 1988, Ash and Wilson 1992, Davis 1992, Craik 1993) as well as the nature of fashion representations (Brooks 1989, Evans and Thornton 1989, Lewis 1996, Nixon 1996). This work has been framed by a number of theoretical perspectives: Marxist materialist analysis (Leopold 1992), structuralism (Barthes 1985), semiotics (Hebdige 1979), psychoanalysis (Flügel 1930, Lewis and Rolley 1997, Nixon 1996, Silverman 1986), social psychology (Soloman 1985, Tseëlon 1997) and post-structuralism (Entwistle 1997a, 1997b, Nixon 1996, Wilson 1992).

I want to explore the various approaches that have been adopted in relation to fashion. Three approaches can be discerned *across* the literature, defined not by discipline but by the kinds of question they ask and the theoretical and methodological approach taken. The first starts out by asking such questions as, why wear clothes?, questions that tend to lead to simplistic answers. A second approach within the literature attempts a more sophisticated analysis, exploring the relationship of fashion to 'modernity'. While broad in scope, these theoretical approaches do not provide an account of how fashion is *experienced* and *practised* in everyday dress. They provide a theoretical account of *fashion* which results in the neglect of *dress* as practice. They also often fail to address they way in which fashion is intimately connected to the body, treating fashion as a social and communicative phenomenon but not a phenomenon of the body. The third approach is less concerned with theoretical explanations than with examining specific dress practices in a culture. This concern with practice can be found in some recent anthropological literature (Barnes and Eicher 1992, Freeman 1993, Hoodfar 1991, Weiner and Schnieder 1991), which examines the cultural signific- ance, meanings and practices around adornment, as well as in social psychology (Cash 1985, Ericksen and Joseph 1985, Tseëlon 1992a, 1997), which looks at what people do and mean by their dress in daily life. However, they are of limited value to an account of fashion in the west.

Theoretical Approaches I: 'Why' Questions and their Answers

Early explanations of dress and fashion, and indeed many contem- porary accounts, have tended to start from 'why' questions: why do we wear clothes? They may also ask questions about the nature of fashion: why a fashion system based on continual change?; why do fashions change as they do?; why the difference between men's and women's fashions? An examination of these 'why' questions is quite revealing of the ways in which fashion has been theorized and can also demonstrate how thinking on fashion has tended to be reductive, producing a theory of dress or fashion which is simplistic in its attempt to be all-inclusive. The net result of such 'why' questions is the reduction of fashion to simple causes and effects and to overly deterministic and reductive accounts.

Theoretical explanations of dress and adornment

In answer to the question why do we adorn?, anthropology has come up with a number of different explanations: protection, modesty, display and communication, each one being progressively more inclusive than the former. Barnard (1996), Polhemus and Proctor (1978) and also Rouse (1989) give good summaries of these different approaches and begin by noting the early influence of the late nine- teenth-century anthropologist Malinowski who posed the narrower question, why do we wear clothes? One answer is that human beings have basic needs, one of the most fundamental of which is to protect the body from the elements. However, this theory is problematic: in some cultures people do not wear clothes and indeed, as Rouse (1989) notes, many are able to survive in extreme temperatures without much protection from clothes. This is true of clothes in the west as well as in non-western cultures: skimpy clothes, for example, are worn for the sake of fashion, often regardless of freezing temperatures. Polhemus and Proctor (1978) and Rouse (1989) therefore note that this explanation ignores the fact that many styles of dress both in the west and in traditional and non-western cultures are not practical and often cause bodily discomfort.

The second explanation that has been put forward is that of modesty: clothes are worn in order to cover the sexual organs. However, anthropological evidence suggests that there is no universal notion of modesty but a high degree of cultural variability, making modesty problematic as a founding principle. As Rouse (1989) notes, modesty and shame are relative to social context. Psychological literature has also asked why we wear clothes and has sought to explain the fact in terms of psychological processes. Flügel's work (1930) in this area constitutes the classic text. He does not reject the two theories of protection and modesty, but proposes that a third might be of more significance, that is the purpose of decoration and display. Clothes are worn not to reduce sexual messages but to make us more sexually attractive. Adapting Freud's psychoanalytic approach, he goes on to suggest that clothes express two contradictory tendencies, that of modesty and exhibition, and also argues that clothes themselves (such as the male necktie) may symbolize the sex organs. In this way, clothes express an ambivalence and this leads him to suggest that 'the use of clothes seems, in its psychological aspects, to resemble the process whereby a neurotic symptom is developed' (Flügel 1930: 20). Clothes, for Flügel, constitute 'a perpetual blush upon the surface of humanity' (1930: 21). A fourth explanation for adornment, that it stems from a universal human propensity to communicate with symbols, has become a dominant theoretical framework, accepted by anthropologists on dress as well as by theorists concerned specifically with fashion. Given its dominance, this explanation of fashion/dress as communication is discussed in more detail below, but first I examine some of the theories put forward to explain fashion.

Theoretical explanations of fashion

There are numerous fashion histories which attempt to find a theoretical explanation of fashion. This literature seeks to explain fashion as a unique system of dress and to understand why such a system exists at all, perhaps also addressing the question of why fashions change the way they do. This propensity to ask 'why' questions of fashion is evident in the now classic *Theory of the Leisure Class*, by the late nineteenth-century sociologist Thorstein Veblen, first published in 1899 and reissued 1953. Implicit in his theory of fashion are two why questions, the first of which is: why a fashion system at all? His answer is one that needs to be historicized, since it could be argued that it tells us more about fashion at the end of the nineteenth century than about the meanings of fashion today. Veblen explains fashion in terms of the characteristics he argues are particular to the leisure class, the new bourgeois class who, he argues, adopt fashion as a tool in the battle for social status. The newly emerging bourgeoisie expresses its wealth through conspicuous consumption, conspicuous waste and conspicuous leisure. Since fashion has no utility, members of this class adopt it as a means to show their distance from function: only the rich and leisured can afford to discard clothes before they are worn out. Dress is a supreme example of the expression of pecuniary culture, since 'our apparel is always in evidence and affords an indication of our pecuniary standing to all observers at the first glance' (Veblen 1953: 119). The second question asked by Veblen is: why do fashions relentlessly change? He suggests that the need for conspicuous consumption and waste may explain the need for fashion to keep changing. However, this alone is not enough, since it leaves unexplained not only the motive for making and accepting changes in style, but why conformity to fashion is necessary. Instead, he goes on to argue that wastefulness is innately offensive, and this makes the futility and expense of fashion abhorrent and ugly. He therefore suggests that the movement of fashion and its being followed by people can be explained as our attempt to escape the futility and ugliness of fashion, with each new style welcomed as relief from the previous aberration until that, too, in all its futility and wastefulness, is also rejected.

According to Veblen, women's dress displays these dynamics more than men's since the only role of the bourgeois lady of the house is to demonstrate her master's ability to pay, his pecuniary strength to remove her entirely from the sphere of work. Veblen's account of the leisure class constructs the bourgeois woman as servile (he compares her role with that of domestic servants); they are passive beings or 'men's chattel' and the clothes they wear are indicative of this. Women's dress was closely linked to fashion and therefore was an important means by which the bourgeois class could conspicuously consume and be fashionably wasteful. The Victorian woman's dress was also an important indicator of vicarious leisure. The bourgeois lady wore clothes that made her obviously incapable of work – elaborate bonnets, heavy skirts, delicate shoes and constraining corsets – testimony to her distance from productive work and of her consumption of leisure. Veblen condemns these traits of fashionable

dress and calls for dress which is based on rational, utilitarian principals reminiscent of the principals of many dress reformers (see Newton 1974 for a summary).

There are a number of problems with Veblen's theory. His account
of fashion and fashion change relies on the idea of emulation (the
limitations of which are examined in more detail below and in chapter
3). His analysis of the bourgeois woman lacks any sense of agency:
fashion is conceived of as an over-determining and negative force in
the life of the Victorian woman. Both Kunzle (1982) and Steele
(1985) offer a rather different view of the Victorian woman's relationship to fashion and revise the standard fashion story of the corset as
oppressive to women (Veblen 1953, Roberts 1977). Steele's account
sets out to consider the role of erotic display in fashion, arguing that
the traditional image of the Victorian woman as sexually and socially
repressed 'needs to be radically revised' (1985: 3). Instead, she posits
the view that 'Victorian fashions revolved around an ideal of feminine
beauty in which eroticism played an important part' (1985: 3) and in
this way there is more continuity between the nineteenth and twentieth centuries than previously thought. Kunzle (1982) goes further
than this, arguing that the wearing of the corset by the Victorian
woman was not a sign of her servile status, but that instead the female
tight-lacer was a sexually and socially assertive woman. Both Kunzle
and Steele see the Victorian woman as an active subject and support
their argument by historical evidence of what Victorian women did in
their daily practice (although Steele takes issue with Kunzle's evidence
of tight-lacers, taken from the correspondence of corset fetishists,
which, she suggests may have exaggerated for the sake of erotic effect).

It is also worth noting at this point that Veblen's account of
women's relationship to dress, if ever appropriate, is now significantly
out of date. As I have argued elsewhere (Entwistle 1997a, 1997b) the
entry of women into the professions has brought with it a shift in
the public/private, production/consumption dichotomy, which had
women confined to the home and the realm of consumption. It also
brought with it a shift in the terms operating around female dress. As
a player within the productive world of work, and a wage earner in
her own right, the career woman is no longer 'man's chattel' and her
dress no longer about vicarious display of leisure. The entry of
women into the professional job market resulted in the emergence
of dress that was not incapacitating but indeed almost 'rational', at
least in its principal aim of enabling women to get on in the world and
not be encumbered by fussy and feminine dress.

Despite the problems with Veblen's account it provides a good
example of an early sociological study and one that is still influential

today. Many of his ideas can be traced through the work of other theorists of fashion and indeed, as Wilson (1985) notes, in general Veblen's ideas have gone largely unchallenged by fashion writers. This may have something to do with the fact that he is one of the few social theorists to have treated fashion with any seriousness. One sympathetic reading of Veblen comes from the work of Bell (1976), although his analysis produces a far less negative picture of fashion and does not condemn fashion as ugly or irrational. A similar line of argument can be traced through the work of Baudrillard (1981), who argues that

> fashion continually fabricates the 'beautiful' on the basis of a radical denial of beauty, by reducing beauty to the logical equivalent of ugliness. It can impose the most eccentric, dysfunctional, ridiculous traits as eminently distinctive. This is where it triumphs – imposing and legitimating the irrational according to a logic deeper than that of rationality. (1981: 79)

Wilson takes issue with Veblen's and Baudrillard's account of fashion as wasteful and futile. In condemning fashion, Veblen assumes that the world should be organized around utilitarian values; this is a world where 'there is no place for the irrational or the non-utilitarian; it was a wholly rational realm' (Wilson 1985: 52). A further problem with Veblen, according to Wilson, is his causal account of fashion change. His theory that fashion is constantly changing in an attempt to get away from ugliness and find beauty is reductive and over-deterministic. In his assertion of utility in dress, Veblen attempts to 'explain away' fashion as essentially useless, unnecessary and irrational, thus failing to acknowledge its ambivalent and contradictory nature as well as the pleasures it affords. The same is true of Baudrillard, whose account, according to Wilson, is 'over simplified and over-deterministic' in that, he, like Veblen, 'grants no role to contradiction, nor for that matter to pleasure' (1985: 53). Moreover, Baudrillard's attack on consumption *per se* is ultimately nihilistic, producing an account of individuals as caught up in a 'seamless web of oppression' (1985: 53).

The problem of causality is one that dogs several other classic accounts of fashion and dress. A number of theorists begin by asking why questions: why does such a seemingly 'irrational' system of dress exist and why do fashions change in the way they do? Many theories have developed to explain fashion's dynamics in terms of a logic inherent to the fashion system. Three theories in particular have become quite influential as explanatory frameworks: the theory of emulation or 'trickle-down'; the theory of *Zeitgeist*; and the theory of 'the shifting erogenous zone'. All three attempt to explain fashion by reference to a singular force and are highly problematic, in that in seeking to find the 'causes' of fashion, they tend to be reductive and mechanistic.

Veblen (1953) and Simmel (1971) are the most famous proponents of the theory of fashion as emulation, according to which styles start at the top of the social hierarchy with an elite class opting for a distinctive style of dress; the classes below, seeking to emulate the status of this class, gradually adopt the style and fashion thus 'trickles down'. By the time a particular style has been adopted by the working class, the elite, in order to maintain their distinction and status, have moved on to another style, thus fashions continually shift. Georg Simmel (1971) argues that fashion expresses a tension between uniformity and differentiation: it expresses the contradictory desire to fit in and connect with a group, and simultaneously to stand out and assert an individual identity. According to Simmel, adopting extreme and new styles of dress is one means by which the elite differentiate themselves from the rest but, given their high social status, the things they choose to wear become desirable and are copied by the social class below them in an attempt to emulate their status. Once the style has 'trickled down' to the lower classes, it can no longer serve to differentiate the 'leading edge' elite who have to move on to adopt another, often more extreme style to maintain their status position. This oscillating rhythm produces fashion with its logic of constant innovation.

Emulation has come under attack by a number of theorists (Campbell 1989, Partington 1992, Polhemus 1994, Wilson 1985). Rouse (1989) outlines three main criticisms of this approach: first, change does not occur because the lower classes begin to wear the clothes of the rich; second, there have been occasions when fashions from working-class and other low-status groups such as black youth have become influential; and third, that the 'trickle-down' theory is dependent upon a time lag between styles worn by the rich being adopted by the lower classes, which, given today's production turnover, is no longer the case. Partington (1992) attacks emulation more radically in her account of working-class women and Dior's 'New Look'. She suggests that working-class women did not emulate this look but adapted it in their own way, which was not a 'watered down' or less creative version of the 'real' thing. McCracken (1985) has attempted to re-evaluate the emulation model, updating it by examining power relations between the genders. His account looks at the professional and business woman's emulation of the male business suit at work. He argues that this new breed of professional woman wanted the same status as men at work and, in order to achieve it, emulated the suited look long established as the uniform of men in business. However, in order to develop this argument, he has to 'prove' that the dominant group (i.e. men) is now altering its style as more women start to wear the suit. This seems patently not the case: McCraken provides little evidence to substantiate this point. The main issue, however, is that emulation as a model for explaining dress is too mechanistic and too simplistic. (Further discussions of emulation and its problems are offered in chapters 3 and 7.)

The question of why fashion changes as it does is answered by some authors with reference to *Zeitgeist* (e.g. Ditcher 1985). This approach argues that fashion responds to social and political changes. It is an explanation of style that has become part of everyday 'folklore', evident in the commonly cited idea that hemlines drop during economic depressions, as was the case in the 1930s, and rise in times of economic boom, as in the 1960s. Wars are given great importance in this approach. During the First World War, for example, women went out to work in greater numbers than before, and it is assumed that this resulted in the abandoning of the corset and the long hobble skirts of the preceding period; and it is in terms of this explanatory framework that commentators interpret Dior's 'New Look' as part of the 1950s move to make women more feminine and decorative after the masculinizing influence of the Second World War. However, there are numerous problems with this approach, one being that it tends to over-simplify fashion: as Wilson notes, 'such statements are too obvious to be entirely true, and the history they misrepresent is more complex' (1985: 46). The 'New Look' can in fact be traced back to *before* the outbreak of the Second World War: Bell (1976), for example, argues that Vivien Leigh's dresses in the film of *Gone with the Wind* (1939) anticipated Dior's post-war look. The quantitative study of women's fashions from the 1600s to the 1930s conducted by Richardson and Kroeber (1973) is perhaps the most exhaustive attempt to correlate fashion change with social change. In examining fashion plates of over three centuries, they could not find any conclusive evidence to suggest that social changes influenced any particular dimension of the female silhouette. Instead, as Bell suggests, dress often fails to mirror social climate: while some connections might be established for some of the time, the connection is 'not one of mechanical causality' (1976: 102). If we try to pin changes down to political and social movements, we will always find exceptions to the rule because fashion cuts both ways. Bell also goes on to say that if we allow *Zeitgeist* theory a free hand it becomes almost a supernatural hypothesis, one of metaphysical rather than social proportions.

A third strand in answering the question of why fashions change as they do focuses on attempts to explain why women's fashions change so rapidly. Laver (1969, 1995) argues that there is a single rule governing women's fashions, namely the 'seduction principle': women's dress is primarily about the enhancement of their sexual attractiveness to men. On the other hand, men's dress does not change as rapidly as women's and is governed instead by the 'hier-archical principle': it is about the enhancement of their social status. The rapidity of change in women's fashions is explained by Laver through the theory of the 'shifting erogenous zone'. At different times, women's clothes display a particular part of the female body but, in order to keep men's desire, the emphasis must continually shift. Thus, for example, he argues that men became tired of the emphasis on female legs in the 1920s so shifted attention to the female back in the 1930s, hence causing a shift in women's fashions.

As a number of authors testify (Bell 1976, Hollander 1994, Polhe-mus and Proctor 1978, Rouse 1989, Steele 1985, 1996, Wilson 1985), there is a definite link between dress and eroticism. Wilson, for example, argues that 'it seems so obvious that dress must bear some relationship to sexuality that the assumption goes virtually unquestioned' (1985: 91). Even in societies where few clothes are worn, it is common to dress up for ceremonies in ways that serve to enhance sexual appeal. Fetishistic dress, as I demonstrate in chapter 6, is also testimony to the power of clothes to incite sexual desire and indeed in the west many items of clothing, for example corsets, and such fabrics as leather and rubber have become closely associated with sex (Kunzle 1982, Wilson 1985, Polhemus 1994, Steele 1985, 1996). However, while there is an undoubted link between dress and sexuality, Laver's account (1969), which places eroticism as the prime mover of women's fashions, is inadequate. As Wilson argues, it is very difficult to determine what erogenous zone clothes display: 'trousers might reveal the leg or the bottom', for example? (1985: 92). She also suggests that there are a number of instances of women's dress, such as their dress for work, which seeks to 'muffle' sexuality, not enhance it, demonstrating that eroticism and display do not explain all fashion. Polhemus and Proctor (1978) also suggest that the theory of erotic attraction cannot take account of many styles of dress which are not erotic. For example, it fails to explain the fashion for combat trousers for women in the late 1990s; these garments seem to be neither obviously erotic nor particularly reveal-ing of the body.

Problems with 'why' explanations   Among the problems with historical
accounts and theories that take 'why' questions as their starting-
point is the fact that the literature is over-simplistic and methodologically naive. It tells stories of fashion as a self-evident, unfolding
narrative of change explained by a single motivating force: status
competition (Veblen 1953); 'the shifting erogenous zone' (Laver
1969); the 'neurotic impulse' or 'perpetual blush on the face of
humanity' (Flügel 1930). This kind of theory results in the organization of fashion history in terms of narratives that are unilinear and
reductive. A further problem is that, more often than not, fashion is
depicted as 'ugly' and 'irrational' or indeed trivial and vain, thus
producing theories that are heavily moralistic. Since fashion literature
traditionally tends to focus on women, these macro-theories have
therefore often produced simplistic, moralizing and patronizing
accounts of women's involvement in dress: for example, Laver's
account (1969) produces women as passive victims of the 'male
gaze' (Mulvey 1975); Veblen's account of women's relationship to
fashion constructs them as 'exquisite slaves' and victims to the irra-
tionality of fashion.

However, perhaps a more general and fundamental problem with
all these 'why' questions is that they result in macro-theory which
attempts to explain the fashion system in an all-inclusive way. As
demonstrated above, each theory has its limitations primarily because
each attempts to find an all-inclusive explanation of adornment or
fashion. This kind of approach to dress and the fashion system
reduces to singular cause and effect what is actually a complex
phenomenon. The literature fails to recognize fashion as a socially
constituted practice which cannot be understood in isolation but as
part of a wide range of other social forces, in particular class, race and
gender. Moreover, the 'why' approaches with their propensity to
over-generalize, fail to give an account of agency on the part of
women and men. There is no account of dress practice: the theorist
sits at a distance, interpreting fashion without seeking to grasp the
meanings given to it in daily life or indeed the ways in which it is
transformed and resisted by people in practice.

In contrast to these theories, the argument put forward here is that
dress needs to be understood as a situated practice that is the result of
complex social forces and individual negotiations in daily life. An
approach to dress which adopts the framework of situated practice
opposes crude reductionism and rejects any attempt to isolate fashion
as an all-powerful and determining force. Instead, the fashion system
sets parameters around dress but within these parameters are many

practices of dressing that are dependent upon a variety of other social structures. A consideration of dress from this perspective involves investigating experiences and practical understandings of fashion as well as the factors which mediate it. It would counteract the tendency to make generalizations about *all* dress which 'grand theory' tends to do.

Dress and fashion as communication   This discussion has so far examined the problems associated with many of the universal explanations of adornment from anthropology, as well as the limitations of a number of classic accounts attempting to explain the specific dynamics of the fashion system. However, as indicated above, one explanation of all forms of adornment, traditional and modern, is that they stem from the human propensity to communicate through symbols. The idea that humans share a fundamental need to communicate has now become widely accepted as the dominant explanatory framework among anthropologists of dress and theorists of fashion. Anthropology has provided evidence to indicate that all human societies modify the body through some form of adornment and that this, along with language, is posited as a universal propensity. The idea that dress is communicative is adopted by theorists such as Barnard (1996), Davis (1992), Lurie (1981), Polhemus and Proctor (1978), Rouse (1989) and Wilson (1985) and used to explain the purpose of fashion in modern societies. This explanation is more fruitful than other theories for dress, adornment and fashion: clothes and other adornments may be worn for instrumental purposes or for protection but they are also part of the expressive culture of a community. It follows that if clothes are expressive or communicative aspects of human culture, then they must be meaningful in some way. One clearly discernible approach to the issue of meaning in fashion/dress has emerged from structuralism and semiotics, as has a more nebulous body of work that explores the communicative aspects of fashion and consumption within modernity and postmodernity. The latter ranges from historical works that examine the emergence of fashion and the role played by fashion in modernity to accounts of the significance of fashion in late modern life, an approach which focuses particular attention on the role of fashion in the construction of identity.

One example of the approach to fashion as communication draws analogies between fashion and language, considering the way in which fashion operates 'like a language'. The language-like nature of fashion and dress is considered by such theorists as Davis (1992), Polhemus and Proctor (1978) and Rouse (1989) but is carried to extremes in the work of Lurie (1981). She suggests that fashion has a 'grammar' and a 'vocabulary' like spoken languages, with dress being theoretically larger than verbal language, extending to hairstyle, the way the body is held, how it walks and so on. There are sartorial equivalents of 'anarchic words', taboos (e.g. dresses for men) and 'slang words' (e.g. jeans), while accessories like earrings and hats can be compared to adjectives.

There are a number of problems with this direct application of language models to fashion. Davis (1992) suggests that clothing can be thought of like a language but suggests that the more ambiguous language of music is better suited to capturing the equally ambiguous nature of clothes. He therefore argues that the idea of language should be applied to fashion metaphorically and not literally, and goes on to suggest that the idea of a code is particularly useful: a code is 'the binding ligament in the shared understandings that comprise a sphere of discourse and, hence, its associated social arrangements' (1992: 5). There are social codes of dress but these are very context bound, and there is no equivalent to a sentence in dress and no way that dress can give as precise a message as a spoken sentence. Clothes, then, for Davis are meaningful but their meanings are ambiguous and imprecise. Their real power comes from their ability to suggest, evoke and resist a fixed meaning. Tseëlon (1997) also demonstrates the ambiguity of clothes. Having asked a group of women to come to a focus group dressed in a way that 'expresses who they are', she compared the intentions of the women with the interpretation made of them by others: the result was considerable misunderstanding and misinterpretation. It would seem, therefore, that if the meanings of dress are not as clear or precise as verbal language, Lurie's analogy becomes untenable. This inability of clothes to be 'read' effectively is noted by Campbell (1997), who criticizes the very premise that fashionable dress is communicative. He suggests that the considerable misunderstanding involved in reading the dress of others reflects the difficulty of fixing *any* meaning to clothes.

However, while the direct application of language models to fashion is problematic, the structuralist model and its method, borrowed from the structural linguistics of Ferdinand de Saussure, has become a dominant framework for considering fashion, particularly within cultural studies. Structuralism is interested in meaning and how meaning in communication systems is possible. Saussure proposed that signs gain their meaning not from anything intrinsic to them, but from their ability to stand in for things. The sign comprises two elements, the signifier (i.e. the sound or image of the sign) and the signified (i.e. the concept associated with it). Signs gain their identity from one another through their difference to other signs, and meaning (in language or any other sign system) comes from the way in which signs combine with other signs. While Saussure developed his theory in relation to language, he saw the potential of his approach for the study of all signs systems and prophesied that a 'science of signs', which he called semiology, would develop. Such a 'science' would provide a method for understanding meaning in all communicative practices, including dress. Semiotics draws upon Saussure's system of language but moves from looking at written communication to non-verbal phenomena. The focus of semiotic accounts has been to explain *fashion* as a system rather than everyday *dress*, and to address *fashion texts* rather than *practices*. The reasons for this focus of attention are purely methodological. Roland Barthes, who played an influential role in establishing semiology (or semiotics), provides a classic structuralist account of fashion in *The Fashion System*, (1985) and demonstrates very clearly the structuralist's methodological concerns. Barthes recounts his decision to focus on the written fashion text, as opposed to its visual representation or the real garments worn, in his search 'to reconstitute step by step a system of meaning, in a more or less immediate manner' (1985: x). He says it is the 'structural purity' of the fashion text that governed his choice: real clothing and its representation are burdened with practical problems but the magazine's text offers the best possibility of studying a slice of fashion at a given moment:

> only written clothing has no practical or aesthetic function: it is entirely constituted with a view to a signification: if the magazine describes a certain article of clothing verbally, it does so solely to convey a message whose content is: *Fashion*; . . . written clothing is unencumbered by any parasitic function and entails no vague temporality. (1985: 8)

Barthes therefore recognizes the limitations of this choice in terms of a sociology of fashion, suggesting that an analysis which looks only at the written system may disappoint sociologists because it does not deal with fashion as an institution and may indeed tell us only about semiology. The structuralist approach as Barthes develops it effectively 'brackets off' other equally important aspects of the fashion system, such as its industrial and commercial aspects, as well as how it is incorporated into everyday practices of dress. The structuralist approach, governed by methodological concerns, is thus propelled towards texts rather than practices. The 'structural purity' of the text comes from its being a 'frozen' or 'static' moment, whereas social action is complex and dynamic and difficult to capture. As

Barthes' account testifies, it is much easier to study a slice of text than it is to study the complex mechanisms of an industry such as the fashion industry, or the complex and nebulous negotiations which make-up everyday dress practices. The relative ease of the structuralist method, which can indeed be done from the armchair, makes it a popular choice with theorists. Fashion literature of this ilk has focused on 'reading' photographs, magazines and advertisements as texts. Evans and Thornton (1989), for example, attempt to re-evaluate theories of female narcissism and theories of masquerade through women's magazines and fashion photographs. In one chapter they analyse six fashion photographs and proceed to analyse semiotically the internal arrangement of the elements in the photograph. In a similar vein, Brooks (1989) analyses the way in which Helmut Newton orchestrates 'the look' within his fashion photographs. Moving beyond semiotics, Nixon (1996) draws on psychoanalysis and Foucauldian post-structural analysis (as well as empirical work on marketing and advertising practices) to examine the organization of the look in style magazines for men, focusing in particular on fashion photography and the various representations of the 'new man' popularized in the 1980s.

In his analysis of youth subcultures, Dick Hebdige (1979) draws directly upon the Saussurian tradition in order to talk about the 'signs' adopted by the subculture to create meaning within, and give identity to, the group. His semiotic analysis moves from written texts as in Barthes' analysis to the uses of objects by youth subcultures. Hebdige uses this concept to suggest that subcultures 'steal' or 'appropriate' objects from mainstream culture but in doing so 'inflect' them with their own meaning. A humble object such as a safety pin with its associated domestic meanings is inflected with subversive and aggressive meanings when worn through the nose of a punk. In this way, Hebdige gives an account of the meaningful role played by 'style' within youth subculture. Although Hebdige's account focuses not on fashion texts but 'real' garments and their uses within social groups, this account of style remains a structuralist one by virtue of its methodological approach. Hebdige *textualizes* subcultural dress practice: he reads the body/style of the subculture *as if it were a text*. Such textualism makes no distinction between reading a fashion magazine and reading the body of a punk or a mod. This ability to textualize everything serves to 'bracket off' real live bodies as they are lived and experienced. The structuralist method, in seeking to find the relations between elements in a structure, puts a distance between the theorist and the subjects under investigation, since semiotic analysis can be done in the armchair or office and does not require entering the field of action itself (Bourdieu 1989).

This 'bracketing off' of the world beyond the text is a deliberate epistemological and methodological stance taken by structuralists, who claim that we cannot know the world beyond its representations. This stance effectively displaces the idea of embodiment and the individual and can give us no account of experience or agency. It can therefore tell us nothing about what sense people make of fashion, what pleasures it affords, or how fashion structures the experience of dress and the clothing decisions made in everyday life. There is a further problem with this method as with other studies of fashion which focus on texts, and that has to do with the position of the theorist who, in 'reading' representations remains at a distance from actual practices. In his critique of structuralism, Bourdieu (1989, 1994) argues that structuralism maintains a position of distance from the world but assumes a position of superiority; the implicit claim of the structuralist is that he or she knows more, has greater understanding and insight, than those they observe. Thus, Hebdige's work on subcultures does not give us an account of what people do and mean by their dress: his analysis does not consider what subcultural participants say about their dress. Instead we are offered Hebdige's interpretation of their dress and what it means. The structuralist reading assumes that there is an objective meaning that can be discerned from the surface and which the method of structural analysis can unlock.

Structuralism, however, is not entirely responsible for this focus on texts. Contributions to the study of fashion within art history and film theory have been equally concerned with texts rather than practices. Gaines and Herzog (1990) explore the meaning of the dressed body in texts, mainly film texts, while Hollander (1993) explores 'how clothes in works of art have been connected with clothes in real life' (1993: xi). Hollander suggests that the formal qualities of art are important in illuminating the way in which clothes should be worn and how the body should look in them: so much so that 'the way clothes strike the eye comes to be mediated by current visual assumptions made from pictures of dressed people' (1993: xi). However, while Hollander's focus on art to illuminate dress, although not unusual (it is the standard approach within art/costume history) is problematic because she extends her analysis of the representations to suggest how these representations may have influenced the way clothes and nakedness are perceived in general. Bell (1976), for example, advises caution in relying on paintings and fashion plates, since the painter might have exaggerated the dress, and the person depicted might have chosen to wear particularly elaborate dress for the purpose of the painting. Paintings therefore do not necessarily tell us what dress would have been worn in everyday life. It is also problematic because the clothes depicted in art tend to be the clothes of the elite, not those of 'ordinary people'. For this reason, de la Haye (1988) and Taylor and Wilson (1989) focus not on paintings but on other sorts of representation in order to examine fashions through the ages. A further problem with focusing on art images, or indeed any image, is noted by both McDowell (1992) and Bell (1976), who argue that visual information is just one part of clothing: what we lack in these historical records is the sensual *sound* and *feel* of clothes. Hollander's claim that 'the clothed figure looks more persuasive and comprehensible in art than it does in reality' (1993: xi) points to a methodologically driven quest not unlike Barthes' desire to investigate the workings of the fashion system by looking at fashion journalism. The body in art might present a static, tidy, more 'comprehensive' image than in reality and might therefore be easier to study. However, clothes in everyday life are not like art, nor do they pretend to be: clothes in everyday life take on the form of the body and in doing so get crumpled, creased, ripped and so on. Textual approaches therefore do not tell us of the many other aspects of fashion and dress.

I do not wish to suggest that these textual approaches are in themselves invalid since they serve the purpose of illuminating the way in which clothes are represented, albeit in idealized form. However, what is problematic is the dominance of approaches which focus on texts to the exclusion of other issues concerning fashion and dress, as well as the tendency to extend the analysis of texts beyond the text itself, as Hollander (1993) does. By textualizing fashion and dress these approaches can sometimes be reductive; if practices are reduced to texts, the complexity of fashion and dress and the way in which it is embodied is largely neglected. Studies of fashion and dress in terms of how they are lived and experienced are equally valid but have found little place within historical or contemporary literature. The study of fashion/dress as situated bodily practice moves away from looking solely at texts, although such structuring influences as paintings and fashion magazines are not to be ignored. It looks at how people take account of their involvement with fashion and the way they dress in particular social situations. A concern with subjective accounts necessitates a move into the 'field' of action itself rather than maintaining a position of distance occupied by structuralism. The notion of situated bodily practice also recognizes dress as an experience of embodiment and the outcome of practical actions taken by individuals on their bodies.

Theoretical Approaches II: Fashion and the Condition of Modern Life

Another body of literature on fashion has emerged which examines its communicative abilities and its role in modern and late or postmodern life. The works of Finkelstein (1991), Giddens (1991), Sennett (1977), Simmel (1971) and Wilson (1985, 1992) have all attempted to understand fashion as an integral aspect of modernity and/or postmodernity. While these approaches are discussed in detail in chapters 3 and 4, it is worth noting some important points about this literature here. There are a number of themes which unite these accounts: they focus on the nature of identity under conditions of rapid change, exploring the resources for the self that modernity opens up in order to cope with these changes and examining the role played by dress in the presentation of the self on the modern social stage. These accounts deal with sociological concerns in that they examine the fashion system not from the point of view of human psychology, or from the idea of disembodied sign systems, but examine the social forces at work within a system of dress and situate fashion within the context of the development of modernity.

Wilson makes a strong case for considering fashion in terms of modernity in *Adorned in Dreams* (1985). She is critical of the various theories put forward to explain fashion (emulation, *Zeitgeist*, fashion as language, psychoanalysis and so on) as generally reductive, missing 'fashion's purposive and creative aspects', its 'tantalising and slippery essence' (1985: 58). She proposes instead that the concepts of 'modernism' and 'modernity' capture this essence. Fashion, she suggests, has an affinity with modern art and a number of fashion designers have purposively borrowed from modern art. The concept of modernity is mobilized because it 'seems useful as a way of indicating the restless desire for change characteristic of cultural life in industrial capitalism, the desire for the new that fashion expresses so well' (1985: 63). Fashion is also part of the modern experience because it is central to the experience of the modern city; dress is one 'technique of survival' in a metropolis that brings one into contact with strangers.

The theme of display and self-presentation in the city is also central to Richard Sennett's analysis of *The Fall of Public Man* (1977). In his account, the development of the bourgeoisie and the increasing separation of public and private that ensued during the late eighteenth and nineteenth century have eroded the public life of the individual. Over the course of the eighteenth century and with the rise of Romanticism, the public sphere was eroded by the intrusion of the private sphere and this was coupled with the injunction to be 'authentic' in public. This can be traced through the kinds of dress worn at the time. Up until around the mid-eighteenth century, appearance was not seen to express the self, but instead to be a performance 'at a distance from the self'. The eighteenth-century aristocratic figure, both male and female, would have worn highly elaborate dress, heavy make-up and flamboyant wigs but this striking impression did not attempt to present the individuality of the person. The elaborate dress would set the body (and thus the identity) of the wearer at a distance as 'costume' does in the theatre: the body was a 'mannequin'. Appearance was all about play and performance and this enabled individuals to live fully in the public world. However, as Romanticism took hold, challenging artifice and celebrating 'natural' and 'authentic' man, the sense that dress and appearance should be related to one's identity emerged.

The modern individual, then, is one who is aware of being read by his or her appearance (as discussed in chapter 4). This theme is also pursued by Joanne Finkelstein (1991). Like Sennett, she is interested in the development of 'authenticating narratives' that link one's appearance with identity. While the physiognomic theories popular in the nineteenth century might now seem quaint, Finkelstein argues that they have not disappeared: the common form they take is reading people by reference to their body, dress and overall appearance. Given that people are aware of the significance given to their appearance, more and more are choosing to manipulate it through cosmetic surgery or dress; it is also true that we are increasingly aware that appearance can be 'inauthentic' or artificial. The modern world, says Finkelstein, is thus a strangely contradictory one.

As I argue in chapters 3 and 4, increasing importance has been attached to the body and this can be traced back much earlier than the eighteenth century and could be deemed part of a longer 'civilizing process'. Elias (1978) points to the way in which the body became a site for marking out status and distinction in European court societies. In the court, social roles and status were indicated by the degree of bodily control, good manners and gentility exhibited, and knights could rise or fall on the degree to which they managed their bodies and maintained a 'civilized' appearance. Elias maintains that this civilizing process is never ending. It could be argued that the processes identified by him are the pre-history to Sennett's and Finkelstein's analysis of the different emphases placed upon bodily appearance in the seventeenth, eighteenth and nineteenth centuries. In contemporary society, not only are bodies bearers of status and distinction, as Bourdieu (1984) points out, but the body has increasingly come to be seen as the container of the self, signifying 'individuality' and 'authenticity'. Featherstone (1991b) catalogues the social and cultural changes that have brought about the 'performing self', which he argues emerged in the early twentieth century. He examines the extension of new forms of representation into everyday life, in particular photography and Hollywood films, arguing that these have, along with the cosmetics industry, placed increasing attention on bodily appearance and health, youth and beauty. According to Featherstone, this has brought about a modern self that is acutely interested in how it appears to others; appearance has become important in the pursuit of happiness and fulfilment. Shilling (1993) pursues a similar theme when he talks about the emergence of a number of 'body projects' in the late twentieth century, such as dieting and body building, which attempt to gain control over the appearance of the body and which are thought to enhance one's ability to achieve greater personal satisfaction out of life.

Another attempt to understand the nature of modernity and its impact upon the self centres on one important aspect of modernity noted by Bauman (1991), Davis (1992), Finkelstein (1991) and Giddens (1991), namely, ambivalence. The modern or postmodern world is a social maelstrom characterized by a loss of certainty, a world where 'all that is solid melts into air' (Berman 1983). For the modern self, this fragmentation results in anxiety and a crisis in identity, although not all individuals experience the modern as threatening or alienating. It is in such a world that fashion opens up possibilities for framing the self, at least momentarily, since fashion is always moving, never stable. As Davis (1992) argues, fashion provides symbols, however ephemeral, for fixing identity while simultaneously playing with the instability of identity. Baudelaire's *flâneur* (Baudelaire 1986; see also Benjamin 1989) and the dandy are examples of the modern self (discussed in chapter 4) who exploit the freedoms of the city and traverses its avenues and boulevards to see and be seen. However, clothing in the modern world is deployed to deal with the ambivalence although, as Davis (1992) argues, fashion does not produce permanent symbolic solutions, only temporary ones. The way in which identity is the site for work is a theme explored in the work of Giddens (1991) and Beck (1992). Although they do not deal specifically with dress, both posit the idea that modern identity has become a 'reflexive project'. The modern self is increasingly aware of itself, including its appearance, and able to intervene and act upon it.

These theories of modernity are insightful, offering accounts of how identity in contemporary society is constructed. They are particularly useful for understanding how fashion develops as a technique of dressing, employed self-consciously to construct an identity suitable for the modern stage. This literature on fashion and modernity is of considerable value in terms of understanding and historicizing practices of dress today. However, one problem is its failure to ground these ideas in empirical work on practices of the self. Tseëlon (1997) is one notable exception to the theoreticist tendency. She attempts not only to interpret the ways in which femininity has been constructed in Christian and other texts, for example but has also explored the way in which these ideas have framed women's understandings of their appearance and impacted upon their strategies of dress. She has therefore stepped into the field itself, interviewing women about their self-presentation and clothing choices, and therefore comes closest to understanding dress as 'situated practice'.

Empirical Approaches

The two broad theoretical approaches examined above tend to theorize but not to investigate dress in everyday life empirically. The two bodies of literature that have conducted empirical work on practices surrounding dress are anthropology and social psychology.

The ethnographic approach adopted by anthropology has resulted in detailed and grounded accounts of the meanings and practices of dress within particular cultural contexts. For example, work has been conducted on the construction of gender among the British community in colonial India (Callaway 1992), the meanings surrounding maternity wear (Bailey 1992), the meanings given to cloth in different cultures (Weiner and Schnieder 1991), and the practices of veiling in Egypt by women white-collar workers (Hoodfar 1991). These studies all pay close attention to the culturally specific meanings and practices of dress within a particular context. Hoodfar, for example, shows how veiling practice in Iran is very different from that of women in Egypt, demonstrating the complexity of this practice.

While it would be inappropriate to generalize across all these studies, since their value comes precisely from the fact that they deal with the specificities of dress in different contexts, one thing they do share is an interest in the local practices surrounding dress. These accounts are quite different from structuralist accounts of fashion in that they are concerned with the meanings of dress as they are understood and lived by a group. Unlike the semiotician, the ethnographic researcher does not stand outside or at a distance, but builds up a picture of dress practice from observation and engagement. Since they are accounts of dress practices in non-western cultures, however, they are not intended to contribute to the understanding of dress in the west. For this, one has to look to social psychology, where some detailed studies have been carried out.

Social psychology is interested in dress in terms of how it is utilized by the individual and what role it plays in interpersonal communication. Tseëlon (1997), for example, is concerned with how individual women dress and explores the constraints on their choices. There is also a small body of literature on the issues at stake in female professional dress. Two studies on female professional dress are brought together in a collection edited by Soloman (1985): Cash (1985) and Ericksen and Joseph (1985). These studies adopt a (rather crude) methodological framework of hypothesis testing, starting with a particular 'problem' or question. For Cash the problem is 'the impact of grooming style on the evaluation of women in management'; for Ericksen and Joseph it is 'achievement motivation and clothing preferences of white collar working women'. Ericksen and Joseph propose that 'achievement motivated white collar working women wear business like costumes more than their non-achievement motivated counterparts' (1985: 357) and this hypothesis is then tested by large-scale questionnaire-based surveys and the testing of images of women in different kinds of outfit. Such psychological studies are, however, highly problematic. The framework of hypothesis testing is flawed: the methods are naive and there is no critical reflection upon the methodology, which is taken to gain access unproblematically to the 'truth' of female white-collar dress. Such accounts are also flawed in that they do not give any account of the subjective meanings of dress. These approaches are therefore of little sociological relevance to a study of fashion and dress.

This chapter has set out to examine the literature on fashion, dress and adornment and has sought to point out the strengths and weaknesses of various approaches. It has also explored the complex relationship of fashion and dress and examined how the various bodies of literature distinguish between both. I have argued that, in general, early theories of fashion and fashion change tended to be reductive and mechanistic while the literature on modernity has avoided such over-simplistic accounts, framing the role played by fashion in contemporary culture by giving a more complex account of modern society. However, these accounts tend to be theoreticist and do not address the way in which dress is lived and experienced. A further problem with much of this literature is the tendency to neglect the essentially embodied nature of dress. Wilson (1985) has acknowledged the body to some extent in her account of fashion, recognizing that dress is 'incomplete' without the body. However, in general, the tendency to theorize has resulted in a neglect or 'bracketing off' of the body and embodiment. As argued in chapter 1, the body and embodiment are crucial to the understanding of fashion and dress. Fashion is an important contemporary site for discourses on the body and plays an important role in framing particular practices of dress, along with a host of other social factors. I also argue that dress is a necessary aspect of socialization and from babyhood, individuals are called upon to turn to and act upon their bodies in particular ways. Discourses on fashion and practices of dress therefore form an important component of culture, crucial to the micro-order of daily life (imagine what would happen if you walked into your local supermarket stark naked) and crucial to one's relationship with self and others. A sociology of dress as situated bodily practice aims to give an account of dress within everyday life that is not reductive or theoretically abstract, but theoretically complex and empirically grounded.

3

Fashion, Dress and Social Change

In order to understand fashion it is necessary to consider what sort of social conditions are necessary for its emergence and what place it occupies within modern culture. Fashion has been embedded within the culture of Europe for many centuries, a feature of European modernity which, while seemingly trivial, 'touches on every issue – raw materials, production processes, manufacturing costs, cultural stability...and social hierarchy' (Braudel 1981: 311). As well as analysing the particular social conditions for its emergence, it is also important to consider how fashion has been thought and written about since it has attracted the attention of many writers, intellectuals, moralists, clergymen and historians who have discussed, criticized and often condemned fashion and in doing so, given us some idea of its place within the unfolding modern society. Fashion has been accorded significance in the development of class: as Fernand Braudel argues, 'subject to incessant change, costume everywhere is a persistent reminder of social position' (1981: 311). In particular, it has been seen to play a part in the challenge to old hierarchies and power structures made by a newly emerging capitalist class. Sumptuary laws and discourses on luxury and taste illustrate the threat fashion posed to the old aristocratic order which saw its own power and influence diminished by the *nouveau riche*. Fashion has also been seen to articulate gender and sexual difference, gradually becoming associated with femininity and frivolity; a fact which may go some way to explaining why it has been attacked and condemned as well as marginalized within much social theory.

This chapter aims to give an historical account of fashion but not in terms of a straightforward chronology of fashionable dress as there are plenty of histories which give a detailed account of fashion changes over time. Instead, the chapter focuses on the recurring themes in the literature on fashion, exploring the relationship between fashion and social change, as well as suggesting how the body and its relationship to dress has been understood at different times. In order to do this some chronology is needed to explore the social, industrial and technical conditions required for the development of fashion at particular times. It is also necessary in order to situate debates about fashion, dress and the body within their historical context, to examine what historical circumstances frame these discourses at particular moments.

Fashion and Social Change

Before embarking on this historical excursion it is necessary first to consider what constitutes good fashion history, and indeed, to reflect on the relationship between fashion and society. Common sense dictates a link between the two but precisely how is it formed? What sort of society produces a fashion system or systems? What historical, social, technological and cultural conditions are necessary for the continual development of fashion? And what of fashion's relationship to the surrounding culture – does it, as some would argue, move with and reflect the *Zeitgeist*?

To a social theorist interested in the uses, meanings and practices of fashion and the relationship of fashion to everyday dress, fashion history is a source of some disappointment. Traditional accounts of fashion have tended towards description as opposed to analysis or explanation. These histories focus on the details of dress, the development of the buttonhole, the changing shape of the corset, the dropping and raising of hemlines, in order to provide a chronology of fashion and fashion change. Christopher Breward (1994), who is critical of such histories, argues that they neglect the context and meanings of dress. However, he does suggest that criticisms levelled at such histories are sometimes unwarranted and perhaps unfair. Fashion history arose out of art history as one means of authenticating paintings and this explains the emphasis on chronology and the attention to detail. He also notes that such rich and painstaking detail often provides invaluable documentary evidence. However, he argues that fashion needs to be placed in the context of historical, technological and cultural change and this requires going beyond the terms of aesthetics.

Breward (1994) is also aware of the problems of historical evidence used by historians of fashion, namely, visual and literary representations. While sculpture, paintings, engravings and literary texts are important sources of information, one needs to be careful when connecting the dress they describe with the prevailing culture. The interpretation of historical evidence requires sensitivity to the fact that representations of fashion and dress are not neutral descriptions. For example, paintings of royalty and gentry in their finery present idealized versions of dress, flatter the sitter and generally provide a representation of him or her congruous with their status and power. Representations of peasants might idealize peasant life, as in Romantic literature and painting, or might portray them as idle or debauched, as in the paintings of Brueghel.

A further problem that needs to be addressed when considering the relationship of fashion to society is that of causation. As argued in chapter 2, when fashion histories do try to explain and analyse fashion change there is a tendency for the historian to ask 'why' questions and seek out the causes of fashion by reference to some all-inclusive force: the *Zeitgeist*, the 'shifting erogenous zone', emulation. Of these, theories of emulation have been the most influential and have become very much embedded within accounts of fashion (McKendrick et al. 1983, Veblen 1953, Simmel 1971). For this reason, such theories will be given greater attention in the following chapter (and in chapter 7).

The question of why fashion changes as it does is answered by some authors with reference to *Zeitgeist* (e.g. Ditcher 1985). This approach argues that fashion responds to social and political changes, reflecting and reproducing these changes. However, there are numerous problems with this approach. One problem is that such accounts tend to over-simplify fashion which focuses on those styles that seem to correspond with social change while neglecting styles which do not. However, dress often fails to mirror social climate, as Bell (1976), Wilson (1985) and Steele (1985) argue. Valerie Steele suggests that fashion 'has an internal dynamic of its own that is only very gradually and tangentially affected by social change within the wider culture'; she goes on to say, 'fashion is not a power unto itself, but the principal dynamic of fashion is an internal one . . . Roots of change in fashion *precede* the great event – be it the French Revolution or the First World War' (1985: 5).

Events such as wars might contribute to an understanding of how and why certain styles get adopted on a wide scale but they do not explain how such styles originated. Fashion does not directly or simplistically reflect the times; the fact remains that it is always and everywhere situated within a society and culture. How then can one analyse the relationship between fashion and social and cultural life in a way that avoids the problems discussed above? There are a number of significant questions to consider: what stimulated the development of fashion in Europe and what conditions have served to promote its spread to more and more of the population? To put it another way, what, if anything, can fashion tell us about the society in which it emerges? Can it shed any light on the forms of social order in modern society, for example, formations of class and gender or other forms of identity in modern society? Given that clothing is intimately linked to the body, what is the relationship of fashion styles and fashion change to changing notions of embodiment and changing discourses on the body, appearance and identity? There are no simple answers to these questions precisely *because* fashion is embedded within culture and cannot be isolated as an independent variable. Indeed, one further problem with fashion histories is that they are often prone to isolate fashion change from the rest of the society in which it is found. A sociological approach to the study of fashion is one that situates it within context and looks at the social, political, technological discourses and practices surrounding it, as well as at the prevailing aesthetic discourses framing it. Breward (1994) provides an excellent account of fashion which situates it firmly within a range of social and cultural developments, as does Steele (1988). The following summary and analysis of fashion owes much to their insights. In addition, numerous histories of consumption have brought together economics, politics and culture to suggest some of the ways in which the idea of fashion and the extension of fashionable commodities became an important feature in the development of modern European consumer culture. This literature focuses primarily on the eighteenth century, when a 'consumer revolution' is said to have occurred. However, the idea of fashion goes back much further and we will begin by discussing its emergence in medieval society.

The Beginnings of Fashion

Stylistic innovation has not always existed in Europe and it is by no means universal even today, despite the efforts of global capitalism to extend the reaches of its markets. Very particular social and historical conditions promoted the emergence of fashion and these conditions cannot be said to exist in all places at all times. The development of medieval and Renaissance court society, the expansion in trade across the globe, the emergence of new social classes, and the growth of city life, all played a part in the development of a system of dress based upon continual change. While pinpointing exact dates is always difficult, if not impossible, it is possible to identify a number of general periods as significant in the development of fashion. One can go back as far as the fourteenth century to find the first traces of fashion although 'one cannot really talk of fashion becoming all-powerful before about 1700' (Braudel 1981: 316) and it is not until even later that fashion could be said to be widely available to all, working classes included. However, the *idea* of fashion may have been around longer: the medieval historian Orderic Vitalis (1075–1142) condemned what he saw as the foolishness of fashion, arguing that 'the old way of dressing has been almost completely thrown over by the new inventions' (in Braudel 1981: 317). Braudel argues, however, that Vitalis was probably exaggerating since the shape of clothes 'did not fundamentally alter' during this period and it was some centuries later before fashion as we would recognize it developed. One important contrast between the dress that emerged in medieval Europe and that worn by the 'ancients' is between 'fitted' and 'draped' clothes. Modern clothing falls into the first category and requires stitching, while dress in ancient civilizations was generally made out of simple lengths of fabric tied in elaborate ways. The draped cloth would have hung from the shoulder or the waist and was considered a mark of civilization: indeed tailored clothing was considered 'barbaric' in Roman times (Laver 1995).

The key to the emergence and development of fashion seems to be social change: fashion emerges in societies which have some social mobility rather than a fixed and stable class structure. For Braudel, as for other historians and writers on fashion (Bell 1976, Breward 1994, Wilson 1985), a society that remains stable is less likely to exhibit changes in dress than one which sees social mobility. It is for this reason that feudal society in Europe did not exhibit fashion as we know it today. As Braudel puts it, 'if a society remained more or less stable, fashion was less likely to change – and this could be true at all levels, even the highest in established hierarchies' (1981: 312). So, for example, in ancient China the dress of the mandarin remained constant from Peking to Szechuan for many generations (Braudel 1981) while the kimono hardly changed for centuries in traditional Japanese society, which Braudel describes as 'conservative'. Steele does not entirely agree with this argument: 'far from having "ancient" and "unchanging" costumes, many eastern cultures were characterized by intense (if restricted) fashion competition' (1988: 19). However she concedes that in both east and west during the thirteenth and early fourteenth centuries, the choice of clothing was restricted according to rank and that the movement of fashion was kept in check because of a resistance to movement in hierarchical societies. It would therefore seem that limited stylistic change might occur in ancient societies but fashion in the modern sense of constant stylistic change exists only where there is more fluidity in the class hierarchy. Thus, as Steele argues, 'from the fourteenth century onwards, in both the courts and cities of Europe, there was an inexorable movement toward fashion-orientated behaviour' (1988: 19).

The fashionable society for Braudel is the society which desires to shape and modify the world, breaking with tradition and seeking the new. Innovation, which he argues is 'the source of all progress', stems from a 'restlessness which may express itself in such trifles as dress, the shape of shoes and hairstyles' (1981: 24). However, he does not see fashion as 'trivial', but notes that 'the future was to belong to the societies fickle enough to care about the changing colours, materials and shapes of costume' (1981: 323). This restlessness could be found initially in Italy, probably the birthplace of fashion 'where it is closely associated with the rise of cities – and with the rising middle class' (Steele 1988: 17); this according to Steele (1988), was part of a broader cultural Renaissance, although the court in Burgundy and France acquired important positions within the world of fashion around the same time (Bradley 1955). The demise of the feudal system during the fourteenth and fifteenth centuries more or less coincided with the emergence of new merchant classes, whose wealth stemmed not from inherited land, but from trade, often on an international scale, with a concomitant effect on the promotion of fashion. It would seem that during the fourteenth century there was a sudden change in dress styles, particularly for men, and a speeding up of style changes among the nobility. Between 1300 and 1500 men's and women's dress continued to become looser and simpler, but there was also the beginnings of fitted dress, pulling in tighter to the body (Breward 1994). Around 1350 the tunic worn by upper-class men shortened dramatically and, together with tight hose on the legs, revealed more of the male form than ever before, much to the dismay of the old and the conservative, who considered it scandalously indecent (Braudel 1981). The chronicler Guillaume de Nangis notes how 'men, in particular, noblemen and their squires, and a few bourgeois and their servants, took to wearing tunics so short and tight that they revealed what modesty bid us to hide' (in Braudel 1981: 317).

This style of dress seems to have originated from military dress, which had developed a short plate of armour over the chest in place of long chain mail (Steele 1988). Women's dress also changed, fitting closer to the body and becoming quite elaborate, while a low *décolletage* provided further cause for outrage. The fact that clothing is by its nature close to the body, the 'mere flesh' that is the seat of desires and longings both gastronomic and sexual, has not surprisingly given rise to much religious condemnation over the centuries. The body in Christian teachings is the source of distraction from Godly thoughts and is to be mortified and chastised into submission. Luxurious dress, dress which reveals parts of the body, and changing fashions which attract the eye and distract the soul, are therefore condemned, particularly, by the Puritans of the Reformation. Fashionable dress has therefore been a matter for much moral discourse and, with the development of more modern notions of sexuality, is increasingly condemned as sinful. However, although seeming to deny the body, as Breward (1994) argues, asceticism draws attention to the body (hence also bodily desires and sexuality) in a similar way to the cut of cloth, except that the emphasis is negative as opposed to positive. (For further detail on the debates about dress, sexuality and gender, see chapters 5 and 6 below.)

Throughout the fifteenth century, dress became more and more exaggerated: large hats, long sleeves and long, trailing gowns. However, while the standard narrative of the birth of fashion tends to consider the link between the end of feudalism and the emergence of a new class system, Breward (1994) cautions us from taking this for granted. This kind of descriptive history comes from representations depicted by and for the rich and places a high degree of emphasis upon status. Thus, argues Breward, if one can say that a moment for the birth of fashion can be found in the fourteenth century it describes the emergence of fashion only for the very rich; 'what is missing from such a narrative is any explanation or description either of variety within such a system' when it is likely that other systems of clothing continued 'which while not dominant in terms of wealth and status, must have presented similar shifting codes and styles' (1994: 23). In accounts of peasant dress, it is the functional rather than the symbolic aspects that dominate, although Breward also draws attention to the concern with colour and quality.

Numerous social, cultural and technological changes encouraged the development of fashion for the elite. Breward notes how the manufacture of garments from preparation of raw material to alterations in garment was largely in the hands of women until the late Middle Ages. This arrangement was broken down by the emergence of male-dominated guilds and systems of apprenticeship for weavers and other textile workers which laid the foundations for the development of fashion. This proto-capitalist organization moved the production of clothing out of the home and 'preceded speeding up of fashion change in the following century' (Breward 1994: 30–1).

Thereafter, female labourers were consigned to unskilled production and would, in later centuries, find themselves in 'sweated' working conditions (see chapter 7).

The expansion in the trade of cloth as well as numerous technological developments, such as the spinning-wheel, also helped to stimulate fashion in Europe, increasing the choice and availability of different sorts of fabric. The Crusades of the eleventh, twelfth and thirteenth centuries brought Europe into contact with Eastern civilizations, and there was considerable excitement about the new silks and furs. According to Said (1985) the European encounter with the 'exotic Other' played an important part in the formation of the identities of both Occident and Orient over the next few centuries, as well as shaping the destiny of many countries whose natural resources were plundered for cheap raw materials and commodities which would become increasingly common in the households of Europe. Over the course of the fourteenth and fifteenth centuries, trade routes criss-crossed Europe and beyond, carrying silk and cotton from Italy and wool from England to different corners of the continent. This expansion in world trade played its part in the establishment of fashion: 'the dramatic evolution of fashion from the mid fourteenth century is certainly resonant with the heightened language of commerce and a new material worth that arguably takes clothing into the sphere of a "modern" fashion system' (Breward 1994: 22). Italy of the fourteenth century with its trade in silks and cotton could be described as 'proto-capitalist': according to Steele (1988), the structure of Renaissance city-states in Italy enabled the development of fashion and helped to disseminate it in a way that would not be possible in a remote place. Breward further argues that the fashionable body is closely associated with the growing city 'as focus of social interaction and display and an allied sense of cosmopolitanism' (1994: 35). (The relationship between fashion and city life is examined in chapter 4.) In addition to the newly emerging city, the court also provided a platform for fashion and the court society, most notably in seventeenth- and eighteenth-century France, and was to take on particular significance in the setting of fashions.

Class, Status and Power in Late Medieval and Early Modern Culture

During the fourteenth and fifteenth centuries, power across Europe became increasingly concentrated on the courts, which sought to tame and co-ordinate territorial domination. While court societies developed, there was a progressive reduction of violence and factional fighting as power became increasingly monopolized within the hands of noblemen and, more importantly, monarchs:

> royal courts were centres of national power, arenas where the struggles and alliances between monarchs and nobility were played out. Increasingly, as kings tried to reduce the military might of their most powerful subjects and as nobles came to accept humanist ideas that valued learning and taste as much as martial prowess, courts became centres of culture and refinement. (Brewer 1997: 4)

The courts played an important role in the 'civilizing process' by engendering new codes of corporeality. The 'animalistic' functions of the body were progressively constrained: codes and rules were developed for eating and sleeping and even for defecating and reproduction, functions which had previously been openly conducted and discussed, but were now increasingly 'hidden away' as they became subject to shame and embarrassment. Life at court demanded greater emotional control than had existed in early medieval society and instituted more and more finely differentiated codes of behaviour. This development is detailed by Norbert Elias in the first volume of *The History of Manners*, entitled *The Civilizing Process* (1978). Elias's evidence is taken from the writings of various fifteenth- and sixteenth-century social commentators, in particular Erasmus, whose popular treatise on manners 'On Civility in Children', published in 1530, details the sorts of body management required at court. The prohibitions he records about eating, sleeping and other such matters (don't blow your nose on the tablecloth; don't throw your bone in the communal pot after gnawing at it and so on) shed light on some of the ways in which ('uncivilized') bodies must have behaved at the time and illustrate the sorts of constraints increasingly imposed upon bodies over the course of the 'civilizing process', a process which for Elias (1978) is never ending.

During the shift from medieval to Renaissance court society the body increasingly became the bearer of social value, carrying information about a person's social status. The court societies of this period enjoyed relative social mobility: a courtier or knight could catch the eye of the king and curry favour by illustrating good taste, manners and deportment. As Elias puts it:

> To keep one's place in the intense competition for importance at court, to avoid being exposed to scorn, contempt, loss of prestige, one must subordinate one's appearance and gestures, in short oneself, to the fluctuating norms of court society that increasingly emphasise the

difference, the distinction of the people belonging to it. One *must* wear certain materials and certain shoes. One *must* move in certain ways characteristic of people belonging to court society. Even smiling is shaped by court custom. (1978: 231–2)

In such a society as this, based on relative social mobility, new relationships between clothing, appearance and identity emerged and fashion played an increasingly significant role in the life of the court. According to Breward, the pervasiveness of fashion had direct impact on the emergence of the individual's 'sense of self-knowledge': in late medieval society 'the body was prioritized as the dwelling place of the soul' (1994: 34). Increasingly, in the court, and also in the city, appearance was used as a 'classifying tool', a means of marking out class distinctions in which dress played a crucial part. Notions of 'good taste' and refinement were emphasized and embodied in the courtier 'in his manners and elegant comportment – the gesture of a hand, the subtlety of a bow, a witty remark – but also in the objects with which he surrounded himself' (Brewer 1997: 4).

For Breward (1994), this courtly society and the fashions emerging out of it, emphasized symbolic display which put the body at a distance from the clothing worn. Beneath acres of elaborate fabric the body was hardly visible: clothes caught the eye because of their richness and grandeur, not because they revealed the body. 'The existence of skin and the concrete conception of the body were largely forgotten in the presence of the coverings of wool and fur... The envelope assumed the role of the body' (Vigarello in Breward 1994: 34). The relationship between body and clothing is also described by Sennett (1977), who argues that up until around the mid-eighteenth century the body of the court aristocrat was something like a mannequin (see below). Well-established conventions of dress would indicate one's position within the class structure or one's membership of a guild, rather than articulating individuality or inner feelings. Thus, elaboration, artifice or even unnaturalness came to characterize styles of dress that put the body at some distance from the clothes.

The spread of fashion during the Middle Ages was very uneven. Only the rich could afford to participate fully in fashion and this created some uniformity in dress among the elite across Europe, although cultural variations did also emerge. Peasant dress changed little, but affluence among merchants and traders enabled them to participate slightly in fashion. From Italy, fashion spread to the court of Burgundy, the most splendid in Europe, prefiguring the stature of Versailles (Steele 1988). The Burgundian dukes under the house of Valois (1364–1477) were far wealthier than their counterparts in

Versailles or Paris and this was reflected in dress. Certain colours, in particular red and purple, were restricted to the ruling class, although this was progressively challenged. Such sumptuary laws indicate the link between fashion and social class: fashion not only emerges in societies with looser class structures, but itself becomes a site of class conflict:

> by the fourteenth century, status had come to be based less on the traditional standard of birth than on visible and acquirable markers of social identity, such as civic offices, land holdings, houses, household furnishings, coats of arms, seals and apparel. As a result, the regulation of these material status signifiers came under increasingly greater scrutiny. (Sponsler in Emberley 1998: 46)

Sumptuary laws aimed to regulate consumption from food to clothing and took a number of forms, ranging from Acts of Parliament to proclamations from monarchs and local ordinances. Beginning in the Middle Ages with Edward III (1327–77) almost all monarchs in Britain until the seventeenth century introduced some legislation on consumption (Emberley 1998). Thus as Slater notes: 'the *ancien régime* inherited a feudal idea, if no longer quite the actuality, of a social structure comprising fixed and stable status: a world in which social position is ascribed by birth and is fixed as part of a cosmological order' (1997: 29–30).

Increasingly during the late Middle Ages and through the Renaissance, those at the top end of the class structure sought to police and regulate fashion, while those lower down periodically challenged or simply flouted such regulation. Among the motivations behind sumptuary laws was a concern to preserve class distinctions, enabling identification of persons at a glance. They also served to preserve certain commodities for the wealthy, restricting symbolic displays of wealth to the property and land-owning classes. In addition, sumptuary laws attempted to restrict the import of luxury goods from abroad and so protect the interests of merchants at home. However, these laws do not describe what people actually wore and it is difficult to know to what extent such laws were enforced or followed. What they show is the competing interests at work in the area of consumption and how class and status had become matters of concern requiring political intervention. As status became more fluid and more accessible, it follows that clothing became the target of political elites attempting to regulate such status. For this reason, 'clothing laws are crucial texts in the dynamics of social change and social control in late medieval England' (Sponsler in Emberley 1998: 46). Fashion tells a tale of class struggle, albeit heavily mediated. Many condemnations of fashion can be explained as reactions by some intellectuals towards the breakdown of traditional order and the loss of their own power and status as the *nouveaux riches* became able to purchase the same signifiers of status without the inherited right to do so.

Over the course of these centuries concern about fashion was expressed not just in terms of extravagance, which had previously been seen to break down the social order of the classes, but also with the breakdown of moral order. In her analysis of sumptuary legislation on furs, Julia Emberley argues that 'the hierarchy of furs and social positions created by these regulatory acts also influenced notions of sexual propriety among different classes of women and contributed to the construction of feminine and masculine genders and sexual differences between men and women' (1998: 9). In terms of sexual morality, the distinction between the 'respectable' and the 'fallen' woman was particularly significant. A British parliamentary ordinance of 1355 attempted to police this distinction, forbidding prostitutes to wear fur. It read: 'no known whore should weare from henceforth any hood, except reyed or striped of divers colors, nor furre, but garments reversed or turned the wrong side outward upon paine to forfeit the same' (in Emberley 1998: 54).

Fashion in the Renaissance Court

While medieval Europe became increasingly fragmented, different centres of fashion rather than a single capital came to be developed (Steele 1988). In particular, fashion began to take on a distinctly nationalist character, with styles of dress becoming associated with different European courts. Italy maintained its importance as the home of the Renaissance but after 1492 and Columbus's discovery of the Americas, Spain became particularly influential in political and economic terms and also, not surprisingly, in terms of fashion. England under Henry VIII had grown in importance as a trading nation and this new prosperity served to enhance her status abroad. Catherine of Aragon and her entourage are credited with introducing the Spanish farthingale skirt to the English court and it was worn by all but peasant and working-class women. However, this transmission of fashions from abroad was sometimes commented upon and sometimes seen as a problem. The English dramatist Thomas Dekker (*c.* 1570–1632) commented in his *Seven Deadly Sins* that

> the Englishman's dress is like a traitor's body that hath been hanged, drawn, and quartered, and is set up in various places; 'his cod-piece is

in Denmark, the collar of his doublet and the belly in France; the wing and narrow sleeve in Italy; the short waist hangs over a Dutch butcher's stall in Utrecht; his huge slops speak Spanishly' . . . And thus we that mock every nation for keeping of one fashion, yet steal patches from every one of them to piece out our pride. (quoted in Braudel 1981: 321)

The simile of the 'traitor's body' in this quotation highlights a concern that the consumption of goods from abroad threatened the body politic of the nation; it was treachery against the trade interest of one's own country. As Slater puts it, 'the health of the body politic is represented by the healthy household of the sovereign. Consumption will tend to deplete this wealth by drawing on imports' (1997: 176). This mercantile line of thought is not surprising given the importance of trade to England at this time. London had established itself by the mid-sixteenth century as a major trading port, which developed through the seventeenth and eighteenth centuries, and therefore also as a centre for consumption and style.

As such cities as London and Paris grew wealthier – and, indeed, as the population of cities increased – it became more and more difficult to know the class of people one met. By the same token sumptuary laws became ineffectual: how can one know when a person is dressing above his or her station in a city of strangers? According to Sekora (1977), sumptuary laws responded to fears about breakdown of economic order or morality if members of the lower classes consumed goods above their basic needs or station in life. Breward (1994) notes that there is some evidence to suggest that by 1560 the concerns of clergymen and moralists about the breakdown of order was having an effect on the enforcement of sumptuary laws. This contrasts with accounts of unbridled fashion consumption during the same period but for Breward these two accounts are not in contradiction – sumptuary laws were always difficult if not impossible to enforce and suggest the prevalence of fashion rather than its suppression. If, as Breward suggests, there was some attempt to enforce such laws more vigorously in the sixteenth century, this would suggest that fashion had indeed become more widespread and therefore more threatening.

The nature of elite modes of dress at the end of the sixteenth century is encapsulated in the notions of elaboration, excess and artifice. Great importance was attached to appearance and its manipulation in the Renaissance and there was an emphasis on art and creativity in the construction of outward appearance. The style of dress for men and women 'polarised into aggressive masculinity, accentuated at the shoulders and throwing emphasis on to the narrow hips, muscular legs and padded codpiece, contrasted with an angular femininity, exemplified through a balanced, symmetrical pairing of bodice and skirt' (Breward 1994: 44).

Men's and women's clothing was elaborate and stiff – for both sexes the neck was particularly encumbered with stiff white collars. Slashing and embroidery could be found on all wealthy male and female garments. This style remained the same until the early seventeenth century though changes in cut and colour made fashions 'seem to take on their own self-contained momentum' (Breward 1994: 52). These minute details in dress seemed to preoccupy the Elizabethans. Clothing was governed by complex codes both hidden and blatant which could be decoded only by those with genteel refinement: 'the importance of overt and indirect symbolism in dress to Elizabethans across the social scale is difficult to over-estimate' (Breward 1994: 63). Dress was not about individual choice but 'recognition and comprehension of a complex set of formal visual codes' (1994: 65). For example, there was a highly developed language of colours in heraldry and coats of arms were one means of marking out family status. For Breward, the overriding emphasis on the symbolic and the high degree of artificiality and elaboration in elite dress lend an archaic quality to current perceptions of Elizabethan dress, derived mainly from paintings. In portraits of Queen Elizabeth I, for example, her dress is so elaborate as to obscure the body altogether:

> the exaggerated sleeves and the gigantic skirt efface between them all other indications of a human body...the effect of the richly lined oversleeves is of a sumptuous casing which, without attributing to the Queen anything so specific as broad shoulders (she had, indeed, no *bones* at all), extends the dimensions of the figure to make of the arms an anatomically improbable, embracing, encompassing semi-circle. (Belsey and Belsey 1990: 11)

The body is lost in the clothing which bears little relationship to it; the line and contours of the limbs almost completely obscured.

Historical evidence from portraiture and etiquette books has isolated the mid- to late sixteenth century as 'a significant moment of change in relation to attitudes towards individuality and a new sense of self' (Breward 1994: 69). According to Greenblatt, 'in the sixteenth century there appears to be an increased self-consciousness about the fashioning of human identity as manipulable, artful process'; although the word 'fashion' had long been in use 'as a term for the action or process of making, for particular features or appearance,

for a distinct style or patter…it is in the sixteenth century that
"fashion" seems to come into wide currency as a way of designating
the forming of a self'. This fashioning 'may suggest the achievement
of…a distinctive personality, a characteristic address to the world, a
consistent mode of perceiving and behaving' (1980: 2). Greenblatt
cites the poets and writers of this period, such as Spenser and
Shakespeare, as embodiments of the new self-fashioned gentleman.
In manuals on etiquette and manners one finds further evidence of a
new concern with the body, its decoration and deportment: the

Miniature of Queen Elizabeth I by Nicholas Hilliard (1547–1619), showing how the body
was a mere mannequin to the heavy and elaborate clothes which obscure and abstract it.
Reproduced with the kind permission of the Trustees of the Victoria and Albert Museum.

'gentleman's body emerges as a totality to be continuously and minutely governed according to principles of grace and decorum' (Bryson 1990: 141). Such fashioning was not restricted to men: Elizabeth I was particularly artful in her construction and representation of herself as a great, almost mystical being, a virgin queen and mother to England. Indeed, as Greenblatt notes, her ability to turn her 'potentially disastrous sexual disadvantage' (1980: 167) into a cult of secular virginity is evidence of her extraordinary ability to fashion her identity. George Gower's portrait of her at the time of the Spanish Armada is among those to proclaim 'the sovereignty and the right to rule: the splendour of her appearance, her vision and her *self*-control are evidence of the majesty and the authority which inhere in the person of the Queen' (Belsey and Belsey 1990: 15).

Moralists complained that overt concern with fashionable dress indicated vanity and unfettered individualism incompatible with class and duty. This was more marked in the city than in the country, where traditions were more likely to encourage people to 'know their place' in the social hierarchy. Contemporary pamphlets and treatises focus on declining standards in metropolitan centres and illustrate the sorts of concern expressed by some in the sixteenth century about fashion and sartorial display (Breward 1994). For example, excessive interest in clothing is singled out by some writers as a moral problem that upsets the 'natural' order of things, both the 'natural' hierarchies of class and the moral propriety of a good, God-fearing society.

Judaeo-Christian attitudes towards the body have also left an indelible mark on the progress of fashion. Nonconformists from the time of Martin Luther to Oliver Cromwell reacted against what they saw as the excesses of Rome and condemned sartorial extravagance. The sombre clothing of the Reformation continued in Protestant countries, particularly in Holland, and was carried to the New World, where it was embodied in such religious communities as the Shakers. However, with the growing influence of Spain, the Spanish style, dark, formal and highly elaborate, swept through much of Protestant Northern Europe as part of the Counter-Reformation. It was adopted by most European courts; the marriage of Mary Tudor to Philip II of Spain in 1554 ensured its widespread adoption in courtly circles. There were many who resisted the style as wicked and excessive, objections being at their strongest in Germany.

During the final decade of the Elizabethan period another feature developed, that of naturalism in dress. People sitting for their portraits in the 1590s 'are beginning to want to see themselves depicted less as symbols and more as vehicles of human emotions and feeling'

(Strong in Breward 1994: 68). This is manifest in the sitters' untidy appearance and a preference for pastoral settings which 'signifies most of all . . . the ability of clothing to reflect a new sense of "private self" as much as it symbolised public status and history' (1994: 69).

Fashion in the Seventeenth Century

The seventeenth century was one of massive political and religious upheaval. The Thirty Years' War exposed the tension between Catholics and Protestant states which struggled for dominance not just in Europe, but the colonies abroad. The reign of Charles I represented the 'English apotheosis of . . . Renaissance kingship' (Brewer 1997: 5). The court was as rich and extravagant as it was large and sprawling and was the focus of rituals, displays, ceremonies and tableaux, some of which were performed by the king and queen themselves before an audience of courtiers (Brewer 1997). Male and female clothing was rich and elaborate – the padding, starch and drapes of varying textures from velvet through to lace obscured the body. The contrast between this and Oliver Cromwell's rule is sharp and the Civil War is often seen as a clash of straight-laced Puritans and Roundheads and flamboyant Cavaliers and Royalists. The Puritans under Cromwell swept away the luxurious and decadent styles of James I and Charles I and introduced sombre, undecorated dress: face patches, for example, were banned. In their ideology, moral rectitude was closely linked to plain dress and can be seen most clearly in the austere style of the Quakers. However, these are simplistic characterizations and it makes more sense to look at wider social and political changes, in particular the evolution of the private sphere and developing ideas about the individual which informed attitudes to appearance and consumption. According to Campbell (1989, 1993), the Puritans, while seemingly anti-fashion and anti-consumption, brought about a change in attitudes which helped to promote modern hedonism and consumption, thereby stimulating the consumer revolution of the eighteenth century.

The return of the monarchy with the Restoration of Charles II in 1660 did not see the restoration of calm, but continuing religious and political strife. Charles II tried to emulate his father's opulent kingship and even looked to emulate the splendour of Louis XIV in France, but his court was 'a weak copy of the extravagant absolutist regime across the Channel' (Brewer 1997: 8). Dress remained opulent but elements of informality crept into both male and female dress. Gender divisions were lessened by the similarity of some aspects of dress: deep lace collars, long hair dramatically curled and high heels were worn by both sexes. The most distinctive development in male dress was the integration of doublet, jerkin and breeches into a unified whole, the tunic or coat; and a similar integration of female dress took place in the final decades of the century in the form of the mantua – based on night-dress – which linked the top or bodice to the skirt to make an entire gown (Breward 1994). These developments served to make the line of clothing more fluid and the body's contours more apparent.

As the balance of power shifted towards Holland and France, dual fashion paths developed in the French court and the Dutch bourgeoisie. The Dutch carried the stark black and white Catholic style of the Spanish into the next century – transforming it into a Protestant, bourgeois and urban style, suited to Calvinist religious ideology (Steele 1988). This style extended to the nineteenth century, becoming the 'uniform' of the bourgeoisie all over Europe, part of an attempt to redress the excesses of the aristocracy. Although the stark dress of the Dutch continued to dominate some parts of Europe, during the mid-seventeenth century the French court emerged as a powerful force in fashion. The court of Louis XIV established France as the supreme trend-setter among the elite in Europe, a position retained by that country until the mid-twentieth century. Although only five when he ascended the throne in 1643, 'when Louis came of age he ushered in an era of unprecedented extravagance and splendour, and Paris very shortly became the fashion capital of the world' (Bradley 1955: 193). Luxury, excess and elaboration, along with splendorous texture and colour, were to become the style of Versailles, not only in terms of dress, but in the architecture and interiors of the grand palace itself. Louis XIV, known as the 'Sun King' for his emblem of the sun and snake, was aware of the symbolic nature of clothing. As early as 1665 he recognized the potential importance of fashion to French industry: various attempts were made to protect French textiles from the rival luxury fashion industries in Italy and Holland, in particular, the promotion of silk weaving in France to challenge that of the Italians (Steele 1988); the heavy duties on foreign fabrics and precious metals along with incentives to help French manufacturers also served to stimulate the French fashion industry (Yarwood 1992). However, as Steele puts it, 'economics alone does not explain the shift from international Spanish black to modish French fashion' (1988: 23); more important than state support, argues Steele, was the power of the French court, consolidated by the marriage of Louis XIV to the Spanish infanta, Maria Theresa, in 1660 and leading to the triumph of French

Baroque splendour in the seventeenth and eighteenth centuries. While black and white remained dominant in other parts of Europe, particularly among Spanish noblemen and Dutch and English Puritans, sumptuary legislation in Louis XIV's court kept fashion in check and established complex codes of etiquette: clothing was restricted and regulated, gold and silver trimmings, for example, being reserved for the king's family and some favoured courtiers. Despite the rigid rules, which actually slowed down the pace of change in fashion, the styles of the French court were copied across Europe. In these days before the fashion magazine, fashion dolls transmitted the latest court fashions and acted as 'ambassadors'.

In contrast to the over-elaborate and formal style of court dress, often slow to change, a more genuinely modern fashion was emerging in the city of Paris (Steele 1988). Thousands of tailors worked to produce clothes for court but towards the end of Louis' reign, younger princesses and ladies revolted against the court style in favour of the new styles originating in Paris. Steele notes how on one occasion in 1715 the Duchesse d'Orléans and the Princesse de Conti presented Louis XIV with the newest fashion from Paris, to which he gave his approval. On the King's death that year, however, fashion came to be determined between individual ladies and dressmakers and this served to accelerate the pace of fashion. Nevertheless, with such figures as Mme de Pompadour and Mme du Barry and later Marie Antoinette as fashion setters for courtly, aristocratic dress in other European courts, the French court retained its prestige. The dominance of French, especially Parisian, fashion remained unchallenged until the mid-twentieth century.

Dress, Class and Social Identity in the Eighteenth Century

Compared with sixteenth- and seventeenth-century court society, the society emerging in the eighteenth was increasingly urban in style. London came to occupy an important place within the imagination, which is not surprising given that 'one in ten English people lived there; one in six spent part of their working life in the metropolis. Ten times larger than any other English city, it dwarfed the other British capitals . . . and with nearly 750,000 inhabitants at the mid-century, was the largest city in western Europe' (Brewer 1997: 28). The eighteenth century was an era of great sociability, when cities 'developed networks of sociability independent of direct royal control, places where strangers might regularly meet' (Sennett 1977: 17).

One might encounter others in the new pleasure gardens of Paris and London, or in the new streets that were developing for pedestrians, or in the numerous coffee bars and cafés where one could spend hours reading, chatting or simply observing others. Coffee-bar clubs like the influential Kit-Cat Club flourished between 1690 and 1720, encouraging regular discussions on literature, art, theatre and politics (Brewer 1997: 40). John Brewer notes how 'the Kit-Cat Club exemplifies the shift that took place in the early eighteenth century from court to city, from raffish courtier to polite man-about-town' (1997: 41). This shift can be perceived in the changing style of portraiture introduced into England at the time by Godfrey Kneller, who painted the portraits of the Kit-Cat Club members. 'There is none of the grand self-absorption of the court portrait; these are men engaged with society' (1997: 41–2).

'Society' became an object of attention and discussion for an increasing number of urbanites as well as the gentry in small provincial towns. Members of 'society' would go visiting, promenading and shopping, in settings ranging from pleasure parks and gardens, such as the Vauxhall or Ranelagh Pleasure Gardens, to theatres, exhibitions, grand shops, masquerades and balls held at assembly rooms across the country. These settings had their 'season' – Bath and London were visited at different times in the social calendar by the gentry living in the provinces. Although these activities were primarily the focus of attention for a small privileged set, activities such as promenading, once the preserve of the elite, were taking off as popular pastimes among wage labourers in the big cities, and the theatre, once a restricted form of entertainment, opened up to a wider audience than ever before (Brewer 1997). As Brewer notes, one's ability to participate in such cultural activities depended not just on having the price of a ticket, but on looking 'respectable'.

Patterns of consumption began to change with the increase in wealth and many historians have argued that there was something of a consumer revolution during the eighteenth century (Brewer 1997, Brewer and Porter 1993, Campbell 1989, McKendrick et al. 1983, Slater 1997, Weatherill 1993, 1996). With incomes rising 'it is likely that many had surplus disposable income; as this translated into higher consumer demand, growth in manufacturing was stimulated' (Porter 1990: 205–6). The commodities purchased were likely to be beyond necessity: table linens, silverware, pottery, clocks and furniture, along with personal adornments such as bonnets, parasols, handkerchiefs, gloves, perfume, watches. This expansion in consumer goods, alongside an expansion in 'society', opened up more opportunities for social display. The audiences at public settings 'made publicly visible their wealth, status, social and sexual charms' (Brewer 1997: 69) and the new consumer durables became a popular means to transmit such charms.

It is no surprise then that around this time the idea of emulation came to preoccupy social theorists and has since been put forward as an explanatory model to account for the consumer revolution in the eighteenth century (see in particular McKendrick et al. 1983). Theories of emulation propose that fashions start at the top of the social ladder and percolate down as the 'lower orders' consume elite fashions in an attempt to copy or emulate their 'betters'. Emulation was seen by contemporary philosophers and moralists as a problem since it was said to disrupt the natural or cosmological order of the universe wherein status is fixed and ordained by God. As the modern society of commerce swept away the old agrarian order, it brought with it new sources of status not dependent upon land and blood but money. New social groups – merchants, industrialists, the new middle classes – could afford to purchase, 'above their station', luxury items once exclusive to kings and nobility. In the eyes of traditionalists, this was seen as 'a form of sin, rebellion and insubordination against the proper order of the world, and represents moral, spiritual and political corruption' (Slater 1997: 69; see also Sekora 1977). Discussions about luxury, the control of sumptuosity illustrate this preoccupation with maintaining the boundaries of class and status in the face of change. However, while emulation is seen by some intellectuals as a sin and therefore a problem, it comes to form the basis of modern sentiment. Emulation for Adam Smith (Smith 1986) is the source of modern virtue since it is through the selfish pursuit of riches and status that the general wealth of a nation is increased. Moreover, for Smith, emulation encourages greater sympathy and sociability among people.

Emulation theories have since formed the backbone of many discussions of the eighteenth-century consumer revolution and they remain a dominant explanatory framework for understanding fashion ever since. For Slater, emulation is not a single theory but part of a vocabulary of modernity, 'a pre-occupation for western modernity from its start' (1997: 157). The idea of emulation, also known as the 'trickle-down' model, has been proposed by different theorists as an explanation for the extension of fashion in the eighteenth and nineteenth centuries (McKendrick et al. 1983, McCracken 1985, Veblen 1953), although Braudel (1981) also links it to the very origins of fashion in the fourteenth century. Veblen (1953) and Simmel (1971) are two of the commonly cited proponents of this framework and they both refer to fashionable dress in their accounts (see chapter 2).

In providing a neat and tidy account of fashion and fashion change, emulation has been immensely popular. However, emulation as a concept is very problematic. For one thing, this theory assumes rather too much based on little or no evidence (what is 'human nature' after all and how can we prove emulation to be 'natural'?). An example of how difficult it is to establish emulation as the basis for consumption can be illustrated by examining one 'fact' commonly noted by social commentators in the eighteenth century to support the idea, namely, that of the lady's maid who wore the grand clothes of her mistress. The maid in her finery was seen by some as a problem, an illustration of naked social ambition on the part of the maid to climb the social ladder or be mistaken for a lady. However, the sight of a servant girl's grand clothes may not, however, be traceable to her desire to emulate her mistress, as thought by some social commentators in the eighteenth century. First it should be noted that it was common practice for a mistress to pass 'hand-me-downs' to her female servants and these gifts would have been seen as part of her wages (Fine and Leopold 1993). Second, it is also true that maids often sold on clothes bequeathed to them in wills in the lucrative second-hand clothing market, 'the preference for cash (from selling hand-me-downs) over the pleasures to be had from keeping and wearing the master's old clothes' suggesting 'a definite limit to the allure of emulation', according to Fine and Leopold (1993: 126). Even when the clothes were kept and worn, Colin Campbell argues that we cannot assume this as evidence of emulation; to do so is to assume intentions which are not apparent in the mere act of wearing the fancy clothes. Indeed, even if emulation is the intention, he argues, we do not know what it is exactly she is emulating and why. In other words 'to dub an activity "emulative" is in this sense merely to begin the process of understanding' (Campbell 1993: 41). There may be a whole range of reasons why a maid would wear the clothes of her mistress, as Campbell notes:

> does the maid's intention to compete with her mistress in the style and opulence of her dress merely imply a desire to rival her in fashionableness or does it stem from a more general ambition to be considered her social equal? Is she seeking, through this emulative conduct, to impress her fellow servants, her family and friends, her mistress, any strangers she meets on the street, or indeed herself? Does this striving to impress stem from envy of her mistress, from a need to boost her own feelings of self-esteem, or from naked social ambition? (1993: 41)

The flaw in this theory for Campbell is that it confuses consequence with intention. It also illustrates the problem with reading dress of others from a theoretical distance. As argued in chapter 2, theories of fashion tend to abstract it from the social context, resulting in general statements about fashion/dress without testing these against actual practices. In other words, they are reductive: too much is assumed on the basis of too little evidence. Fashion and dress in such theorizations are divorced from the body and from the practices of dress in daily life which are complex and over-determined. Other critiques of emulation theories point to its mechanistic view of social class and status (Slater 1997) and its assumption that only the elite innovate, when certain evidence would suggest that working-class styles can in fact 'bubble up' to become the latest style (Partington 1992, Polhemus 1994, Wilson 1985). Further problems arise from the lack of specificity in the theories: it is hard to identify who the 'elite' trend-setters might be at any one time – are fashions set by court, king and aristocracy, or by the new bourgeoisie? If the former classes for the seventeenth or eighteenth centuries, why would the new bourgeoisie take over in the nineteenth century, as is sometimes claimed? Campbell (1989) argues that the increased propensity to consume came from the bourgeoisie not because of a desire to emulate the aristocracy, but because of a change in attitudes towards consumption. Indeed, he suggests that far from being emulators, the middle classes of the eighteenth and nineteenth centuries were setters of taste: empirical work on probate inventories shows a greater concern with fashion in households of urban tradesmen than landed gentry living on great country estates (Weatherill 1993, 1996).

Emulation theories fail to explain fashion and why the idea of 'fashion' and 'fashionability' extended through so much of the population in the eighteenth century to encompass all aspects of life (and lifestyle, although this concept is a twentieth-century one). Art, literature, music, interior décor, along with dress, styles of hair and make-up, were caught up in the universe of fashionable society of the eighteenth century. 'Society' was overtly concerned with fashion and the urban and provincial gentry would have kept their eye on what the 'fashionable set' was doing, where they were going, how they decorated their houses, and what they were wearing. Indeed, 'provincial towns put on London airs' and developed their own equivalents to the pleasure gardens of Ranelagh or Vauxhall, or the theatres of Drury Lane (Porter 1990: 223–4). In the literature of Jane Austen and in the diaries of rich ladies, concern with fashion is overt. Anna Margaretta Larpent, wife of Chief Inspector of Plays in the Lord Chamberlain's office, represents one such cultured lady (Brewer 1997). She took her refined activities, such as reading, art, theatre and concert going, very seriously as part of an overall project of self-improvement and, although she might protest at the superficiality of some of those she encountered – 'how horrid is the life of (too many) people of fashion, one might forget they had souls' – but as Brewer notes, 'this did not prevent her from pursuing these pleasures' (1997: 70). Indeed, as he argues, 'in this culture of display, vanity, pride and greed as well as the finest clothing were on show' (1997: 73). Even those who professed not to care all that much about fashion, such as Elizabeth Shackleton (1726–81) of Alkincoats in Lancashire, were interested to know of the latest London styles in dress and interior décor (Vickery 1993). It was not just women who were caught up in the consumer revolution, although commentators at the time and historians of consumption since have tended to assume this. Affluent men of fashion would have done their share of shopping, buying their own snuffboxes, handkerchiefs and gloves as well as supervising the purchase of large consumer goods for the home such as furniture (Vickery 1993).

According to Porter (1990) and McKendrick et al. (1983), advertising helped to fan the flames of the new consumer revolution, although it alone cannot account for the spectacular explosion of demand for new commodities, which must reflect a change in attitudes towards consumption (Campbell 1989; Weatherill 1993). Campbell argues that the birth of consumer culture came with the birth of modern hedonism among the Puritan bourgeoisie. This is far removed from the ethics of envy and imitation that traditional histories and theories of emulation emphasize. As discussed in chapter 4, modern hedonism involves the use of the imagination to control external stimuli. This produces both the longings and dissatisfactions associated with modern consumption. Modern consumerism, according to Campbell, is 'anything but materialistic'; the 'basic motivation is to experience in reality the pleasurable dramas which they have already enjoyed in imagination' (1989: 89). So as Breward (1994) suggests, the servant girl dressing like a lady encodes goods with dreamlike properties and escapism rather than envying the style.

None of these new modes of sociability entirely swept away old privileges or hierarchies of class and status – indeed, the increased affluence for some served to heighten the division between 'haves' and 'have nots' (Porter 1990) – but they did see a progressive challenge to such hierarchies. Sumptuary laws provide a good example of the contrast between the old and new order: while the laws remained on the statute books, few arrests were made since 'people in very large cities had little means of telling whether the dress of a stranger on the street was an accurate reflection of his or her standing in the society' (Sennett 1977: 66). Sennett provides further evidence of the contradiction between the desire to fix class identity and the impossibility of doing so. The new social classes, not just merchants and traders, but those in offices of government and private finance, occupied an ambivalent position: their identity was not underpinned by tradition and they could not be located within the existing class hierarchy. So while laws on dress were unenforceable, attempts were made to 'bring order to the mixture of strangers on the street' (1977: 66) with the establishment of costumes for different occupations. However, these too were unenforceable since people had no way of distinguishing impostors, given that people would take to the streets wearing the costume of a particular profession or guild whether they belonged to it or not. It would seem that 'whether people were in fact what they wore was less important than their desire to wear something recognisable in order to be someone in the street' (1977: 67). So a shipping clerk going for a walk wearing the dress of a butcher is wearing a costume and in doing so is observing a convention. 'Codes of dress as a means of regulating the street worked by clearly if arbitrarily identifying who people were' (1977: 68).

How did the clothing of this period relate to the body? For much of the eighteenth century, public dress for aristocratic men and women was highly elaborate. For women, skirts were full and long, sometimes slashed to reveal the petticoat, and richly decorated with ribbons, jewels and buttons. The dress worn in public was as elaborate for men as for women: breeches and waistcoats in luxurious fabrics such as velvet, brocade, taffeta, satin or damask would have been decorated with lace or embroidery and would have been brightly coloured in apple-green, wine – red, orange and violet. Ribbons and garters would have adorned the costumes of both men and women and make-up and patches worn to add lustre to the complexion. However, as Sennett notes, while such finery attracted attention to the wearer, it 'did so by the qualities of these adornments as objects in themselves, and not as aids to setting off the peculiarities of his face or figure' (1977: 69). The body, he suggests, was like a mannequin. Men and women wore wigs, which, along with large and ornate hats would have totally obscured the natural shape of the head and would have been the real focus of attention, not the individual beauty of the face. The surface of the body operated in a similar way – the increased exposure of women's breasts over the course of the century was intended as a showcase for the jewels worn around the neck.

As public life expanded, with many more occasions for sociability than before, there was a significant change in the relationship of the body and dress. Whereas in the seventeenth century, dress for the

Les Adieux, after Moreau le Jeune, *c.* 1777. Eighteenth-century fashionable dress was elaborate and excessive. Dressed for the opera, this fashionable woman has to pass through her opera box sideways to accommodate her large skirt. Reproduced with the kind permission of the Trustees of the Victoria and Albert Museum.

elite was elaborate at all times, whatever the occasion, by the mid-eighteenth century a division had opened up between public and private dress. 'On the street... clothes were worn which recognisably marked one's place' while in the private realm clothes were 'more natural [and] the body appeared more expressive in itself' (Sennett 1977: 66). A common metaphor to describe this division between public and private, and one that Sennett draws on, is the stage: in public one was 'on stage', playing a role which might or might not be 'authentic'; at home, one was 'backstage' and could relax, wearing loose dress and concentrating on 'comfort'. For women, this might mean wearing a négligé. In public, a different standard of bodily

presentation was demanded and dress played its part in this performance, marking out roles, conventions or status which might or might
not relate to the actual status or identity of the wearer. This performance was accepted for what it was – a more or less convincing
appearance, as that of an actor's might be. As Sennett suggests:

> at home, one's clothes suited one's body and its needs, on the street
> one stepped into clothes whose purpose was to make it possible for
> other people to act as if they knew who you were. One became a figure
> in a contrived landscape; the purpose of the clothes was not to be sure
> of whom you were dealing with, but to be able to behave as if you were
> sure. (1977: 68)

Conventions of dress, speech and interaction in the eighteenth century were taken as straightforward social conventions, not as symbols
behind which lies some inner truth (as they are today). For Sennett,
this element of playfulness with one's public appearance and identity
is a positive thing, enabling one to be artful and expressive and enjoy
open social interaction. Indeed, Sennett argues that people are more
sociable when there are tangible barriers such as social conventions
between them. However, when one treats things as symbolic, as
embodying a hidden meaning, the playfulness of conventions is lost
and so too the freedom it allows in terms of sociability. 'Human
beings need to have some distance from intimate observation by
others in order to feel sociable. Increase intimate contact and you
decrease sociability' (1977: 15). Such a concern with inner reality
results in a more psychological view of the other, a questioning of the
inner reality of the other often leading to mistrust. The result is that
the public arena is considered to be 'dead public space' and leads to a
search for truth and intimacy which ultimately results in a retreat into
the private sphere. Sociability, enjoyed in and of itself when governed
by social conventions, is consequently viewed as unsatisfying and
without meaning. Sennett is therefore critical of the Romantic concern with authenticity which invaded the public realm in the nineteenth century and in doing so, he argues, it diminished the
possibilities of an active and artful social life. (Discourses on authenticity inspired by Romanticism and the rise of bourgeois individualism are discussed in chapter 4.)

As Sennett's focus is primarily on Paris, he does not draw attention
to the differences in styles of dress across Europe. In England, a
country style of dress became popular over the course of the eighteenth century; this was distinctly informal compared with the elaborate dress of the French, still heavily influenced by the formality of the
court. The *habit à l'anglaise* grew in popularity in France towards the

end of the eighteenth century, possibly reflecting the current republican admiration of liberal England. Ironically, the informal English country style was in fact adopted by the English aristocracy in the eighteenth century (Steele 1988). Tensions between the older formal French style and the English country style had repercussions both in France and abroad. In France, the 'Macaroni' style (as in the song 'Yankee doodle-dandy') became associated with the ultra-modern young noblemen in France; this style spread to England, where it was adopted by some of the more conservative aristocracy. The fashion was foppish, elaborate and considered effeminate; some condemned its tight short coat as obscene. The Macaroni style was censured in France on the grounds that a country with such feeble people who sported it could not defend itself. Partly as a result of this condemnation and growing nationalism, the fashion in men's dress changed as people began to see sober dress as a reflection of patriotic values, country and city (as opposed to court) life and enterprise (as opposed to gambling and frivolity) (Steele 1988).

During the eighteenth century the city emerged as an alternative space to the court for fashion (Brewer 1997). Rules of court gave way to urban society and city life. This expansion of industrialization and the city coupled with the growth in the urban bourgeoisie continued into the nineteenth century, undermining the power and privilege of the aristocratic elite. Such a dramatic shift in power and such sweeping social changes brought with them changes in the relations between public and private life, the effects of which we are still feeling today. Romanticism, with its powerful critique of industrialization and urbanization, became an increasingly popular antidote to the new modern life. As discussed in the next chapter, this helped to upset the balance between public and private life that had been carefully maintained in the eighteenth century and to promote new relations between appearance and identity.

Fashion from the Nineteenth Century Onwards

Fashion thrives in a world of social mobility, a dynamic world characterized by class and political conflict, urbanization and aesthetic innovation, so it is not surprising that fashion flourished in the nineteenth century, when social upheaval reached a new zenith with the French and the Industrial Revolutions. The frenetic pace of change continued into the early twentieth century, most notably in further social and political unrest that culminated in the two world wars. As the term 'modernity' captures the idea of a society in dramatic transition, it is equally applicable to the accelerating rate of changes in fashion during this period. Thus as Breward notes, 'if there is one major theme amongst many in which . . . a discussion of Victorian clothing can be situated, it is this problem or idea of "modernity" ' (1994: 146). Wilson also draws on the concept of modernity to consider fashion in the nineteenth and twentieth centuries because it 'seems useful as a way of indicating the restless desire for change characteristic of cultural life in industrial capitalism, the desire for the new that fashion expresses so well' (1985: 63). Modernity invokes a number of developments: industrialization, the growth of capitalism, urbanization, the rise of privatised individualism and the development of 'mass' culture, to name but a few.

Capitalism emerged out of revolutions which shook western Europe in the first few decades of the nineteenth century: in Britain it took the form of a social revolution sparked off by industrialization and fuelled by bourgeois individualism and liberalism; in France, it took the form of a bloody political revolution which threw off the shackles of the *ancien régime*. In both cases, a new capitalist class emerged to challenge preconceived ideas of power and wealth: their wealth was tied to factories, capital or merchandise rather than land or blood and brought them into conflict, at least in status terms, with the old aristocracy and nobility. Except in France, for the most part the challenge was fought out obliquely less with swords than through symbols, of which dress was one of the most significant. The nineteenth century was an era dominated by 'capital'; 'new money buys landed estates, it can wear the clothes of court and "society", it can indulge in the leisure pursuits of the aristocracy' (Slater 1997: 70). In the history of European fashion so far, trends had been set by the royal and aristocratic dress worn at court, but by the late eighteenth century, in both Britain and France, changing fashions had come to be set by the new bourgeoisie. Steele notes how, after the Revolution of 1792, women's dress became increasingly that of 'undress', with new lines from the Directory (from 1795) to Consulate (1799–1804) and Empire (1804–15) inspired by classical design (1988); such dresses as chemises were possibly also influenced by French colonial involvement in the Caribbean, where women wore simple straight dresses. The common story that the Revolution brought about the fashion for the chemise is too simplistic. According to Steele, the simplicity of this dress compared with the over-elaborate Bastille style do not correspond neatly: the chemise had in fact made appearances *before* the fall of the Bastille. One portrait shows Marie Antoinette in a simple dress which caused outcry at the time and was removed from public view. The portrait was painted by Elisabeth

English walking dress, 1807, showing the classical straight lines of the Regency period. Reproduced with the kind permission of the Trustees of the Victoria and Albert Museum.

Vigée-Lebrun, whose own style of dress was simple (she hated the elaborate court dress at Versailles). After the pared-down elegance of Regency fashions, women's dress became ever more fussy with 'Romantic' dress: a profusion of lace, frills and ribbons. By the mid-nineteenth century, skirts were wide and heavy, the crinoline cage being introduced in the 1850s. Men's dress changed comparatively little, though it lost much of its decoration and the dominant colours were sober in contrast to the commonly worn pinks, reds, mauves and yellows worn by eighteenth-century aristocratic men. Discourses on fashion draw attention to the sharp distinctions between men's and women's dress during the nineteenth century, when women became increasingly associated with 'frivolity'. The standard history has tended to equate the restriction of women to the family with the restriction of her dress of whalebone corset and cage of crinoline, accepting without qualification the notion of a masculine renunciation of fashion. The story is, of course, more complex than that (see chapter 5) but the striking image of the Victorian period is one of marked gender division.

Industrialization changed the nature of fashion: the development of new technologies for producing clothes, such as the sewing machine, was spurred on by new demands for cheap mass-produced clothing, particularly for men. Furthermore, wars stimulated a demand for uniforms and new industrial work (on the railroads of the United States, for example) demanded cheap, strong clothes. To this day, men's clothing remains more industrialized than women's, which has remained modelled more on *haute couture* than mass production (Fine and Leopold 1993, Leopold 1992). This shift in the production of clothing to factories altered the structure of the fashion system, which had hitherto been based on a 'putting out' method. As discussed in chapter 7, this resulted in the emergence of the sweatshop, the harsh, inhumane and often dangerous factory.

Increasing urbanization also helped stimulate fashion, providing an expanded stage for the display and transmission of clothing, and providing a useful cloak of armour for city life (see chapter 4). The increasing anonymity of the city brought with it new possibilities and new problems: new opportunities for social encounters, particularly for late nineteenth-century women, who were able to visit 'respectable' places such as department stores and cafés in the city. It also brought with it problems on both a macro- and a micro-level: fears about social order grew with the expansion of the city and some intellectuals expressed fear at the emergence of a 'mass' society, an anonymous and sometimes violent 'mob' society. There is a close link between the burgeoning new capitalist class and Romanticism as an aesthetic and intellectual movement which both prioritize the individual and celebrate individual isolation, as well as seeking refuge in the imagination as a place apart from the horrors of modern life. Romanticism privileged a peculiarly privatized individual whose retreat and isolation enabled him to find 'himself' in among the debris of modern life. These developments placed a new emphasis upon the self and stimulated the rise of privatized individualism.

How do all these developments relate to fashion and dress? In such a world as this, fashion takes on new significance; it is the means by which people negotiate their identity, move through the city unnoticed (or noticed, depending on the style) and comes to serve almost as 'armour' protecting the individual. Fashion can be used to give oneself impressive 'individual' identity, while simultaneously being capable of signalling commonality since it enhances uniformity. These dualisms, between conformity and individuality, between private self and public appearance, introduce themes which have dominated debates about fashion and dress. A further dualism, between artifice and authenticity, has played a significant part in academic debates about fashion as well as informing a 'commonsense' understanding of fashion: does fashion conceal the 'authentic' self and serve as 'artifice'? This questioning stems from a Romantic concern with self and authenticity.

While fashion was a protective 'armour' for some, it was a tyrannous, irrational force for others. The growth of dress reform movements during the nineteenth century led to the fashionable dress of the day being condemned, on various grounds. These movements were often associated with political campaigns, such as socialism or feminism, which were set on eradicating social and political inequalities. Many of the reform movements advocated the devising of a 'uniform' as one way to encourage equality; as the 'tyranny of fashion' encourages competition between individuals, it should be eradicated. Fashion was criticized by some (e.g. Veblen 1953 and Flügel 1930) as frivolous, useless, unnecessary or just plain ugly. Veblen's functionalism led him to see fashion as essentially useless; it was also tyrannous to women who were constrained by heavy and elaborate dress. As discussed in chapter 5, other dress reformers were associated with feminism and called for women to wear trousered dress rather than heavy skirts (Newton 1974). However, it was not just female dress that was criticized: Flügel was associated with the Men's Dress Reform Movement and argued that men's dress was similarly constraining and oppressive.

The belief in a progressive style of dress is very much a product of late nineteenth-century faith in progress and Utopia, and, in some cases, science (Newton 1974). Some dress reformers were concerned with health and hygiene and many were associated with 'water-cure' medicine and advocated looser dress on the grounds that it was more 'hygienic' and 'natural' (Luck 1992, Newton 1974). The Aesthetic Movement in England reacted against what its adherents considered the ugliness of fashion and advocated a more 'natural' style of dress. A certain strain of Romanticism runs through these attitudes to dress and it relates to the simplistic view of the body and 'nature'. Aesthetic dress, as worn by those associated with the Pre-Raphaelites, assumed that a 'natural' form of dress could be devised when in fact no dress is ever 'natural' since whatever its shape or form, it is always an expression of culture and represents an attempt to modify the body in some

Photograph of Jane Morris (wife of William Morris), wearing Aesthetic dress 1865. In contrast to standard Victorian female dress of the day, Morris wears her dress without a corset and a profusion of skirts and decoration. Posed by Gabriel Dante Rossetti. Reproduced with the kind permission of the Trustees of the Victoria and Albert Museum.

way. One final point to note about dress reform, however, is that not all dress reformers were progressive (Kunzle 1982, Steele 1985). Some were actually conservative, for example those who opposed the corset in the nineteenth century on the grounds that it damaged women's reproductive organs and thus her child bearing capacities.

This chapter has looked at the development of a modern fashion system and at how fashions have changed in response to a complex range of social forces. The simplistic assumption that fashion reflects the spirit of the times has been challenged but this is not to say that fashion is unaffected by shifts in social life. When considering how and why fashions change, it is not enough to isolate a single spirit or feeling associated with the times and look for modifications in dress that might correspond. Dress is tied up to social life in more than one way: it is produced out of economic, political, technological conditions as well as shaped by social, cultural, aesthetic ideas. Fashionable dress does depend to some extent on particular social and economic circumstances, as discussed in this chapter. However, the forms of dress are not reducible to the social or economic.

4

Fashion and Identity

Introduction

Fashion and dress have a complex relationship to identity: on the one hand the clothes we choose to wear can be expressive of identity, telling others something about our gender, class, status and so on; on the other, our clothes cannot always be 'read', since they do not straightforwardly 'speak' and can therefore be open to misinterpretation. This tension between clothes as revealing and clothes as concealing of identity runs through much of the literature on fashion and fits into broader thematic concerns with identity described by Sennett (1977), Finkelstein (1991) and others. These theorists examine the ways in which identity can be said to be 'immanent' in appearance and yet, how it can also be mistaken, hidden behind a 'disguise'. This tension is felt particularly strongly in the modern city, where, without tradition or established patterns for recognizing others, we mingle with crowds of 'strangers' and have only fleeting moments to impress one another. Thus,

> when we encounter a stranger as initially mysterious and inaccessible, we refer to clothing styles and physical appearance, in the absence of any other means, as a reliable sign of identity. Clothing is frequently seen as symbolic of the individual's status and morality, whether actual or contrived. (Finkelstein 1991: 128)

Anonymity increases the emphasis placed upon appearance and indeed, with the development of large sprawling cities in Europe in the nineteenth century, two strategies for dealing with the anonymity of the city begin to pull in opposite directions: the idea that character is immanent in appearance (Finkelstein 1991), an idea that pulls one in search of the authenticity of the 'other', the 'truth' behind the appearance; and an alternative desire for artifice and play with appearance, through fashion and disguise, provoked by the anonymous nature of the city. The contradiction between these two strategies serves to heighten the drama of the city and focuses attention on the body and on dress as indicators to be read for hidden meaning. In the figures of the dandy and the Romantic one finds the contradiction between artifice and authenticity played out through styles of dress. For Campbell (1989), the figures of the dandy and the Romantic in the nineteenth century represented two divergent practices of dress and consumption which co-existed. The dandy style was an older aristocratic style of dress which articulated a concern for individual distinction, a never ending concern to appear 'distinguished', while the Romantic style represents a more familiar desire within contemporary culture, namely to be an expressive individual and be 'true to oneself'. Thus the dandy style emphasized the artifice of appearance, the self as performed and perfected through self-conscious use of dress and the body, while the Romantic style was concerned with authenticity and the self as 'genuine' and 'natural'.

This tension between artifice and authenticity, between the self as constructed and self-styled and the self as natural and authentic is one that recurs in contemporary literature. As Finkelstein (1991) argues, there is a fundamental contradiction running through our contemporary readings of appearance and identity: while we look to read the other through appearance and hope we can do so accurately, at the very same time we are aware that 'appearances can be deceptive'. This awareness of the problematic nature of appearance does not stop us from attempting to control how we look and calculate our appearance in order to 'put our best face forward' or 'make a good impression', and we employ a whole host of strategies to enhance our appearance. Fashion and dress are the tools for this calculation, but various health projects, such as diet, fitness exercises and cosmetic surgery all contribute to the appearance of the body as well. Featherstone (1991a), Giddens (1991) and others have argued that these body projects are an indication of the way in which the self in late modern culture is increasingly a 'reflexive self' who is increasingly called upon to think about and act upon the self in particular ways. This theme can also be found in Foucault's work (1988) on 'technologies of the self', in which he examines the historically specific ways we are called upon to make ourselves particular sorts of human beings. Different styles of dress can be said to form part of these 'technologies of self'. In this respect, the dandy and the Romantic could be said to be two nineteenth-century 'technologies of self' both derived from particular styles of dress as well as owing much to different social and political allegiances.

However, the options open for the performance of identity are not unconstrained. How we perform our identity has something to do with our location in the social world as members of particular groups, classes, cultural communities. The clothes we choose to wear represent a compromise between the demands of the social world, the milieu in which we belong, and our own individual desires. 'Fashions are bonds that link individuals in a mutual act of conformity to social conventions' (Finkelstein 1991: 122). This tension between social structure and individual agency is a familiar one to sociologists and is described succinctly by Simmel in his account of 'individuality and social forms' (1971). As one of the few sociologists to consider fashion, Simmel accords it some degree of importance in modern society as a phenomenon which exhibits the contradictory desires for social imitation and individual differentiation. Fashion embraces not only the desire to imitate others and to express commonality, but to express individuality. In other words, while dress signals our membership to particular communities and expresses shared values, ideas and lifestyle, at the same time we do not want to be 'clones' dressed in identical fashion to our friends. In order to understand how fashion and dress are linked to identity, Simmel's analysis, with its emphasis on these contradictory tendencies is pertinent here.

Simmel's analyis points to the essentially social nature of dress: individuals are located within communities and their style of dress expresses this belonging. Thus, a further theme when discussing identity in relation to the fashioned body is how fashion and dress articulate group identities, in particular, how they are deployed in order to mark out distinctions between classes and groups of people. This issue touches on questions of status and how status is embodied through fashion, dress and deportment and returns us to discussions of how the body has come to be the bearer of social status. This theme is discussed in chapters 1 and 3 (in particular through the work of Elias 1978 and Bourdieu 1984, 1994). The importance of the body as the bearing of status and distinction is a theme also explored by Bourdieu (1984, 1994). In his analysis of class, status and power, he argues that the body holds a crucial place as the mediator of this information through inscriptions, tastes and practices he refers to as the 'habitus'. Bourdieu's account looks at how this battle for distinction is a battle for power – economic, social and symbolic – since to acquire distinction potentially raises one's stakes: a Sloane Ranger at a Swiss finishing school who cultivates certain manners and cultural knowledge, stands to increase her socio-economic position by 'marrying well'.

It is impossible to talk of status and status competition without talking of class. At one time, indeed until as recently as the early twentieth century, class was visible through particular uniforms or styles of dress: butchers, bakers, milkmaids, coal miners, were clearly identifiable through dress. However, even in the nineteenth century new social classes were already pushing forward and competing for status, old and fixed ideas of class were fast disappearing. In contemporary western culture class is no longer so readily apparent to the eye through dress alone but this is not to say that social divisions are no longer apparent through styles of dress: it is still the case that dress can mark out divisions between different groups, and this is particularly true in the case of youth subcultures. Subcultures use dress along with other popular cultural artefacts to mark out differences of taste, lifestyle and identity. However if distinction is about setting oneself apart, it is also always about signalling to others that one is similar to them. Thus the particular manners and bodily dispositions of a Sloane Ranger signal her belonging to a particular class. These themes can be applied to look at how other social groups, such as subcultures, deploy cultural goods to distinguish themselves from each other and from 'mainstream' culture. Further, the Sloane Ranger and the member of the youth subculture illustrate the tension described by Simmel (1971), between imitation and differentiation: both set themselves apart from others through bodily style and dress *while also* showing their membership of a particular cultural community by dressing in a similar way to their class or subcultural group.

In this chapter, I explore the themes relating to identity in some detail, examining the complex ways in which fashion and dress are linked to social identity. These tensions and contradictions were most visible in the nineteenth century, heightened by the rapid social changes in social life at this time. I therefore consider the characteristic features of the world described as 'modern', paying particular attention to the city as the stage *par excellence* for sartorial display. I then explore in detail the themes outlined above: imitation and differentiation; artifice and authenticity; body, dress and social status.

Modernity: Imitation and Differentiation

During the nineteenth century there was an unprecedented population explosion in the capitals of Europe; in England increasing numbers of peasants were displaced by the enclosure system and moved to London in search of work. The increasing industrialization of work severed the urban populace from the rhythms of nature and, as more and more people went to work outside the home, to factories, to coal pits and to offices, the working day did not have to begin at dawn and end at dusk. These developments changed the geography of social life: cities became bustling and congested, dirty, noisy, often dangerous places to live and work; they also provided an 'expanded stage for the public drama of modern life' (Steele 1988: 135) and fashion flourished on such a stage. In such an environment 'strangers' meet with no more than fleeting moments to make an impression on each other. Thus increasing anonymity led to greater emphasis on appearance as the means by which to 'read' the other.

The intensity of this environment brought with it new pressures and new possibilities. Simmel characterizes the society emerging in the nineteenth century as 'modern': it is highly abstract and complex in structure, reaching an apotheosis with monetarization. During the nineteenth century there was a quantitative rise in material culture – the extension of the world of goods, of consumption, shopping and symbolic display – all of which offered new possibilities for individuals to recognize themselves as consumers 'who have come to determine their own development in this world of goods' (Miller 1987). Simmel sees modernity as inherently contradictory: it simultaneously opens up new opportunities for individualization not possible in traditional, rural communities, and also closes down possibilities for social coherence. Problems arise when the world of objects outstrips individuals' attempts to come to terms with it; when subjects do not appropriate objects in ways that relate to their projections but confront the world as alien. As Simmel argues, 'our freedom is crippled if we deal with objects that our ego cannot assimilate' (1971: 462). The excessive array of objects for purchase always threatens to overwhelm us. He explores the contradictions of modernity, arguing that modern life exhibits a desire for *generalization*, 'of uniformity, of inactive similarity of the forms and contents of life', and for *differentiation*, 'of separate elements, producing the restless changing of an individual life' (1971: 294). These two antagonistic principles are expressed through adornment which 'creates a highly specific synthesis of the great convergent and divergent forces of the individual and society' (Simmel 1950: 344). Fashion articulates a tension between conformity and differentiation: it expresses the contradictory desires to fit in and stand out: 'fashion is the imitation of a given example and satisfies the demand for social adaptation . . . at the same time it satisfies in no less degree the need of differentiation, the tendency towards dissimilarity, the desire for constant change and contrast' (Simmel 1971: 296). The idea that fashion is always about the differentiation of a particular group is generally linked to the theory of 'trickle-down' and emulation which, as argued in chapters 2 and 3, is flawed in terms of fashion. However, without accepting the proposition that fashions develop at the top or that emulation is the key motivation of fashion, one can still argue that what is 'fashionable' or in today's parlance, 'trendy' or 'hip', has always to be differentiated from the mainstream. Once a style becomes widely adopted, it is no longer 'different' and thus no longer 'hip'. At any one time, one or more group may be associated with 'hip' and be responsible for setting a trend. Today this group is often likely to come from the street, from youth subcultures rather than from an elite at the 'top' of the social strata. Fashionability thus depends upon distinction or differentiation which, once copied universally, is negated. A trend-setting group whose identity depends upon being 'hip' will therefore move on to adopt another style. This process is a highly commercialized one today, the fashion industry being constantly geared to find 'new looks' each season (a new colour, line of skirt, shape of jacket). The speed at which this happens and the concomitant effect on the interconnections between designers, fashion buyers, journalists and 'street' cultures is examined in chapter 7.

Pertinent here is the way in which fashion could be deployed for particular groups at particular times and used to differentiate that group, making it visible and its members identifiable. The same can be said for all dress, even that characterized as 'anti-fashion' or 'oppositional' to mainstream fashion. For example, the dress of various nineteenth-century Utopian movements, based often around a 'uniform', 'gave the members a "family likeness" and marked their difference from outsiders, thus acting as a powerful indicator of shared values and community boundaries' (Luck 1992: 202). In the twentieth century the dress of rebellious youth subcultures similarly served to mark out and distinguish an identity for these groups. Dress is therefore the means by which identities are marked out and sustained. While this has always been the case, certainly in relation to class identity, it is important to note that modernity opened up new possibilities for the creation of identity: it unfixed individuals from traditional communities, placing them in the 'melting-pot' of the city, and it extended the commodities available for purchase to an ever widening circle of people, thereby providing the necessary 'raw material' for the creation of new identities. As the nineteenth and twentieth centuries progressed, one's identity depended less and less on a fixed place in a stable social order: one's group affiliations could be 'elected' and one's identity 'invented' in the modern world.

Fashion as Artifice

Industrial capitalism and urbanization not only changed the contours of the landscape of the nineteenth century, it transformed social and temporal relations. Class conflict was a marked feature of the period. City life had its own rhythm and pace quite unlike that of the country: industrial life shifted the rhythm of the day and reordered the relationship between private and public life. As discussed in the previous chapter, the intimate life of the home and the public life of the street and 'society' had been held as separate and distinctly different realms in the eighteenth century. Public roles as performances put a discreet distance between self and 'other' and between public and private life, thereby enhancing the sociability of people. However, according to Sennett (1977), the nineteenth-century urban, industrial bourgeoisie altered this harmonious relationship. Partly as a result of the shocks administered by industrialization and partly as a result of changes in morality, the public sphere came to be seen as 'dead space': space which was alienating and lacking in spiritual or moral virtue. It became a place to escape *from* rather than, as in the eighteenth century, a place of virtue and pleasure to be enjoyed and valued. The nineteenth century was the era when the privatized family became the bedrock of social life, the refuge of meaning and authenticity. In this 'intimate vision of society' people came to expect psychological benefits from their experience of the world; precisely because so much of life in the public realm doesn't reveal psychological rewards, it is experienced as impersonal, empty and alienating. This sets the scene for the emergence of the city as a place of danger, filled with 'strangers' who by virtue of their strangeness are unknowable and therefore potentially threatening.

In the large cities that sprang up during the nineteenth cenutury, individuals were brought into contact with an ever increasing number of 'strangers'. In such an alienating environment, surrounded by unfamiliar faces, appearances were the only means of reading the 'other'. In such a world as this, fashion becomes central to the experience of the modern city; according to Wilson (1985), dress can be a 'technique of survival' in a metropolis that brings one into contact with strangers. Thus, as she argues, 'the nineteenth century urban bourgeoisie, anxious to preserve their distance from the omnipresent gaze in the strangely inquisitive anonymity of the crowd where "anyone" might see you, developed a discreet style of dress as protection' (1985: 137).

However, appearances can be therefore deceptive and indeed, as Wilson notes, mystery, suspense and disguise preoccupied the Victorian era, an era which gave birth to the murder mystery, the detective novel and the thriller. The most famous of nineteenth-century sleuths, Sherlock Holmes, was preoccupied with uncovering mysteries and secrets and deployed his powers of deduction to penetrate the appearance of things and people. However, as Sennett (1977) notes, the ability to read the appearance of others and to fix their identity was made more difficult by the mass production of clothing, particularly with the growth in mass-produced patterns, which blurred the lines that demarcated recognizable class identities. In the nineteenth century, one might wander around the city in the disguise of a lady, as did the mistress of diarist Arthur Munby. A servant to Munby, Hannah mostly wore the garb of the nineteenth-century female servant – simple dress, coarse apron and shawl, and plain bonnet. But later, once secretly married, she could pass for a lady, although not without gloves to hide her tell-tale rough hands. When a country rector's wife introduced herself to Hannah (who was dressed as a lady outside the church) and later left a card at their residence, Munby and Hannah were obliged to pay her a visit which would require Hannah to masquerade as a 'lady' in company. For this tense meeting Hannah 'wore her pretty broad hat of black felt, with a violet veil wrapt around it; it made a picturesque background for her shining hair and sweet loving face; and she wore a dress of pale grey with black ornaments; and grey gloves, which she was on no account to take off' (Munby in Hudson 1974: 373). The meeting passed off well enough except for Hannah's farewell: an accidental 'Goodbye *Ma'am*'. But in general, dressed appropriately Hannah could attend lectures with Munby in her 'disguise' and no one could tell that her 'station' in life was as lowly as a maid. Other disguises were perhaps even more 'deceitful', such as the character Munby encountered on Oxford Street: 'I saw before me, striding along in company with an Italian organgrinder, a tall young man in full Highland costume; wearing a Glengarry bonnet, a scarlet jacket, a sporran and a tartan kilt and stocking, his legs bare from knee to calf. It was not a man – it was Madeleine Sinclair the street dancer' (Munby in Hudson 1974: 131).

Cross-dressing has been common throughout history and in chapter 5, the role played by dress in the construction of gender is examined in more detail. In this chapter it is appropriate to discuss how some instances of cross-dressing illustrate the uncertainty and instability of appearances in the modern city. Fashion serves to protect one from prying eyes and enables one to put a distance between self and other – it is the 'armour' of the modern world. It opens up possibilities for disguise, for the construction of a self which is 'artificial' in the sense of being a work of artistry.

Such a world also demands a particular attitude (Simmel calls it 'blasé'), which involves a mode of being and a style that enables one to cope with the 'heat' and frenzy of modern life in the city. Rather than registering shock, disapproval, dismay at the sights and sounds of the city, the individual strikes a pose of cool indifference and observes without seeming to observe. Dress and the 'blasé attitude' are techniques for survival in the city; both serve as shields against the eyes of strangers. The *flâneur* who idles along the streets of the city, yet always on the lookout, strikes such a pose of nonchalance. The *flâneur* was distinctly Parisian in character, who 'lived on the boulevards, and made the streets and cafés of Paris his drawing room' (Wilson 1991: 54); as Baudelaire put it, to 'be away from home, and yet to feel at home; to behold the world, to be in the midst of the world, and yet to remain hidden from the world – these are some of the minor pleasures of such independent, impassioned and impartial spirits' (1986: 33).

The ability to walk the streets freely was an option more open to men than to women and the *flâneur* was generally a dandy, a man of aristocratic disposition. However, Wilson (1991) suggests that the prostitute was a *flâneur* whose street-walking put her in an ideal position from which to observe the city. For Baudelaire, the painter Guys Constantine exemplified the *flâneur*, although he went beyond that of indifferent observation to be a 'passionate spectator' able to capture the fleeting beauty of the street (Steele 1988). This 'painter of modern life', this *flâneur*-painter, was an acute observer who is aware of shifts in fashion: 'if a fashion or the cut of a garment has been slightly altered; if buckles or bunches of ribbons have been dethroned by rosettes...his eagle's eye will already have perceived it' (Baudelaire 1986: 35). In this respect, 'fashion was the key to modernity' for Baudelaire (Steele 1988: 90). It was essentially about the continual desire for the beautiful; 'an ideal towards which the restless spirit of mankind is incessantly spurred' (Baudelaire 1986: 63). The painter who depicted his subjects in older costume and not the contemporary styles of the day betrayed a certain laziness, but the true painter of modern life was one who could capture the transient ephemera of modern life in addition to the eternal and unchanging elements of beauty.

Fashion and Authenticity

While some adopted disguise and artifice as methods of 'hiding', this posed problems for others: how could one be sure of the veracity of the people one encountered? As Sennett (1977) argues, until around the mid-eighteenth century the problem of the veracity of appearances produced congenial sociability and one accepted the other at face value; in the nineteenth century it produced suspicion and unease. The 'intimate society' of the nineteenth century sought to probe *beneath* the appearance, to find the 'inner truth' of the 'other'. This attitude encouraged the idea that if there is an inner reality, then it should relate to one's outer appearance. As Sennett notes, 'when street clothes and stage costume come to be seen as having something to do with the body, as they did with house clothing of the mid-eighteenth century, they will also come to appear to have something to do with the character of the person wearing them' (1977: 72).

In other words, as clothing began to connect more closely to the body and individuality of the wearer, it was read for its 'authenticity'. Arguably, the pressure of clothing to reveal the 'authentic' intentions of the wearer was greater for women in the nineteenth century who, according to Halttunen (1982), were constructed as the moral guardians of Protestant, bourgeois culture and therefore had to be 'honest' and 'true'. She argues that the connection between inner sentiment and outer appearance was most clearly articulated by advocates of 'sentimental' dress popular in the mid-nineteenth century. Sentimental dress, which threw off the excessive decoration apparent in female dress from 1815 to the 1830s, drew attention to the body and face of the wearer: bonnets, for example were plain and simple and drew close to the head, so framing the face and its features.

The idea that character is immanent in appearance became increasingly popular in the nineteenth century, although the idea stretches back much further. The desire to find inner truth behind the mask of appearance is tied to the cult of Romanticism as much as it is tied to the rise of the urban bourgeoisie. Romanticism as a philosophical and aesthetic movement stretching back to the eighteenth century prioritizes the 'natural' over the social or cultural and challenges what it sees as the artifice and superficiality of appearances. In such a moral universe as this, dress and appearance are thought to reveal one's 'true' identity; gone is the eighteenth-century idea that appearances within the public realm can act as a playful façade set at a distance from one's intimate life. Romanticism encouraged a more psychological vision of self and society. It brought with it a new focus on individual uniqueness, explored in the work of philosopher Jean-Jacques Rousseau – a concern with the self which is narcissistic: 'the Romantic is one who discovers himself as centre' (Campbell 1989: 184). The Romantic strives for perfection, having found the world to be wanting, and the 'conflict between sincerity and propriety solidifies into clear cut opposition between self and society... as estrangement became the natural state for artists and romantically inclined intellectuals' (1989: 194). This leaves the Romantic seeking out an escape-route from what it sees as ugliness and inauthenticity.

Alongside the rise of Romanticism, the ascendancy of the bourgeoisie in the nineteenth century accentuated the cult of individualism. Their fortunes created out of their own enterprise and initiative, the bourgeoisie helped to forge the idea that one's fate depended upon one's skills and ingenuity and the nineteenth-century bourgeois male came to epitomize the 'self-made man'. The political-economic philosophy of liberalism further extended the emphasis on the individual and a *laissez-faire* attitude to political and economic fortune. With these philosophies of Romanticism and liberal individualism merging to form part of the 'Protestant ethic', the individual came to be seen as the source of meaning and authenticity. While seemingly 'common sense' this version of the self is a historical creation. Elias (1978) has argued that the idea of the self-contained self, hermetically sealed within an individual body, is a peculiarly modern one. As discussed in the previous chapter, the civilizing process has changed the way we view our bodies and, over the course of the nineteenth and twentieth centuries, this induced a more psychological version of the self.

This process is further examined by Finkelstein (1991) who, like Sennett, focuses attention on narratives on authenticity. While stemming from Romanticism, she argues that these 'authenticating narratives' are also linked increasingly to 'scientific' discourses (this being the age of Darwin and his *Origin of the Species*). Finkelstein looks in particular at eighteenth- and nineteenth-century studies of physiognomy, which produced various theories on how to read a person through the body: 'Physiognomy was a means of calculating and understanding the invisible from the visible; it assumed that the nature of human actions and intentions were recorded in the obvious signs of the face and body' (1991: 28).

Anything from the arrangement of the face, the shape of the skull, the line of the skeleton, even the shape and texture of the eyelashes were supposed to reveal the 'true nature' of the person. These theories led to crude characterizations of people into stereotypes, for example, crooked mouths were thought to indicate a corresponding skew in character and criminality, full lips, viciousness. The nineteenth-century physiognomist Samuel Wells considered that his branch of science enabled individuals to improve themselves: by learning to read character through facial features we could 'reconstruct ourselves on an improved plan, correcting unhandsome deviations, moderating excessive developments, supplying deficiencies, moulding our characters' (Wells in Finkelstein 1991: 32). This is of course an idea full of significance in today's plastic culture, which continues the idea that one's appearance is important in how one is read, and is something that can be changed or modified.

If, as in the nineteenth century, appearance comes to stand as an important indicator of inner character, then the smallest of details can become important in fixing or establishing identity. Dress plays its part in this, indeed, its smallest features are often the most telling. As Sennett notes, a gentleman could be identified precisely because he did not make any great claims to be one: 'one could always recognise gentlemanly dress because the buttons on the sleeves of a gentleman's coat actually buttoned and unbuttoned, while one recognised gentlemanly behaviour in his keeping his buttons scrupulously fastened, so that the sleeves never called attention to this fact' (1977: 166).

However, as Finkelstein (1991) argues, it was not just gentlemen who used dress to fashion a particular identity. In the United States during the nineteenth century there was a movement towards individual self-promotion through dress among upwardly mobile young men. For them, 'how they looked was important not only as a means of business advance, but also as a measure of self-esteem' (Branner in Finkelstein 1991: 114).

Modernity is therefore strangely contradictory: authenticating narratives, such as physiognomy, make claims to know the self from its surface appearance, while at the same time there is a heightened awareness that appearance (such as the cool exterior of the blasé attitude) is constructed and can therefore not be trusted as 'authentic'. While such theories might now seem quaint, Finkelstein argues that they have not disappeared and that we continue to read people by reference to their body, dress and overall appearance. The suspicion as to what is a 'true' appearance is heightened by the fact that appearance is malleable and can therefore be 'inauthentic' or artificial. The significance of appearance meant that people began to be concerned with the control of appearance, and clothing and demeanour were therefore employed as techniques to control how one was perceived. Goffman (1971) recognizes this when he examines people's 'impression management' in social situations. When the body diverges from the norm in any way, whether in terms of proportion, movement or symmetry, it becomes a traitor to social rules and the moral order. 'The aberrant individual will be responded to differently and will be judged in comparison with the limits of normative order' (Finkelstein 1991: 67). In this respect, our outward physical appearance has become an important means for obtaining social status.

This theme is linked to my earlier discussion of debates about the body as the bearer of status (see chapters 1 and 2). Featherstone (1991a) argues that the contemporary body has increasingly become the focus of attention as the prime location of identity. Whereas once the body was subject to controls such as diet and exercise aimed at subduing the flesh and enhancing the spirit, the body in consumer culture is now subject to a myriad of 'disciplining' techniques aimed at manipulating it to 'look sexy'. In addition to endless diet and exercise programmes, there are a range of other forms of body work that can be performed in order to enhance one's physical attractiveness. The aim of all this is the production of the 'body beautiful' and the maximization of pleasure, since the beautiful body is a valued one. Initially promoted through Hollywood and the cosmetics industries, the modern 'care of the self' has become one of the defining features of consumer culture. Rather than imposed upon us, these practices call us to be self-conscious and self-disciplining. Control is produced less by brute force and more by surveillance and stimulation. As Foucault notes:

> mastery and awareness of one's own body can be acquired only through the effect of an investment of power in the body: gymnastics, exercises, muscle-building, nudism, the glorification of the body beautiful ... we find a new mode of investment which presents itself no longer in the form of repression but that of control by stimulation. 'Get undressed – but be slim, good-looking and tanned!' (1980: 56–7)

Thus the body is the source of our identity and, if we keep 'working' on it, can potentially enhance our social status. However, any discussion of social status has to accord some significance to class since, historically at least, class has determined status. The link between body, dress and class identity needs further examination also by virtue of its significance within the literature on fashion and dress and is especially pertinent for any discussion about modernity which saw progressive challenges made to old class allegiances.

Clothing, Class and Identity

In his analysis of fashion Simmel (1971) argues that the elite set out to differentiate themselves from the majority by wearing extreme, modish styles. However, given the demise of the court, who were the new elite in the nineteenth century? How were battles of social class played out through status symbols such as fashionable dress? How did a recognizably modern form of consumerism emerge and what were the factors stimulating it? Finkelstein suggests that during the nineteenth century there was a 'dawn of the self-styled, fashioned individual who was concerned with self-promotion, and who employed clothing and various items of fashion and conspicuous consumption to celebrate his new status' (1991: 114). This individual, like the figure of the Regency dandy exemplified by the socialite George Bryan Brummell, known as Beau Brummell (1778–1840), might therefore come from a humble background but climb the social ladder through elegant dressing and conscious self-fashioning. According to Finkelstein, Brummell ushered in an era when 'social ascendancy and character were no longer needed to be viewed as inherent. In the figure of Beau Brummell, there was the declaration of the self produced modern individual, whose identity was fashioned from material possessions' (1991: 114).

However, while the dandy may have heralded an era of elaborate self-fashioning, he was not a self-made man in the bourgeois sense; indeed, in style he was aristocratic and anti-bourgeois. Nor did his style of self-fashioning resemble modern-day consumption with its hedonistic spirit and search for novelty, but was undertaken with an attitude of stoicism rather than pleasure. Moreover, the dandy was not 'fashionable' in the sense of leading or promoting new fashions. While some elements of dandy style have become established, in particular, the dandy cravat (the forerunner of the modern-day men's tie), the dandy was not an innovator as such.

In his search to find the spirit of modern consumption (and thus modern fashion) Campbell (1993) has analysed different styles or modes of consumption, focusing particular attention on the dandy and the Romantic bohemian. He argues that the dandy represents an older style of consumption, an 'aristocratic ethic' that is at odds with modern-day hedonistic consumption. The origin of modern-day consumption lies with the development of a 'Romantic ethic'. Whereas the dandy's dress was based upon an older, aristocratic attitude to appearance which privileged a mannered and artificial performance of the self, the Romantic bohemian seeks to be authentic and natural. The figures of the Romantic bohemian and the dandy epitomize these two distinct styles, although, in the case of the artist dandy, there are important overlaps between the two styles. They also represent two strategies for dealing with the contradictory nature of modernity. The dandy is a figure who emphasizes the performative nature of modernity, the possibilities it opens up for self-creation through appearance. In this respect, the dandy celebrates artifice over authenticity, the latter being of central concern to the Romantic bohemian. However, as we shall see, the dandy is an inherently contradictory character and thus this distinction, while useful, is a crude one.

The dandy

> The man of wealth and leisure, who, even though weary of it, has no other occupation than the pursuit of pleasure; the man brought up on luxury and accustomed since his youth to the obedience of other men; the man, in short, who has no other profession but that of elegance, will always have a distinctive appearance, one that sets him utterly apart. (Baudelaire 1986: 54)

Dandyism originated in Britain towards the end of the eighteenth century, reached a peak during the Regency period and lasted through much of the nineteenth century. In France the dandy style of simple, elegant English country costume was adopted by new republicans and some artists as well as by disaffected aristocrats, or *Incroyables*. The style was, according to Wilson (1985), 'highly erotic', the tight breeches and finely tailored jacket calling attention to the male form, as did the lack of make-up, perfume and 'foppish' decoration. As Wilson points out, however, the term 'dandy' is sometimes confused with the 'fop', or eighteenth-century aristocrat known for his vanity, elaboration and rather effeminate appearance. However, the dandy style was quite the opposite of this and introduced a style of masculinity that is more recognizably modern. The term 'dandy' is frequently used even today to describe a man who takes particular pride in his appearance, but dandyism, as the poet Charles Baudelaire defined it, goes much beyond this:

> dandyism is not . . . an immodest interest in personal appearance and material elegance. For the true dandy these things are only a symbol of the aristocratic superiority of his personality. In his eyes, therefore, which seek, above all, *distinction*, the perfection of personal appearance consists in complete simplicity – this being, in fact, the best means of achieving distinction. (1986: 55, emphasis added)

A French, dandified *Incroyable*, 1815, dressed in clean-cut, elegant costume popularized in Regency England by Beau Brummell. Reproduced with the kind permission of the Trustees of the Victoria and Albert Museum.

As a figure who made it his occupation to be a man of leisure, who prided himself on his aesthetic superiority, seeking distinction through the exercise of his exquisite taste, the dandy is a contradictory character, part modern hero, part aristocrat. On the one hand, the dandy was a new kind of social climber, a truly modern figure, whose status depended less on blood and inheritance than on good manners and impeccable taste; on the other he represented 'the last gleam of heroism in times of decadance' (Baudelaire 1986: 57), rejecting modernity and harking back to an older, English aristocratic style. Frequently without occupation, with no regular source of income and generally no wife or family, the dandy lived by his wits. In this sense, then, there is also something Romantic about the dandy

whose attachment to dress and style in general draws on the idea of
the individual as creative and self-creating as well as original. The
figures of socialite Beau Brummell in Regency Bath and Baudelaire in
mid-nineteenth-century Paris represent two versions of the dandy.
They also demonstrate a new shift in male dress; as Finkelstein
(1991) argues, the dandy is an important figure in the development
of modern fashions for men, his appearance marking a distinctive
break with the masculine style of the *ancien régime*. In contrast to the
elaboration of aristocratic male dress of the eighteenth century, with
its colour, embroidery and decoration, the dandy fashioned an
appearance of stark simplicity. Brummell, the archetypal Regency
dandy, summed up the formulae for dandyism as 'no perfumes . . . but
very fine linen, plenty of it, and country washing. If John Bull turns
round to look after you, you are not well dressed; but either too stiff,
too tight, or too fashionable' (Laver 1968: 21). Although representing a different, distinctly Parisian version of the dandy, Baudelaire's
dandyism similarly rejected eighteenth-century elaboration and colour in favour of a pared-down style based largely on black, offset only
by a flash of brilliant white at the neck and possibly a pair of pink
gloves.

The elegant simplicity of the dandy did not come without considerable effort. Brummell would spend hours each day at his toilette,
shaving and scrubbing until his skin all but shone, preparing his linen
and perfecting the knot in his cravat. For Baudelaire, the dandy
aesthetic was almost a religion, demanding conscious effort and
painstaking care akin to monastic rule. However, as Campbell
notes, the dandy's style was based not only on dress which had to
be 'perfect but understated', but on 'all gestures and expressions of
feeling, whilst an emphasis upon refined and subtle conversation led
to a premium being placed upon wit. To attain this ideal of refined
behaviour was successfully to display a superiority of self' (1993: 51).
The body was therefore the most important 'tool' for the dandy: the
style depended not just on wearing particular clothes, but on managing bodily demeanour, gesture and mobilizing wit to win status, and,
in Brummell's case, approval from the Prince Regent (later George
IV, at one time a companion) and 'society' as in exclusive Regency
social circles.

The look represented not only a new style for men, but a new
relationship between surface appearance and political and social
allegiance. It was during the Regency that a 'new balance was being
struck in which the external appearance, particularly for men, was
becoming a significant index of political and social interests' (Finkelstein 1991: 112). According to Baudelaire, dandyism appears 'in

periods of transition, when democracy is not yet all-powerful, and the aristocracy is only partially tottering or brought low' (1986: 57). The period of the dandy was indeed one of political instability: the turn of the century was characterized by revolutionary social and political turmoil and in such an environment, the old class order, particularly in France and Britain, was fast fading. In this atmosphere, 'the fate of an individual could be decided because of his or her political allegiances, the individual could increase his or her social security by demonstrating a disinterest in any political questions' (Finkelstein 1991: 112). And so it was that 'a certain number of men, detached from their own class, disappointed and disorientated, but still rich in native energy, formed a project "a new sort of aristocracy", based on superior indifference and the pursuit of perfection' (Baudelaire 1986: 57). In his quest for the best starched linen and elegantly knotted necktie, the dandy made visible his distance from more 'substantial' issues such as politics and demonstrated a greater concern with his individual social standing, as did Brummell. Social climbing or 'distinction', as Baudelaire puts it, was the ultimate aim. Although Brummell's social background was humble and his income by no means large, he came to be known throughout Regency Britain for his exquisite taste and elegance. His social standing thus depended upon the degree to which he could mobilize his body, his appearance, manners and deportment on which his fame rested. Matters of dress were important to the dandy because they revealed one's sense of taste, and hence 'one's essential quality of self' (Campbell 1993: 52). Therefore, as Finkelstein argues, Brummell's emergence on the social scene heralded an era when 'fashionability became increasingly common as a means of self-promotion'; an era when identity could be forged out of material objects (1991: 114). As Campbell notes, it was not so much fashionability that was prided, but 'his ability to create and maintain an overall image of refinement' (1989: 168). Brummell's self-fashioning depended largely on his famous cravat, and Finkelstein finds it fitting that his identity was forged from a decorative piece of clothing, an item of conspicuous style through which 'Brummell could declare his primary interests were in his own elegance and sense of aesthetics' (1991: 114).

Baudelaire's political allegiances were characteristically difficult to pin down: he had fought in 1848 on the side of the revolutionaries against the monarchy, although he later dismissed his actions as 'intoxication'; while he attempted to live the life of an aristocrat, in many respects he resembled the bohemians of the Left Bank, even though he sought to distance himself from them: as Steele notes, his clothing was 'designed to set him apart from the bourgeoisie, the bohemians *and* the conventionally elegant aristocrats' (1988: 83). In other words, in style he resisted any firm political allegiance, as did Brummell's. Baudelaire's fascination with the dandy is expressed most clearly in his homage to the painter Guys Constantine. However, his depiction is not without contradiction, since he notes how the true dandy is coolly indifferent, unlike the passionate Mr G, with his keen involvement in modern life (1986: 57). Also, the true dandy was a man without paid employment, which means that the artist-dandy, like Baudelaire himself, is a rather corrupted version. However, in the artist-dandy Baudelaire describes, one finds an essential feature of all dandyism, namely, the 'burning need to acquire originality' (1986: 56). The dandy's road to originality was a road that led away from the natural and authentic to artifice and performance. A highly mannered style, not only in dress but in deportment and rhetoric, held the key to superiority. And all manner of artifice could be employed. Although Baudelaire did not think women capable of dandyism, his depiction of female beauty is based on the same idea of artifice. Artifice is the privilege of culture which is, according to Baudelaire, of a higher order than nature and, with this in mind, he sings the praises of cosmetics which enhance a woman's beauty; 'the lamp-black that outlines the eye', 'the rouge that emphasizes the upper part of the cheek' all serve to represent a distinctly modern desire to exceed nature (1986: 64). Hence 'artifice ... can but be a servant only to beauty' (1986: 64). For Baudelaire, artifice was an ennobling thing in itself since it severed one from nature; embellishing and improving on nature.

It would therefore seem that the dandy is the antithesis of Romanticism which seeks out the authentic and celebrates the natural. However, in developing a 'cult of oneself', the artist-dandy has something akin to the Romantic about him, although there are important differences. Romanticism, in its celebration of the individual, indulges the senses and in doing so emphasizes pleasure, in stark contrast to the cold 'melancholy' of dandyism. In this respect then, dandyism for Campbell represents a version of the 'aristocratic ideal' which, in harking back to a bygone era of distinction, is reactionary. In order to find the ancestor of modern-day consumption and fashion, one must look elsewhere, to the figure of the Romantic.

The Romantic bohemian

According to Campbell (1989), while seemingly out of kilter with the modern age, the Romantic is crucially linked to the modern spirit of hedonism which, from the eighteenth century onwards, had the paradoxical effect of inducing a new attitude to consumption. The Romantic revolt stems back to the eighteenth century and is fundamentally an attack on modern ideas of empiricism, rationalism and materialism. Above these narrow ideas, Romanticism values 'change, diversity, individuality and imagination' (1989: 181). Creativity was valued and with it, the imagination, the ability to re-create oneself as well as create artworks. It was through the imagination that one glimpsed the possibilities for a perfect world, a 'bohemia', where one could escape from the imperfections of modern life. Although the Romantic ethos was linked to spirituality and not materiality, it laid the foundations for a hedonistic attitude towards the world and the objects in it, 'by providing the highest possible motives with which to justify day-dreaming, longing and the rejection of reality, together with the pursuit of originality in life and art; and by so doing, enabled pleasure to be ranked above comfort' (Campbell 1993: 54).

The desire to seek out the pleasures afforded by the senses drives the Romantic spirit in a never ending quest for novelty and amuse-ment, a 'longing to experience in reality those pleasures created and enjoyed in the imagination, a longing which results in the cease-less consumption of novelty', in other words an autonomous pleas-ure-seeking that is characteristic of modern-day consumption and 'self-illusory hedonism' (Campbell 1989: 205). Bohemianism not only articulates Romantic ideals but is a way of life devised along the principles of Romanticism. Like the dandy, the bohemian might not work, making leisure an end in itself. Unlike the dandy, however, the bohemian seeks out pleasure while relinquishing comfort (the bohemian frequently lives in poverty), and looks for new experiences by which to indulge the senses. This mentality is not, however, limited to the Romantic bohemian, who is essentially an outsider, but spread out across the eighteenth and nineteenth centuries, stimu-lating a new taste among middle classes for novelty which is the basis for modern fashion and consumption. According to Campbell (1989, 1993), there is, therefore, a close link between Romantic bohemian-ism and periods of expanding cultural consumption: the 1890s, the 1920s and the 1960s are the examples he cites. The link is also evident when one considers the place occupied by Paris, which was the spiritual home of bohemianism as well as the fashion capital of the world for most of the modern era. Paris was also the place where one found the most sumptuous and the most excessive department stores of the nineteenth century, temples of consumption and places for imaginary wanderings. It is the Romantic ethic that sent the consumer of the eighteenth and nineteenth centuries to department stores and markets, and a similar impulse drives shoppers to the malls of our own time. It also introduced an unquenchable thirst for novelty and fashion. The new department stores of the nineteenth century were Romantic spaces that opened one's eyes to a dreamlike world of sensory delight; a world of imaginary illusions where the shopper might indulge in the fantasy of owning the objects found there. In setting out their wares in fantastic and sumptuous displays, the department store was born out of the same spirit of self-illusionary hedonism described by Campbell (1989). The fact that more often than not consumption leads to disappointment and disillusionment – how often the object's magic wanes as soon as the parcel is unwrapped at home – is beside the point; indeed such disappointment is a necessary element in the unquenchable appetite of the modern-day consumer. This restless Romantic spirit, this indulgence in dreams and fantasies, is what drives fashion. In order to explore this further, it is necessary to examine the role played by department stores in the propagation of fashion in the nineteenth century.

Therefore, according to Campbell (1989, 1993), in order to find the new 'modern' thirst for fashion one should not look to the aristocracy, whose attitude to consuming objects is derived from a stoicism quite at odds with the playfulness of modernity; one should look instead to the bourgeoisie, the middle classes. Their style, far from emulating the fashions of those higher up the social ladder, was based on a new attitude towards the self, a concern with the imagination and a desire to seek out pleasure and novelty. However, as we have seen, in the figure of the Romantic one finds the emphasis upon 'authenticity', a concern which has become an important feature in contemporary understandings of identity. Instead of the playful artifice of a public self found in the eighteenth century, when public performance was held at a distance from the 'inner' private self, we have, as Sennett (1977) argues, placed an increasing emphasis upon the 'authentic' self locked inside the body and seek to 'read' this through appearance. Psychology, particularly 'pop' psychology, has aided this process, creating the idea of an inner realm of the self whose motives can possibly be read and understood. Modern books on social behaviour, whose topics range from flirting to management and business success, offer advice on how to 'read' the appearance of 'others' through their bodily appearance as well as how to control appearance to 'win friends and influence people'. Identity is therefore thought to be immanent in our appearance even while we are aware of the potential mistakes we can make when relying on surface information such as dress, body, hair, make-up and so on. The potential is there for the conscious manipulation of such tropes.

Fashion and Identity in Contemporary Culture

The above discussion of the dandy and the Romantic highlights some of the themes of fashion and dress in the nineteenth century. As well as illustrating the tension between appearance as artifice and authenticity, the two contrasting figures of the dandy and the Romantic illustrate the link, tenuous and ambiguous though it may be, between different cultural identities (in this instance, class) and dress styles. As Finkelstein (1991) argues, these themes can still be found in contemporary culture and indeed, the ancestors of these two characters, the dandy and the Romantic, can also be traced. Dandy figures litter the twentieth century: according to Hebdige (1979), the mods of the 1960s were typically lower-class dandies, exhibiting an obsessive interest in the finest details of dress. Further, the dandy celebration of artifice and performance runs through a variety of popular cultural styles from glam rock to punk rock. Similarly, Romanticism and a concern to be 'natural' runs through many contemporary understandings of identity, an exemplified in such figures as the hippies of the 1960s and 1970s.

However, the links between fashion and class identity are far less apparent in the twentieth century than they were in nineteenth. In particular, 'high' fashion, once the preserve of a small elite, has been democratized and has extended to more people than ever before. Further, the fashion hierarchy between classes has been inverted with 'high'-status styles no longer necessarily residing at the 'top' of the social ladder but 'bubbling up' from the street, from youth subcultures (Polhemus 1994). There is much evidence to suggest that fashion today emanates from a wide range of sites within youth culture. Distinctive identities are therefore still marked by dress and style but their status challenges traditional notions of status tied to class. In order to examine distinction in dress in contemporary culture we need to bring subcultural style into the picture. In the following discussion, I begin by exploring the links between dress/body styles and class in the twentieth century and then move on to consider the relationship between dress/body in subcultural style. Analysis of the youth subculture also provides an opportunity to return to Simmel (1950, 1971) and explore the way in which style articulates a concern with imitation and differentiation.

Class, distinction and style

At the beginning of the twentieth century, one could still distinguish between working class and upper class by observing their dress: working-class men and women often wore clogs rather than shoes, while the cloth cap was often the symbol *par excellence* of the working-class man as opposed to the top hat of the elite. Although these are obvious clichés, they do illustrate, at least symbolically, the associations between dress and class identities that once existed but have since become obsolete. By the mid-twentieth century, developments in the mass production of fashion, along with the increasing affluence of the working class, had led to fashion being extended to a greater number than ever before, blurring the boundary between the classes in terms of style. Today, class identity is less clearly bound to particular styles of dress than ever. There are, of course, instances of class-specific dress: the Sloane Ranger can be clearly identified by her Burberry, tweed suit and Alice band, for example. However, while *haute couture* has long been associated with a small elite group, in the 1980s designer fashion labels were marketed to an increasing number of people through the 'ready to wear' collections, extending the kudos of *couture* to an unprecedented number of people. Labels such as Christian Dior, Giorgio Armani and Calvin Klein, once exclusive, were opened up to a wider clientele and could be purchased by young urban professionals (the so-called 'yuppies') as well as by working-class children who might not own the real thing but a good replica bought at a market stall. Moreover, today's fashion industry is geared up to produce the latest catwalk styles almost as soon as they are displayed (see chapter 7). The democratization of fashion blurs yet further the distinctions between a fashionable 'elite' and the majority of people.

However, while obvious symbols of class identity have become less distinguishable, smaller details can still mark out distinctions. 'Quality', for example, is the key distinguisher of class: such fabrics as cashmere, linen and leather are associated with 'quality', as are good seams and proper lining. In order to decode these signs one needs to be 'in the know': like all signs, dress depends upon the cultural knowledge of the reader in order for it to be meaningful. However, styles of dress and taste in clothes are only one part of the equation; how one wears these things, indeed, how one 'wears' the body, are equally important. The body is the bearer of social status not just in how it is dressed, but in how it is held, how it moves, how it walks and talks. These bodily dispositions, the *habitus* (Bourdieu

1984), refer to the seemingly natural bodily demeanour we learn as members of a particular family/class. I say 'seemingly' since there is nothing 'natural' about these body styles: they are acquired through family and other cultural institutions such as the school. These acquired bodily traits come to be experienced as natural since we learn them at a very early age and come to take them for granted. The fact that these can convey subtle information about our social class position is evidenced by the fact that at one time the elite and those aspiring to be the elite sent their young ladies of marriageable age to 'finishing school', where they were trained more thoroughly in how to walk tall and graceful, get in and out of a car, eat at a formal dinner party and so on. The supposed 'natural' grace of a lady was thus nothing more than a body style. Here the body is clearly marked out as the bearer of social status.

Subcultural style, subcultural capital

As Simmel (1971) argues, distinction is a characteristic feature of fashion. However, in contemporary culture, distinction does not run along class lines alone but across a wide plane of social identities. In particular, youth subcultures with their distinctive style have become a source of fashion to the extent that, according to Polhemus (1994), such styles now 'bubble up' from street to designers rather than the reverse. Furthermore, subcultures employ dress to mark out distinctive identities both between themselves and mainstream culture, as well as between themselves and other youth subcultures. Thus, as Clarke et al. have argued:

> the peculiar dress, style and focal concerns, milieu, etc. of the Teddy Boy, the Mod, the Rocker or the Skinhead set them off, as distinctive groupings, both from the broad patterns of working class culture as a whole, and also from the more diffused patterns exhibited by 'ordinary' working class boys (and, to a more limited extent, girls). (1992: 56)

Thus, the subculture is a subset of a class culture but is 'smaller, more localised and differentiated' (Clarke et al. 1992: 55; see also Hall and Jefferson 1977). They share some of the same material conditions as their 'parent culture' or class culture, but express their own particular concerns through a distinctive use of style. Because of their distinctiveness, they have attracted a lot of attention. After the Second World War, in Britain in particular, there was a wave of passing subcultures, many of them attracting the attention of the media until they faded away to be replaced by another. 'Spectacular' is the word often used to describe these groups since their use of style and their distinctive patterns of life marked them out as different, exotic, even dangerous. Youth subcultures have been associated with a number of 'moral panics' since the 1950s: teddy boys were associated with excess and with violence; later it was the turn of the mods, rockers and skinheads to be the focus of obsessive media attention as 'deviant', 'violent' or 'hooligan'. The most discussed subcultures have been predominantly working class, male and generally oppositional to mainstream, white, middle-class culture. Indeed, McRobbie (1981, 1991, 1994a) finds this aspect of the research to be problematic since it neglects the experience of girls, who have played only a marginal role in post-war youth subcultures, primarily because they tend to be excluded from a culture which involves 'hanging around' the street late at night.

However, while distinction is one aspect of subcultural style, as Simmel (1971) has cogently pointed out, fashion relies on the contradictory tendency towards similarity; this too is clearly visible in the youth subcultures, which use style to articulate a clear identity to members within the groups as well as to those outside. Michael Brake (1981, 1985) argues that style expresses the degree of commitment to the group, indicating to those outside it the group's opposition to the dominant values. He goes on to note three aspects of subcultural style: image, such as costume; such accessories and artefacts as scooters or motorbikes; gait or postural expression, 'cool' for mods and 'angry' for punks; and lastly, argot, the special vocabulary of the group, and how it is delivered.

The style of the subculture articulates the particular issues or problems that the youth attend to and attempt to resolve. As mentioned above, the style of the mod was, according to Hebdige (1979), that of a lower-class dandy, the painstaking attention to the smallest detail of dress not unlike Brummell's obsession with tying his cravat. According to Hebdige, this style articulated a desire for upward mobility, a longing to 'escape' the monotony of working-class life. Not only did the dress manifest this concern, but so too the 'cool' body style of the mods, which put a 'blasé' distance between them and their immediate environment (high-rise flats in the East End of London, low-status jobs, for example). The term used by Paul Willis (1975, 1978) to describe this 'fit' between the focal concerns of the youth subculture and their overall dress, style, bodily demeanour and leisure activities is 'homology'. The motorbike rockers he examines demonstrate this fit very well: their focal concerns to express a 'hard' masculinity are articulated through dress which is 'hard' or 'tough' (leather being the pre-

Youth subcultural style in Camden market, London, summer 1999. Photograph taken by author.

ferred fabric), while their body posture is one of 'toughness' as opposed to mod 'cool'.

These distinctive styles and patterns of behaviour illustrate the way in which the dressed body can articulate particular identities, making them recognizable to those both inside and outside the community itself. Style then, that combination of dress and the way in which it is worn, is expressive not only of class identity but of subcultural identities. In this respect, style is the 'connective tissue' to which Wilson (1985) refers: it heightens our sense of connectedness to particular groups, making visible our commitment to a particular community. It is linked to class groupings and can articulate class allegiances, as in the case of the Sloane Ranger, or can be the substance which brings together a group that is a subdivision of a particular class. In all cases, the boundary between the inside and the outside of the group is policed in some way: style is one way in which one can tell if the other is a member of the same group. Subcultures depend upon particular forms of knowledge and behaviour and require particular ways of being. This is closely linked to what Bourdieu (1994) termed the *habitus*; subcultures produce their own particular practices which are in part bodily orientations or ways of moving, walking and talking which are worn like a 'second skin' on the body of the skinhead, punk, raver. In her account of club cultures, Thornton (1995) argues that these represent 'taste cultures' who share similar tastes in music, media and values. These club cultures are 'fluid', allowing entry to others for the duration of a single summer or event, and operate with 'hierarchies of what is authentic and legitimate in popular culture – embodied understanding of which can make one "hip"' (1995: 3). She conceives of 'hipness' as a form of 'subcultural capital'; this might not have the legitimacy of middle-class culture but nonetheless operates with its own hierarchies of legitimacy, depending on differentiation from the 'mainstream'. In focusing attention on the forms of knowledge and the hierarchies employed by club cultures, Thornton's account focuses much less attention on style than earlier studies of subculture.

In contemporary culture, the body has become the site of identity. We experience our bodies as separate from others and increasingly we identify with our bodies as containers of our identities and places of personal expression. We can use dress to articulate our sense of 'uniqueness', to express our difference from others, although as members of particular classes and cultures, we are equally likely to find styles of dress that connect us to others as well. This play of difference and similarity is a constant theme in fashion literature, as argued above. In modernity, this tension seems exaggerated since we live in a post-traditional world where identities are no longer as stable as they once were. The anonymity of the city opens up new possibilities for creating oneself, giving one the freedom to experiment with appearance in a way that would have been unthinkable in a traditional rural community, where everybody knows everything about everybody else. The modern or postmodern world where 'all that is solid melts into air' offers up new dangers and new pleasures and this is nowhere more apparent than in the city. The essentially ambivalent nature of this world, described by Bauman (1991), Davis (1992), Finkelstein (1991) and Giddens (1991), is experienced as threatening to some, such as the Romantic who feels alienated from modern life, and exhilarating to others such as the *flâneur* or the dandy who enjoy the freedom of the city and feel at home in its bustling streets. Fashion, dress and consumption provide ways of dealing with the problems of the modern world, characterized by increasing fragmentation and a sense of chaos. Fashion opens up possibilities for framing the self, however temporarily: as Davis (1992) suggests, fashion expresses two contradictory tendencies, taking inspiration from ambivalence and yet also trying to fix identity in the form of an image or style. In other words, as Wilson puts it, fashion 'opens up, yet simultaneously undercuts the possibility of individual self development and of social co-operation' (Wilson 1985: 63). However, as Davis (1992) argues, fashion does not produce permanent symbolic solutions: its symbols are too ephemeral and its ambivalence too deeply rooted. But in the modern world, clothing comes to play a part in how we deal with ambivalence. As Davis suggests, because dress frames our embodied self, it seems 'to serve as a kind of visual metaphor for identity' (1992: 25). Thus, the modern self is increasingly aware of itself, including its appearance, and able to intervene and act upon it. Classes and subcultures employ style, dress, body, posture and so on to create identity self-consciously, both to affirm group affiliation and difference to those on the outside and within. Thus when talking about individuality and identity and the role played by fashion and dress it is important to recognize that identities are socially meaningful. The individual may want to 'stand out' but she or he also wants to 'fit in' with a group.

5

Fashion and Gender

Introduction

According to Wilson, 'fashion is obsessed with gender, defines and redefines the gender boundary' (1985: 117). So while it would seem that today's fashions are more androgynous, even 'uni-sex' clothes display an overriding obsession with gender. Indeed, fashions in androgyny are further evidence of the degree to which fashion likes to play around at the boundaries of sexual difference. This obsession is translated into the dress men and women wear in everyday life which also shows a concern to mark gender difference: in many contemporary situations and on many occasions, there are particular types of clothing demanded of men and women. Clothes draw attention to the sex of the wearer so that one can tell, usually at first glance, whether they are a man or a woman. As Woodhouse notes, 'we expect men to dress to "look like" men and women to "look like" women' (1989: ix). This process starts early: babies, whose sex cannot usually be established at first glance, are very often dressed in colours, fabrics and styles of clothing which differentiate them and announce their sex to the world. Such practices are culturally and historically specific: the common association, pink for a girl, blue for a boy is a recent historical invention: 'in the early years of the twentieth century, before World War I, boys wore pink ("a stronger, more decided color" according to the promotional literature of the time) while girls wore blue (understood to be "delicate" and "dainty")' (Garber 1992: 1). That we now take the reverse to be the 'natural' colours of the sexes points to the fact that such distinctions of gender difference are arbitrary. Thus when we meet someone for the first time 'we *think* we see their sex, but in fact we do not. What we see is their *gender appearance* and we assume that this is an accurate indication of their sex' (Woodhouse 1989: 1). Thus 'seeing is believing' even though people can and frequently do 'cross-dress', sometimes very convincingly.

Practices of dress evoke the sexed body, drawing attention to bodily differences between men and women that might otherwise be obscured. The body is so frequently invoked through clothing that we tend to take for granted that the jacket worn by a man exaggerates his broad shoulders and *décolletage* emphasizes a woman's throat and breasts. However, clothing does more than simply draw attention to the body and emphasize bodily signs of difference. It works to imbue the body with significance, adding layers of cultural meanings, which, because they are so close to the body, are mistaken as natural. It is therefore the case that items of clothing do not neutrally reveal the body, but embellish it. For example, in men's dress, the male suit does not just accentuate male bodily features, but adds 'masculinity' to the body; indeed, until about the 1950s the transition from boyhood to manhood was marked by casting off short trousers and wearing long ones. So significant are clothes to our readings of the body that they can come to stand for sexual difference in the *absence* of a body. Thus a skirt can signify 'woman' and, indeed, is sometimes used (in an insulting way) to refer to a woman, while trousers signify 'man'. The crudest example of this is evident in the icons used to distinguish male and female public lavatories, which almost invariably show men in bifurcated garments and women in a skirt. The fact that women frequently wear trousers does not deter them from entering the door with the female icon, since these icons relate not so much to what men and women actually wear but to the clothing they are typically associated with (Garber 1992). Clothing, in this instance, is the *only* signifier of difference, serving to connote 'femininity' and 'masculinity'. So strong are the connotations that items of clothing can even transcend the actual biological body: the commonly used expression 'she wears the trousers' is used to describe a dominant woman in a relationship who has acquired characteristics normally associated with men. Here 'trousers' signify 'male' and 'masculine'.

It is obvious from these examples that when it comes to clothes we are far removed from the realm of 'brute' biological facts and firmly located within the realm of culture. Clothing is one of the most immediate and effective examples of the way in which bodies are gendered, made 'feminine' or 'masculine'. Thus, any discussion of fashion must account for the way in which it differentiates between two sexes, male and female, and for the way in which is comes to connote 'masculinity' and 'femininity'. Given that our ideas about masculine and feminine are tied not just to sex difference but to sexuality, there is a close relationship between the gendered codes of dress and ideas about sexuality. Indeed, as Butler (1990, 1993) argues, it is impossible to understand gender without understanding the ways in which sexuality is constructed in terms of 'compulsory heterosexuality'. In this chapter, I consider the ways in which clothing articulates ideas about gender and explore the role it plays in constructing 'masculinity' and 'femininity'. The connections between gender and sexuality (in particular, the way in which femininity is conflated with sexuality) are addressed here, but fashion's relationship to sexuality is explored in more detail in chapter 6. Fashion has typically been associated with 'femininity' and it is therefore necessary to consider also how this association has been established historically in the west. One possible explanation for this may lie in the close association of 'woman' with the body evident in much eighteenth- and nineteenth-century social theory, as well as in Christian teachings. However, before examining these themes it is necessary to define the terms; although they are closely linked, sex and gender need to be distinguished from one another and their relationship to sexuality also delineated.

Sex, Gender and Sexuality

Sex, gender and sexuality are often conflated so that there would appear to be a 'natural' and inevitable link between them. As Judith Butler (1990) argues, in western discourse our notions of what makes a man and a woman, i.e. our ideas about *sex* and *gender*, arise out of commonsense understandings of sexuality, generally applied to refer to *hetero-sexuality*. Before we can untangle this complicated knot, it is important to begin by establishing a distinction between all three terms, if only to see how they are inextricably linked.

The distinction between sex and gender has been crucial to feminist thinking of the 'second wave' and is associated in particular with social constructivist feminists, of which Ann Oakley's *Sex, Gender and Society* (1976) is a classic example. The aim of her book is to 'disentangle "sex" from "gender" in the many fields where the existence of natural differences between male and female has been proposed' (1976: 17). She defines sex and gender as follows: ' "sex" is a word that refers to the biological differences between male and female: the visible difference in genitalia, the related difference in procreative function. "Gender" however is a matter of culture: it refers to the social classifications into "masculine" and "feminine" ' (1976: 16).

Thus biological material determines sex, making us male and female, but does not determine the traits of 'masculinity' and 'femininity' which are the products of culture. This distinction is important since it enables one to see how bodies acquire meanings which are not the result of nature but the imprint of culture. So while all cultures mark out a difference between two sexes, not all cultures draw the line in the same place or agree on the characteristics of men and women. The fact that sexual difference is in part a culturally ordained difference has been demonstrated repeatedly by anthropological accounts that show how other cultures interpret sex and 'make-up' gender, of which Margaret Mead's *Sex and Temperament in Three Primitive Societies* (1935) is the classic study. The lack of any universal correspondence between sex and gender means that there is no 'natural' link between the biological categories of 'male' and 'female' and the cultural characteristics of 'masculine' and 'feminine'. Ortner (1996: 18) thus describes gender as a game, or more correctly, a multiplicity of games which take on different 'forms of bodily activity' as well as 'complex rules' according to time and place.

Further evidence that sex does not determine gender in a 'natural' way can be found in studies of hermaphrodites (individuals with characteristics of both sexes) who can go on to assume 'normal' gendered characteristics (masculine or feminine) despite the ambiguity of their biological sex. Studies of hermaphrodites (e.g. Stoller 1968) suggest that the acquisition of 'masculinity' and 'femininity' is not 'natural' or purely 'biological' but is the result of socialization – parental and cultural expectation. Similarly, the existence of transsexuals gives further evidence of the discontinuity between sex and gender. Transsexuals are born with the biological characteristics of one sex but identify with the gender characteristics of the opposite sex. As Oakley notes, 'to be a man or a woman, a boy or a girl, is as much a function of dress, gesture, occupation, social network and personality, as it is of possessing a particular set of genitals' (1976: 158).

Clothing, as an aspect of culture, is a crucial feature in the production of masculinity and femininity: it turns nature into culture, layering cultural meanings on the body. There is no natural link between an item of clothing and 'femininity' and 'masculinity'; instead there is an arbitrary set of associations which are culturally specific. Thus the way clothing connotes femininity and masculinity varies from culture to culture; while trousers are commonly associated with men and considered 'indecent' for women to wear in the west (until the twentieth century that is) they have been worn for centuries by women in the Middle East and elsewhere. Furthermore, the skirt which still potently communicates 'femininity' in the west has no such associations in other cultures where men and women wear sarongs. In the west, the skirt helps to maintain an arbitrary but crucial gender distinction. However, while distinctions of gender drawn by clothes are arbitrary, they often become fundamental to our 'commonsense' readings of bodies. In this respect, fashion also turns culture into nature, it *naturalizes* the cultural order. As Woodhouse notes, 'clothing forms part of a system of social signalling; it is used to indicate belonging . . . above all, it is used to demarcate gender, so that although the symbols change with fashion the gender/sex message remains the same, namely that feminine appearance indicates female sex and masculine appearance male sex' (1989: xiii).

In this way, says Woodhouse, we 'announce' our sex when we dress according to conventions of gender. This supposedly 'natural' link can be found in fashion magazines which frequently proclaim '*vive la différence!*', as if there was a natural, unproblematic difference between men and women that clothing simply reflects. However, the transvestite who masquerades in the clothing of the opposite sex challenges these cultural assumptions. When the masquerade is so convincing that they can 'pass off' their appearance as 'reality', it testifies not just to the importance of clothing in marking out gender, but to the way in which *sex* can be radically discontinuous with *gender*. The two are not fixed and stable as commonly thought, but linked by cultural threads that can be willingly broken.

While a distinction between sex and gender is useful in that it denaturalizes common associations between the characteristics of the body and the characteristics of 'femininity' and 'masculinity', many contemporary feminists are sceptical about the possibility of drawing a clear line between sex and gender (for a summary of this debate, see Entwistle 1998). Such a dichotomy assumes that sex is an unadorned 'fact' of nature, a pre-social state onto which a social meaning is pinned. However, as argued by Butler (1990), biology and nature do no stand outside culture as 'raw facts' which then acquire a social meaning: biology and nature are themselves socially constituted.

The dichotomy of sex and gender is made more complicated by the close association of both with sexuality. Sexuality is extremely difficult to define, as discussed in chapter 6. It is often assumed to be natural, an innate 'force' within us but, like sex and gender, it is a cultural phenomenon. The sexual experiences, appetites and prac- tices of men and women are often said to be derived from their biology, corresponding with the 'commonsense' gender character- istics assigned to them. These associations, while relying on nature, are in fact based in culture. However, rather than seeing ideas about sex and gender as the basis for cultural assumptions about sexuality, Butler (1990) argues the reverse: it is western ideas about *hetero- sexuality* that informs common understandings regarding *sex* (bio- logy) and *gender* (cultural characteristics); sex is therefore not an unadorned 'fact' of nature.

Modern social theory (here 'modern' encompasses the ideas and writings of the Enlightenment thinkers) has tended to see women as closer to the 'animal' or natural world because of women's role in reproduction (see Entwistle 1998, Sydie 1987 for summaries of this). Furthermore, women's bodies were seen by some philosophers to be the source of particular characteristics associated with women: wombs, for example, were also thought to make women's brains smaller, more delicate and less reasonable than men's (Sydie 1987). Thus, for Rousseau, women lacked the capacity of reason necessary to function in the public realm and must therefore remain confined in the private sphere of the home, the sphere of intimacy and emotions suited to their natures as carers of children (and men). When it comes to clothing, these connections between woman, the body and sexu- ality remain strong so that even in the professional workplace they are often seen in those terms. Cases of rape or sexual harassment at work with claims that 'she was asking for it' provide instances of this pairing of woman with the body (Lees 1999, Wolf 1991). This leaves many women anxious about what clothing is appropriate to wear to work, as discussed below.

Looking Back: Dress and Gender in History

Sexual difference has been marked out progressively through differ- ent styles of dress; it has also been marked out through discourses on fashion and finery which have linked them to the 'natural' vanity and weakness of the feminine soul. For centuries woman has been asso- ciated with 'fickle' fashion, vain display and indulgent narcissism. Indeed, this association may explain in part the marginalization of fashion within social theory, why it has been seen as 'frivolous', ephemeral nonsense, unworthy of serious academic attention. Typic- ally, as feminists have pointed out (e.g. Ortner 1974), the things associated with women tend to have lower social status than the

things associated with men and women's pastimes and preoccupations have been trivialized and mocked (Ang 1985, Modleski 1982,
Radway 1987). The characterization of women with the 'triviality' of
fashion and men with more 'serious' business has only recently been
challenged with the rise of the 'new man' whose narcissistic preoccupation with his appearance became the stuff of advertisements and
men's magazines from the 1980s, and whose relationship to clothing
and adornment presented a sharp contrast to the no-nonsense
'wash and go' masculinity, which had dominated much of the nineteenth and twentieth centuries. Therefore when considering fashion
and gender it is worth asking the question: why are women associated
with fashion more than men are?

Femininity and fashion

There is a strong relationship between women and fashion which is
both literal and metaphorical. Women have long been associated with
the making of clothes and women's prowess with textiles was one
means to enhance their reputation as ladies and suitable wives at a
time when they had little economic independence from men. From
the preparation of raw material (spinning, for example), to the sewing
and altering of garments in the home, the manufacture of garments
was for centuries in the hands of women. By the seventeenth century,
needlework was thought to be 'feminine' work, unfit for men to do.
Indeed, as Jones (1996) points out, stitching was thought to be
morally good for women, thought to promote devotion and discipline
and instilled in convent schools during the seventeenth century.
Women also enjoyed some control over fashion as *marchandes de
modes* in the *ancien régime* of pre-Revolutionary Paris. One such
marchande de modes was Rose Bertin, dressmaker to Marie Antoinette, whose power and influence over her famous client 'provoked
considerable censure' and exorcised those who were critical of the
queen's sartorial excesses (Jones 1996: 25). The blame for this extravagance was laid at the door of Bertin for provoking, tempting and
exploiting Marie Antoinette's love of finery. According to Jones, it
was not just the *marchandes de modes* who were thought to have
considerable influence over the spread of 'frivolous' and excessive
fashions, but the shop girls or *grisettes* who sold directly to aristocratic
ladies and whose sexual jealousy of these rich women was said to
'make their rivals "pay dearly" for their pretty clothes' (1996: 44).
Jones argues that by the nineteenth century these concerns about
women's involvement in commercial culture helped to produce new

ideologies of womanhood which swept female merchants 'to the back room, where they could stitch and sew but never command and control' (1996: 48). Women's control over the fashion system as *marchandes de modes* was also gradually broken down by the emergence of the modern male couturier in the person of Charles Worth, who became famous in the 1850s as dressmaker to the Empress Eugénie. As a consequence, female labour was progressively confined to unskilled production and later to 'sweating' and poor conditions of work and pay.

However, at least in medieval times 'woman became entwined with concepts of weaving, textile work and fashion as "feminine" pursuits' (Breward 1994: 33). These associations were 'simultaneously constricting and empowering': restricting in that they confined women to particular sorts of activity, but empowering in that they gave the medieval lady power over purse strings (1994: 33). In medieval times, says Breward 'the management of the wardrobe took on a special significance . . . viewed as a feminine prerogative, specifically concerned with the display of power through a wealth of textiles and the cultivation of physical beauty' (1994: 33). This power, associated with personal and social display and with the management of household expenditure, persisted for centuries as women became progressively responsible for making a home. Women's prowess in this field was seen to enhance the overall status of the household, a theme pursued by historians of the eighteenth century who have examined women's central role in the consumer revolution. As de Grazia has suggested, women's efforts to make a home 'served to define their family's history, to signal their social position to other bourgeois, to differentiate their class from that of aristocrats and workers' (de Grazia and Furlough 1996: 19). Thus, according to Breward, women (especially bourgeois women), 'became well versed in rhetoric of clothing, its growing importance as a communicator of status, taste and gender roles' (1994: 34). This is illustrated in Vickery's study (1993) of the consumption practices of one eighteenth-century lady, Elizabeth Shackleton of Alkincoats (1726–81) who spent much time and took great pride in the artefacts she bought, recording them in her journals and letters. As far as Mrs Shackleton was concerned, shopping was a form of employment most effectively carried out by women; but it was an occupation considered 'unskilled' even though it required time, effort and a good degree of knowledge about commodities and taste. Given that women stood to inherit personal products and not real estate it is not surprising to find them investing in moveable goods, and with no paid occupation and no 'skill', Vickery suggests that it is 'small wonder if, in consequence, she turned to personal and household artefacts to create a world of meanings and ultimately transmit her history' (1993: 294).

Alongside women being associated with the making of clothes, textiles and with consumption, there has existed also a metaphorical association of femininity and the very idea of fashion. According to Jones, 'women had for centuries been associated with inconstancy and change' (1996: 35), characteristics which also describe fashion. It is also the case that, as Breward (1994) and Tseëlon (1997) note, up until the eighteenth century, fashion had been considered a sign of the weakness and moral laxity of 'wicked' women, the daughters of Eve. After this, in the more 'enlightened' eighteenth century, women's association with fashion was explained more in terms of her distinctly 'feminine' psychology (Jones 1996).

In her analysis of the relationship of femininity to fashion, Tseëlon (1997) examines how ancient myths about femininity have informed western attitudes towards women. In particular, she examines the myths of Eve, Pandora, Lilith and the Virgin Mary. She notes that between them, these archetypal figures inform western moral attitudes towards woman and through these 'she is portrayed as disguising behind false decoration, using her beauty and finery as a vehicle to dazzle men to their destruction' (1997: 12). This attitude has taken on a very particular complexion within Judaeo-Christian teachings; from the tales of the First Testament, through the apostolic letters of St Paul, woman has been associated with temptations of the flesh and decoration, just one of the ways in which she can ensnare men. This history of Christian Europe 'bears witness to the fact that even though finery in general was considered a vice, it became conflated with the very conception of the essence of woman' (1997: 12). At the heart of this attitude towards woman was a fear of the body which, in Christian teachings, is the location of desires and 'wicked' temptations which had to be disavowed for the sake of the soul. As a descendant of Eve, woman was perceived to be more susceptible to temptations of the flesh and could also use her body to tempt men from the path of God.

Thus the decorated (female) body is inherently problematic to Judaeo-Christian morality, but so too is the naked, or unadorned body. As Tseëlon notes, in Judaeo-Christian teachings, nakedness became a shameful thing after the Fall and, since the Fall is blamed on woman, then 'the links between sin, the body, woman and clothes are easily forged' (1997: 14). Given its associations with sexuality and sin, it is not surprising that (female) clothing is the subject of such heated debate among moralists and clergy in the medieval period. According to Tseëlon, Christianity countered its fears about woman by attempting to control her sexuality, producing a discourse of modesty and chastity in dress which became encoded into female sexuality. Christian doctrine taught that redemption lay in the renunciation of decoration and modesty in dress, a moral duty born of Eve's guilt. This was carried over to female adornment in general but with the added *frisson* that no amount of modesty can entirely undo the potential sexuality of the female body once encoded as such. Clothes, 'through their proximity to the body encode the game of modesty and sexual explicitness, denial and celebration of pleasure' (1997: 14). So while they veil the body and hide its nakedness, clothes can also enhance the body and draw attention to flesh tantalizingly out of sight. This play of modesty and exhibitionism is a common one in western culture. According to Flügel (1930), who draws on psychoanalysis to analyse clothes, humans have innate but contradictory desires for modesty and exhibitionism which explains the purpose of clothes in the first place. Clothes represent an (inadequate) attempt to resolve this psychic contradiction and as such are a 'neurotic symptom'. Since they cannot effectively do so, they are a continual reminder of our highly developed sense of shame, becoming the 'perpetual blush on the face of mankind' (1930: 21).

If, as Tseëlon (1997) argues, women are more closely associated than men with the body, sexuality, sin and clothing, then it is understandable that they are more likely to be condemned for their dress on the grounds that it is immodest or sexually alluring. One can find particularly misogynistic diatribes on femininity and dress in the medieval writings of clergymen, as well as in the writings of later moralists of the seventeenth and eighteenth centuries. For example, she quotes Edward Cooke, who in 1678 wrote: 'a double crime for a woman to be fashion'd after the mode of this world, and so to bring her innocence into disrepute through her immodest nakedness; because she her self not only sins against shame, but causes others to sin against purity, and at the same time, renders her self suspect' (1997: 16).

From 1100 to the beginning of the seventeenth century, men's fashions were often highly erotic but it was women's immodest display that was the focus of religious and moral condemnation. Only a woman could be accused of seduction in dress. However, by condemning all forms of display, the Church 'has been instrumental in instilling into the female collective consciousness a permanent awareness of the way she appears, and the impact of her appearance on others' (Tseëlon 1997: 13). Little wonder, then, if women have developed a finely tuned self-consciousness about appearance which has nothing to do with their innate 'nature' but is a result of cultural attitudes and pressures. What is striking about this attitude to female display as seduction is that it not only holds woman responsible for her own sexual behaviour, but for man's sexual behaviour too: if a man succumbs to sexual temptation in thought or deed, it is considered her fault for dressing provocatively. This attitude persists in the notion that a woman was 'asking for it' if she was sexually assaulted or raped when wearing a short skirt or revealing dress (Lees 1999, Wolf 1991).

Thus women's fashion and dress has historically been regulated along the lines of gender and sexuality as well as the lines of social, i.e. class, distinction. However these two often converge: as discussed in the previous chapter, sumptuary laws attempted to regulate status but, in the case of women, they also differentiate between the good, gentle wealthy woman and her 'fallen' sister, the prostitute. As Emberley (1998: 9) notes, the hierarchy of furs and social positions created by these regulatory acts also influenced notions of sexual propriety among different classes of women. At certain times prostitutes were forbidden to wear fur as a means of differentiating them from 'respectable women'. However, it is not just sexual morality that is at stake in discourses on women and fashion: women's supposed love of fashion and all that glitters and shines is equally problematic in terms of the general social and moral order. In the seventeenth century and the early eighteenth fears about the spread of luxury sometimes focused on women's supposed insatiable desire and the threat it posed to the family. A tract of 1740, for example, includes the following: 'although her children may be dying of hunger, she will take food from their bellies to feed her own insatiable desire for luxury. She will have her silk fashions at any cost' (Jones 1996: 37). Thus moral discourse gave way to other kinds of rhetoric: 'sartorial offence moved from being defined as a moral transgression to being defined as a social transgression' (Tseëlon 1997: 16). While the former was considered indicative of character flaw, the latter indicates a lack of gentility, education and civility. Moral transgression was also of great concern for both sexes but a woman might transgress moral codes in more ways than a man. By being too highly decorated she might be seen to have fallen prey to the sin of vanity. However, by the eighteenth century, women's excessive interest in fashion was thought legitimate if its aim was to please a husband or attract a suitor (Jones 1996). Indeed, for some philosophers of this period, women's interest in fashion was an inevitable result of their 'feminine' psychology. Women, it was claimed, were peculiarly susceptible to finery 'because of their heightened sense of sight and lively imaginations' (1996: 36).

While men of aristocratic birth were decorated to much the same extent as women, for much of the early modern period this simple fact did not dilute the association of fashion with femininity. Indeed, when male peacocks were criticized it was often on the grounds of 'effeminacy' for showing too great an interest in fashion. Sometimes this criticism was levelled on the grounds that male interest in fashion transgressed the rightful division of the genders. At other times, effeminacy was seen as problematic to the image of a nation. The equation of effeminacy in male attire with the diminution of national interests can be seen in Elizabethan England: in the sermon 'Homily against Excess', which Elizabeth I ordered to be read out in churches such associations are described as follows:

> yea, many men are become so effeminate, that they care not what they spend in disguising themselves, ever desiring new toys, and inventing new fashions . . . Thus with our fantastical devices we make ourselves laughing-stocks to other nations; while one spendeth his patrimony upon pounces and cuts, another bestoweth more on a dancing shirt, than might suffice to buy him honest and comely aparel for his whole body . . . And every man, nothing considering his estate and condition, seeketh to excel in costly attire. (in Garber 1992: 27)

As Garber notes, effeminacy here does not mean homosexuality (as it often does today) but 'self-indulgent' or 'voluptuous' and therefore close to 'womanly' things. Criticism is levelled at the money, time and energy devoted by the effeminate man to the feminine and trivial frivolities of fashion. Similar criticism was directed at the 'Macaroni' style (described in chapter 3), which was popular among young aristocratic men of the eighteenth century. The term 'Macaroni' appeared in an English lexicon of 1764 to describe the style assumed by ultra-fashionable young men of noble birth. It was a rather 'foppish' style, Italianate and Frenchified, and was criticized on the grounds that this type of gentleman had 'become so effeminate and weak, he became unable to resist foreign threats and might even admire European tyranny' (Steele 1988: 31). Men have therefore not been immune to sartorial criticism. The criticism levelled at them at various times has often been on the grounds that they should be 'above' fashion. However, historical evidence illustrates that men have in their own way been under the sway of fashion.

Dress and gender differentiation

If one compares clothing today with the clothing of classical antiquity or medieval and early modern civilizations, it is possible to

Habits de Diverses Nations, steel engraving by Michael Colyn, 1581, showing how gender is not clearly marked in sixteenth-century dress: both men and women wear ornate garments, which obscure rather than draw attention to a sexed body. Reproduced with the kind permission of the Trustees of the Victoria and Albert Museum.

conclude that gender is probably more important today and more clearly differentiated. Indeed, 'until the seventeenth or even the eighteenth century, sexual difference in dress was not strongly marked' (Wilson 1985: 117). Laver (1995) suggests that the more significant division in terms of clothing has not been between genders but between 'draped' and 'fitted' clothes. Draped clothing is the simplest method of using cloth and involves tying a rectangle of material around the waist in the form of a sarong, as in Ancient Egypt, or from the shoulder as in Ancient Greece and Rome. It would seem that in these civilizations, clothing marked out class more prominently than gender; for example, in Egypt slaves were left almost naked as a mark of their low social status.

In medieval Europe sexual difference was marked out more clearly through dress, although class remained a pre-eminent feature. A prohibition on seeing the female leg meant women's costume took the form of a long skirt or robe in contrast to male dress which took the form of tights or breeches emphasizing the leg. This established separate patterns of costume for men and women: male dress in the form of bifurcated garments, tights, breeches and later trousers; and female dress in the form of skirts or such full-length garments as the *cotte*, mantle or gown. In other respects however, male and female dress was remarkably similar. Until around the eighteenth century, as Wilson notes, 'for riding and sport women dressed almost exactly like men, carried purses and daggers suspended from their belts' (1985: 118). Moreover, in terms of decoration there was nothing between the dress of men and women with the nobility of both sexes wearing ornate clothing in rich colours and fabrics, as well as make-up, wigs and perfume. The differences in dress were therefore less significant than one might have thought and 'by the close of the fifteenth century, fashionable dress had become so fantastical and absurd that it was difficult to tell men and women at a distance' (1985: 118). Moreover, tall hats and high heels worn by both sexes would have evened out differences in height between men and women. Later, the differences became more marked, as Breward (1994) suggests, with an aggressive masculinity asserting itself in the sixteenth century in the form of excessive padding around the shoulders, legs and, indeed, the genitals of men as codpieces became ever more exaggerated and elaborate. For all the obvious differences, it is also true that for much of the sixteenth century (and indeed, even the seventeenth) male and female fashionable dress often converged with elaborate ruffs and large puffed sleeves for both men and women. Jewels, ribbons, lace and embroidery also decorated the clothing of both men and women in the seventeenth and eighteenth century.

Over the course of the eighteenth century, partly as a result of the growing power of the bourgeoisie, excessive ornamentation, elaboration and artifice in dress was renounced in favour of a more 'natural' appearance. After the French Revolution male and female dress took on new, more relaxed contours, influenced in part by the classical republics of Ancient Greece and Rome. Wigs went out of vogue for both sexes at the turn of the century (although this was, in part, a reaction to taxes on hair powder) and hair for men became self-consciously unkempt and untidy, snatched back into a ponytail or left loose and wild. This more 'relaxed' style began to influence aristocrats and bourgeois men alike (Steele 1988). A relaxed country costume was adopted by some, but not all aristocrats – breeches, riding jacket, suitable for outdoor pursuits such as hunting and fishing. It was a style of dress that was to influence the dandies of the Regency and Victorian periods of the nineteenth century. Among some aristocrats however, a rather 'foppish' style, elaborate and perfumed, still prevailed.

However, as discussed in chapter 4, the undecorated style for men of the late eighteenth century and the early nineteenth is commonly seen to be more closely aligned to the rise of the bourgeoisie. By the end of the nineteenth century, this style had solidified into a stiff and sombre appearance for men, based largely around elements that would make-up the modern three-piece suit – slim trousers, fitted jacket and waistcoat. This paring down of male dress is referred to as 'the great masculine renunciation' by Flügel (1930), who draws on psychoanalytic theories to analyse fashion and dress. According to him, at the end of the eighteenth century 'man abandoned his claim to be considered beautiful. He henceforth aimed at being only useful' (1930: 111). He suggests that the only importance clothes had for men from this point onwards was the claim to be not elegantly or elaborately attired, but 'correctly' so. The causes of this were primarily of a political and social nature: 'it is not surprising, therefore, that the magnificence and elaboration of costume, which so well expressed the ideal of the *ancien régime* should have been distasteful to the new social trend and aspirations that found expression in the Revolution' (Flügel 1930: 111–12).

According to Flügel, the fraternal, democratic spirit that swept through Europe and North America caused male dress, which had previously emphasized social differences, to emphasize solidarity and *uniformity*; and instead of excessive elaboration, previously separating rich from poor, there took place an increasing *simplification* in male dress. The cries of democracy came from a bourgeoisie who had to work for a living, whose wealth was not the product of inheritance but their own labour. Thus, whereas the aristocracy had shunned all associations with economic activity considered degrading to the dignity of gentleman (the only significant activities being leisured ones, for example riding, and hunting, possibly extending to battle), the bourgeois made work an honourable thing in itself. A renunciation of 'decadent' plumage on the part of the bourgeois male signalled one's commitment to a life of industry, sobriety and work as opposed to a life of aristocratic idleness, sloth and leisure. Kuchta (1996) agrees with Flügel that the 'great masculine renunciation' emerged out of the struggle for political power between middle-class and aristocratic men, but puts it back much further in history, arguing that it had its roots 'in an aristocratic response to the increasing diffusion of fashion in the eighteenth century and to the political culture that emerged after 1688' (1996: 56). In other words, Kuchta suggests it goes back as far as the 'Glorious' Revolution in England

and not the French Revolution of 1789–92 or the Industrial Revolution of the nineteenth century.

The social, political and religious upheavals, Republican sympathies and classicism were woven into female dress of the late eighteenth century and the early nineteenth which took on classical contours similar to that of the ancient civilizations of Greece or Rome. According to Laver (1995) and Steele (1988), women's dress during this period was also influenced by the development of colonies which brought the European powers into contact with the simple dress of so-called 'primitive' civilizations (Steele 1988). In particular, Napoleon's expedition to Egypt 'induced in his compatriots a new wave of Orientalism which made turbans fashionable' (Laver 1995: 156). The dress of the period was indeed simple, a chemise or tunic, which, from 1795 until about 1815, developed successively from the Directory, through to the Consulate and Empire lines. The look was studied 'naturalness', the long line of the body and absence of a corset allowing for greater mobility. Indeed, historians often comment on the visibility of the female body at this time, arguing that 'perhaps at no period between primitive times and the 1920s had women worn so little as they wore in the early years of the nineteenth century' (Laver 1995). This simplicity of line did not last long: early in the nineteenth century corsets began to make a return in the form of long and short stays aimed at keeping a smooth, flat stomach. The classical long chemise was also soon replaced with the re-emergence of bell-shaped skirts. Over the course of the nineteenth century, changing fashions in corsetry and skirts altered the outline of the female body: crinolines, bustles, padding and a succession of different shaped corsets served to raise or lower the waist, flatten the stomach or the hips, raise or lower the bottom, pad out or flatten the bust. The crinoline made its appearance in the 1850s and was welcomed by many women for the freedom of movement it gave after the heaviness of layers of petticoats worn earlier. Among its disadvantages was that it could be a fire hazard, since the skirt could swing quite freely, and that it was also difficult to control in high wind, which created some embarrassing moments for some women. By the end of the 1860s, it was considered ugly and replaced by the long 'Princess' line of the 1870s.

During the Industrial Revolution gender differentiation in the public and private spheres became increasingly exaggerated: work was separated from the home and, although many working-class women went out to work, 'respectable' bourgeois ladies were confined to the home in the role of wife and mother (Davidoff and Hall 1987). The exaggerated emphasis on gender differentiation has been

Photograph of a Victorian woman in a crinoline skirted dress, c.1860. Photograph author's own.

seen to translate into the dress styles of men and women, with many traditional costume histories emphasizing these differences and neglecting some of the ways in which they converged during the late eighteenth and the nineteenth century. For example, dress of the Victorian period has been described as follows:

> men were serious (they wore dark clothes and little ornamentation), women were frivolous (they wore light pastel colors, ribbons, lace and bows); men were active (their clothing allowed them movement), women were inactive (their clothes inhibited movement); men were strong (their clothes emphasised their broad chest and shoulders), women were delicate (their clothing accentuated tiny waists, sloping shoulders, and a softly rounded silhouette); men were aggressive (their

Photograph by Roger Fenton of Queen Victoria and Prince Albert, 1854, showing how gender was increasingly differentiated in mid-nineteenth-century dress. Reproduced with the kind permission of the Trustees of the Victoria and Albert Museum.

clothing had sharp definite lines and a clearly defined silhouette), women were submissive (their silhouette was indefinite, their clothing constricting). Roberts (1977: 555)

Hence, the renunciation of decoration on the part of men is contrasted with the increasing fussiness of women's dress, particularly over the Victorian period when decoration with lace and ribbons seemed to reach a new zenith. The silhouettes of both sexes as well as differences are also noted in terms of colour contrast (the invention of new aniline dyes in the mid-nineteenth century meant that women's dress was seen to be bright, even garish, while men in an age of dandies and industrialization are typically depicted predominantly in black). Finally, commentators tend to associate Victorian women with the relentless movements of fashion, each new season bringing a new line which changes the contours of the female form, in contrast to men whose dress seems frozen, their clothes unyielding to the fickleness of fashion.

The question of how these differences are to be explained is implicitly asked by some theorists, and the tendency is to interpret these rather simplistically. For Laver (1995), the differences can be located primarily in the 'nature' of the sexes; for Roberts (1977) and Veblen (1953), differences of dress reflect the socio-economic positions of the sexes in the nineteenth century; while for Flügel (1930), whose ideas I discuss first, the differences are the result of *both* the natural psychic predispositions of men and women and social and economic conditions specific to the nineteenth century. These accounts tend to gloss over many other aspects of male and female dress at the time, downplaying the many similarities and exaggerating the differences between male and female dress. Thus the fact that women's dress took on many male items of clothing during the nineteenth century is neglected, as is the fact that men's dress did not solidify into the stoical uniform of the bourgeois gent until very late in the century, succumbing to the movement of fashion as well as giving in to some quite vivid splashes of colour for much of the century. Moreover, the discomfort of the tight, fitted male clothes is also generally overlooked. Such explanations, relying on common gendered assumptions, have been quite influential and are therefore worth considering in detail.

Explaining the differences – a 'natural' difference

The idea of a natural difference has been used to explain differences in the dress of men and women in the nineteenth century and the early twentieth, as has the supposed difference in male and female interest in dress. As a psychologist, Flügel (1930) explains male and female dress in terms of psychic drives. He asks why men renounced their fine feathers for the sombre clothes of the nineteenth century and also ponders how men can stand the sacrifice of relinquishing decoration; given their desire for exhibitionism (which Flügel sees as a basic human drive), he wonders where it may have gone. His response draws on the idea that men and women are 'naturally' different. Women, he says, are more narcissistic than men and have a keener sense of sexual rivalry, which makes them more inclined to compete with one another for sexual attention. Therefore, 'as long as individualism is permitted, women struggle with one another for wearing the "latest" or most costly frocks' (1930: 114). Men, on the other hand, have to operate in the social and political world and are therefore more likely to be affected by it. The drabness of their costume has the desired social and political effect of producing 'greater sympathy between one individual and another, and between one class and another' (1930: 114). However, since exhibitionism is a fundamental 'natural' psychic drive, the male will seek some form of compensation for its repression and will do so by displacing this desire to 'show off' onto other things. In this respect, work can act as a form of 'showing off', as can military uniform, which remained highly elaborate and decorative. He suggests that a modification in direction of this desire may occur, shifting men away from passive exhibition to active scopophilia: 'the desire to be seen being transformed into the desire to see' (1930: 118). Thus he suggests that men enjoy a 'vicarious display', in which they can enjoy and feel proud of the splendour of their woman. This displacement involves 'clearly some element of identification with the woman' (1930: 118–19) and may provide complete satisfaction in itself. However, where the projection of exhibitionism fails to satisfy male exhibitionism, 'the man may consciously seek to identify himself with a woman by wearing feminine attire', in other words, he may resort to transvestism (1930: 119).

In his discussion of male and female dress, Laver (1995) comes to similar conclusions as those of Flügel. He also suggests that women are more 'naturally' narcissistic than men and their dress exhibits what he calls the 'Seduction Principle', the aim being to enhance sexual attractiveness. He notes that, 'in general, the purpose of clothes for women has been to make them more sexually attractive and the purpose of men's clothes has been to enhance their social status' (1969: 14). So although men and women wore ruffs around the neck in the sixteenth century and although this was a status symbol for both sexes, Laver argues that for women it was also 'an attempt to exploit the wearer's charms' by drawing attention to her *décolletage*. Thus clothes play a part in attraction to the opposite sex, with men in particular looking for attractiveness in a woman.

These explanations provide examples of how the fundamental sexual differences between men and women, i.e. *'nature'*, are drawn upon to explain differences in behaviour, practices, roles which feminists would argue are based in the *social* world. Rather than describe 'facts', explanations such as these, which suggest women are 'naturally' more narcissistic than men, reproduce social attitudes about men and women. However, these ideas are not so much about biology or sex but *gender*. In particular, these explanations reproduce commonly held myths about women as seducers of men that have their origins in Judaeo-Christian attitudes (as described by Tseëlon 1997). There is in fact, no evidence to suggest that women are any 'naturally' more vain or narcissistic than men and plenty of evidence to the contrary. Indeed, one only has to look back through costume history to find that men took just as much interest in their appearance as women and spent at least as much time and effort. Furthermore, male dress may very well have been closely linked to exhibitionism and erotic display: codpieces worn by men for considerable periods in history are one item of clothing which was all about such display, while the focus on the male leg for many centuries, with tights and breeches, was similarily erotic, drawing attention to the male form. It could also be argued, as Sennet (1977) has, that the *décolletage* fashionable from time to time for women, was not about display of her 'charms' (as Laver 1995 would have it), but before the eighteenth century provided a 'canvas' for the display of fine jewels. By the nineteenth century, when women wore highly elaborate and ornate clothes, it was not because of any 'natural' inclinations but more likely the result of her limited social role. 'One only has to think of what it meant to a Victorian girl to attract a good husband to under-stand the reasons for her narcissistic proclivities. What else could she do, other than concentrate on her appearance?' (Roberts 1977: 566).

There are also specific empirical problems with the idea of a 'great masculine renunciation' at the end of the eighteenth century. For one thing, men did not renounce all colour and finery at this time. Indeed, as Edwards notes, 'the development of the dark modern suit for commerce did not start until well into the Victorian era. Indeed, it was not until the 1880s and 1890s that the stoic uniform of commerce really took off and, even then, the smartness of evening dress in top hat and spats also reached its peak of popularity' (1997: 19). Moreover, once the dark suit became popular, it would have been worn *in addition* to other garments. As Edwards notes, Victorian bourgeois men would have also worn tweed walking suits, hunting jackets, seaside jackets with bright stripes, as well as dinner jackets and velvet smoking-jackets in rich, jewel colours, such as emerald and purple. Even the dandy would not have been predominantly dressed in black until much later in the nineteenth century. The Regency dandy exemplified by Beau Brummell would have worn breeches in a buff, fawn or nut colour, a duck-egg blue or dark blue cutaway coat, a crisp, white shirt, and, on occasion, a canary-yellow waistcoat, pink gloves or a yellow cravat (Laver 1995). It was not until the 1860s that the dandy style, epitomized by the melancholic Baudelaire, became *exclusively* black. Moreover, ornate male dress persisted in military dress, which to this day remains brightly coloured and highly decorated (a fact which Flügel himself recognized). However, what these examples show, and what Edwards argues, is that the history of male dress, interpreted as the unfolding and uniform development of the dark three-piece suit, is misleading, as is the history of male dress that sees it as resistant to fashion. If one considers the male silhouette throughout the nineteenth century, it is possible to see a number of modifications: the introduction of breeches to replace tights in the early part of the nineteenth century and the later evolution of breeches into trousers towards the end of the century. So 'whilst it is true that fashion cycles and changes in overall form were, and to a certain extent still are, faster for women than for men, the more muted changes in decoration, detail and nuance are far more similar for each of the sexes' (Edwards 1997: 15). In fact, as Edwards notes, the overall shape of dress changed little for *either* sex, at least in the Victorian era, when sexual difference was marked by the wearing of either trousers or skirts. Further, while this difference was still quite marked, there was some degree of convergence between men's and women's clothing, with female dress taking on such aspects of male dress as tailored jackets from the 1860s onwards. Indeed, except for the skirt, women's walking outfits from the late nineteenth century through the Edwardian period were remarkably similar to men's.

Explaining the differences – 'social' divisions

While differences between male and female garments can sometimes be exaggerated, it is the case that the early and mid-Victorian fashions were notable for their constant gender coding. A persuasive argument for marked gender difference in the dress of the nineteenth century is put forward by Veblen (1953) and Roberts (1977). They both argue that dress conveys information about the social and economic status of the wearer and suggest that the dress of the Victorian upper class and bourgeois lady symbolized her subordinate position, symbolic of her role as 'man's chattel'. Veblen's account of fashion is based on his overall analysis of the so-called 'leisure class', the newly affluent class that emerged in the United States during the nineteenth century and attempts to re-create an 'aristocratic' way of life in the mercantile 'New World' Republic. This emerging class expressed its wealth through conspicuous consumption, conspicuous waste and conspicuous leisure; in other words, it demonstrated its 'pecuniary' strength by purchasing goods and discarding them when they were deemed out of fashion (rather than worn out) and living a leisured life (much as the life of an old-style aristocrat). Dress is a supreme example of the expression of 'pecuniary' culture, since 'our apparel is always in evidence and affords an indication of our pecuniary standing to all observers at the first glance' (Veblen 1953: 119). He suggests that the need for conspicuous consumption and waste may also explain the relentless movement of fashion. Wastefulness, he argues, is innately offensive and makes the futility and expense of fashion abhorrent and ugly. New fashions are taken up by people in an attempt to escape the futility and ugliness of fashion, with each new style welcomed as relief from the previous aberration, until that, too, in all its futility is also rejected.

According to Veblen (1953), women's dress of this milieu displays these dynamics more than men's, since the only role of the lady of the house is to demonstrate her master's ability to pay, his pecuniary strength to remove her entirely from the sphere of work. Veblen's account of the leisure class therefore constructs this upper class but *nouveau riche* woman as servile and he compares her role with that of domestic servants. These women are passive beings, 'men's chattel', and the elaborate, heavy, impractical as well as restricting clothes they wear indicate this. Their dress is also closely linked to fashion, signifying the ability to consume conspicuously and be fashionably wasteful. Moreover, the Victorian woman's dress was an important indicator of vicarious leisure: the clothes made her obviously incapable of work and were testimony to her distance from productive work as well as her consumption of leisure. Veblen describes the dress of these women as follows: 'the high heel, the skirt, the impracticable bonnet, the corset, and the general disregard of the wearer's comfort which is an obvious feature of all civilised women's apparel' (in Wilson 1985: 52).

Although Veblen's account refers to the United States at the end of the nineteenth century, his analysis has been applied more extensively. Indeed, as Wilson argues, it 'continued to dominate discussions of dress by a variety of writers in the fashion history field' (1985: 53). Roberts's analysis of the Victorian lady's dress (1977) is an example of Veblenesque theorizing. She argues that the heavy and restrictive dress conditioned women into a submissive-masochistic role, making her into an 'exquisite slave' who languished in her subordinate position. Her analysis focuses attention on the symbolism of the corset as the prime indicator of this submissive-masochistic position and she concentrates on the problem of the tight-lacing of corsets.

There are a number of problems with Veblen's account and these problems apply to Roberts's analysis also. Veblen is a functionalist: he begins by asking questions about why fashion emerges and what function it serves to the leisured class, concluding that it is ultimately dysfunctional, i.e. irrational. In doing so, he thereby reduces the role of fashion, failing to understand its more complex cultural and aesthetic role. However, there are further problems with their accounts of women's relationship to fashion which are worth noting here. In Veblen's and Roberts's analysis, women of a certain class are denied any sense of agency: fashion is conceived of as an over-determining and negative force in the life of the upper- and middle-class Victorian woman. Both Kunzle (1982) and Steele (1985) offer a rather different view of the Victorian woman's relationship to fashion and revise the standard fashion story of the corset as oppressive to women told by Veblen (1953) and also Roberts (1977). Steele's account sets out to consider the role of erotic display in fashion, arguing that the traditional image of the Victorian woman as sexually and socially repressed 'needs to be radically revised' (1985: 3). She points to the problem of envisaging nineteenth-century fashions as literally 'enslaving' of women and twentieth-century fashions as 'liberating' when, in fact, the story is far more complex and the continuities greater than one might assume from this crude characterization. Kunzle (1982) goes further than this, arguing that the wearing of the corset by the Victorian woman was not a sign of her servile status, but that instead, the female tight-lacer was a sexually and socially assertive woman, a social climber who used her appearance and sexuality to rise up the social ladder. Both Kunzle and Steele see the Victorian woman as an active subject and their argument is supported by historical evidence of what Victorian women did in their daily practice. (Steele, however, takes issue with Kunzle's evidence of tight-lacers; see chapter 6.)

Victorian dress reform

Women's dress was singled out in the nineteenth century for criticism on the grounds that it was unhealthy (it was said that corsets damaged the spleen and internal organs, particularly the reproductive organs); or unhygienic (long skirts picked up mud, debris and horse manure that were a constant feature of city streets in the nineteenth century). In addition, feminist reformers condemned the way in which narrow shoulders, tight waists, and expansive and awkward petticoats constrained the locomotion of the female body. However, it was not just women's dress that was criticized as constraining; men's dress with its tight collars, fitted waistcoats and jackets was also criticized by those, such as Flügel, associated with the Men's Dress Reform Movement. Furthermore, the dress of both men and women was seen by some to be 'irrational' in that it contorted the body into 'unnatural' shapes and was driven by the 'crazy' rhythms of fashion which were considered not just archaic to a scientific age, but wasteful and unnecessary. These reform movements came from a wide spectrum of society and were motivated by different concerns, some more progressive than others (Newton 1974, Steele 1985).

Various attempts were made in the nineteenth century to find an alternative, less restrictive female outfit. By the early 1850s, a form of dress known as the 'Bloomer' after its most famous proponent, the young American Mrs Amelia Bloomer, was received with much mirth by commentators on both sides of the Atlantic. The 'Bloomer' costume was loosely devised around an Oriental costume – a calf-length full skirt over billowing pantaloons; it was too much at odds with contemporary dress to appeal to many women at the time. Its association with Women's Rights campaigns at the time meant also that many regarded it with suspicion. However, while the Bloomer received much attention, Kate Luck argues that it was not the first occurrence of trousered dress for women, which dates back much further than this and was 'championed by members of a number of different, but overlapping reforming constituencies, most vigorously by socialist communalists and practitioners of water-cure medicine' (1992: 201). She further suggests that among these Utopian groups, trousered dress 'provided a focus for discourses around women's physiological development, professional capacities, the nature of her sexuality, and place in nationalist politics, and, as such, had anticipated most, if not all, of the questions which were to occupy the supporters of bloomerism' (1992: 201).

The first trousers for women were worn by those American women associated with the Utopian movement of the 1820s to the 1860s. A number of such communities, such as Robert Owen's New Harmony, Indiana (1825–8), were established across the United States as an alternative to industrial capitalism and devised their own uniforms. Luck (1992) suggests some possible reasons for the adoption of trousers by the women in New Harmony, not least their practicality, especially for manual work. However, Owen's unconventional views of marriage as an equal partnership between men and women helped to associate trousered dress with sexual impropriety. Furthermore, in the mid-nineteenth century, there persisted a taboo on

Satirical sketch of Mrs Amelia Bloomer, 1851, wearing her famous 'Bloomer' costume.
Reproduced with the kind permission of the Mary Evans Picture Library.

women's legs and trousered dress, in drawing attention to them, was considered by most as 'indecent'. Thus, 'from the mid 1850s, critics of Women's Rights could easily cash in on the identification of trousers with communal socialism and sexual unorthodoxy' (Luck 1992: 211). Trousered dress therefore failed at this time partly because it was seen to challenge a 'natural' and God-given distinction between the genders which deemed that men should wear the trousers. This might, in part at least, explain why the Bloomer costume was so negatively received and ridiculed as 'masculine' in the 1850s by British magazines such as *Punch*. It was also criticized by clergymen such as the Revd Mr Talmadge who 'quoted Moses from the pulpit as the authority who had forbidden women to wear men's clothes' (Newton 1974: 3). Mrs Bloomer's response similarly alluded to Old Testament imagery; 'her comment was that the first fashion was set by Adam and Eve when they assumed fig leaves, and nowhere was it stated that while Adam's were bifurcated, Eve's were not' (Newton 1974: 3). These associations did not stop other nineteenth-century dress reformers from advocating bifurcated dress for women on the grounds of health. However, those who continued to advocate this dress had to fight not just against 'public hilarity at the sight of such an eccentric dress, as has sometimes been supposed'; the real obstacles 'were the shibboleths of unrestrained female sexuality and social liberty' (Luck 1992: 211).

Working-class dress

So far this discussion has considered how gender has been progressively marked out by dress, concentrating on the upper and middle classes of the nineteenth century. In the case of working-class women, however, the gender boundary is to some extent different. For example, bourgeois respectability reproduced a sharp differentiation of gender in terms of dress which was not fully replicated among the industrial working classes of the nineteenth century. Analysis of working-class dress has been neglected, mostly because of a dearth of evidence. There are relatively few surviving examples of working-class costume in pictorial representations; the political economy of paintings, its exclusivity, meant that elite fashions were predominantly recorded and working-class clothes largely neglected. By the late nineteenth century this had begun to change, albeit slowly, and with the development of photography the field of vision extended to include more representations of 'ordinary' people.

One useful resource for the analysis of the (female) working-class dress in the nineteenth century are the photographs and journals of Edward Munby. Although not a photographer himself, Munby developed a passion (a 'benign perversity' as the editor of his journals, Hudson, calls it) for recording working-class women: 'throughout his life he entered innumerable cottages to buy photographs or persuade women to come to the local village photographer's' (Hudson 1974: 77). He would commission local photographers to take pictures of milkmaids, lady's maids, pit women, farm hands and the like, and recorded his expeditions, encounters and photo sessions with these women in his journals. Together his collections of photographs and journals provide a valuable insight into the dress and appearance of working women in the nineteenth century. These women, with their

Photograph of Ellen Grounds, pit worker in Wigan, with Edward Munby, 1873. Trousered dress was acceptable for working-class women at a time when bifurcated dress was still taboo for the respectable lady. Reproduced with the kind permission of the Trustees of The Master and Fellows of Trinity College, Cambridge.

sunburnt faces and calloused hands, were quite the antithesis of the
Victorian lady (in whom Munby showed no interest whatsoever) and
their work clothes quite the opposite of what a 'respectable' woman
would have worn. He describes meeting a pit woman as follows:

> a woman in flannel trousers, waistcoat (with livery buttons, in this
> case) and pink shirt and lilac cotton bonnet . . . about thirty and
> married: hair yellow, complexion golden brown, quite clean . . . A
> quite respectable woman . . . her dress was not noticed in the streets:
> in Wigan, a woman in trousers is not half so odd as a woman in a
> crinoline. Barbarous locality. (Hudson 1974: 76)

Barbarous indeed! Her appearance was quite striking given the standards of dress of the day. In London and in other 'genteel' provincial
towns, trousers would be unthinkable for a 'lady' to wear. Respectability was so closely tied to sexual propriety that to wear trousers
delineating the outline of the legs would be considered improper,
immoral and licentious. However, trousers were common enough
among working-class women in the nineteenth century, especially
those whose work was dirty and hard. When he visited a brewery,
he saw young trainee girls dressed in

> a loose cotton shirt, a waistcoat, and flannel or fustian trousers (petti-
> coats would be in the way, as Mr. S. [the manager] says), with skirt
> pinned up around the waist. Cotton bonnets are worn for the outdoor
> work. Such a dress is very picturesque and serviceable; and being
> perfectly clean – not blackened as at the pits – is extremely becoming.
> (Hudson 1974: 76–7)

Trousers would also have been worn by actresses on the stage,
although such women occupied a marginal status in society and, like
working-class women, were considered not quite 'respectable'. Munby's descriptions illustrate the fact that while dress plays a crucial part
in the gendering of bodies, it does not operate in isolation from class,
occupation and locality. His descriptions of these women also link the
body with dress – he was particularly fascinated by the 'hardness' and
of the working-class female body roughened by heavy labour as well as
by the 'coarseness' of their smocks and pinafores. Thus, exactly how
the difference in terms of gender is marked out is dependent upon the
class position, responsibilities of work and region of birth. A division
between the genders, while strongly demarcated among upper- and
middle-class circles by the wearing of either trousers or a skirt, did not
necessarily carry over into the working classes where this boundary
was, at least for female manual workers, semi-permeable.

Dress and Gender in the Twentieth Century

The twentieth century began with women in corsets and long skirts and ended with them able to wear bifurcated garments in public without risk of shame or censure. This shift was the result of myriad social, economic, political and cultural developments, as well as the inevitable outcome of fashion's relentless search for the 'new'. According to Steele, 'the First World War was in many respects the dividing line between the nineteenth century and the modern era' (1985: 224). However, while female dress of the Edwardian period seems strikingly different to the looser style of dress of the immediate post-war period, one must not assume that the War caused the change in fashion. In fact, while corsets, tight bustles and heavy skirts were replaced by more flowing garments, it is also true that the designs of Paul Poiret from 1908 and 1910 'can be seen as the precursor of the Twenties look' (1985: 213). Indeed, Poiret was himself influenced by dress reform movements before the war. Widening job opportunities for women had given them economic freedom and independence from men and are sometimes seen to have brought about a direct change in women's dress. Steele and Kidwell (1989), for example, argue that as women sought to be accepted in the man's world of business, they often adopted elements of men's clothing, for example suits and neckties, to appropriate some of the symbols associated with masculinity. However, according to Taylor and Wilson (1989), it is too simplistic to equate women in shorter skirts with full social and political emancipation. Women did not achieve the same status as men during this period and, to some extent, 'emancipation' in fashions and social mores (such as women smoking in public, or dating without a chaperone) 'served as a substitute for possibly more solid economic freedoms' (1989: 79). Furthermore, the shift in fashions for women was 'evolutionary, not revolutionary' (Steele 1985: 226). As Steele argues, while fashions may appear to change in step with the times, they are more likely the result of cyclical change *within* fashion than the simple reflection of social, economic or political developments beyond it.

However, attitudes were changing with regard to gender. During the Edwardian era more and more women played tennis, badminton, netball, hockey and the like, thus promoting a more relaxed, less constrained style of dress for girls and women. The look was encapsulated by the 'Gibson Girl', whose 'distinctive S-shaped body dominated the iconography of women into the 1900s' (Craik 1993: 73–4) and whose attitudes and lifestyle represented the outspoken,

Edwardian walking dress in the early twentieth century, showing the convergence that has taken place between male and female dress; the two women in the photograph wear tailored 'mannish' jackets. Photograph author's own.

active woman of the era and marked the beginning of the twentieth century 'cult of youth'. The bicycle also played its part, its growing popularity in the late nineteenth century and the early twentieth, giving women more freedom of mobility and gradually breaking down the taboo on bifurcated garments. However trousers remained socially unacceptable for the 'respectable' woman even in the 'emancipated' 1920s. The transformations in female dress of the early twentieth century are encapsulated in the style of Gabrielle Chanel who, by the First World War, had 'begun to design some of the first modern fashions' for women (Wilson 1985: 40). Chanel's pared-down style of sweaters, simple dresses and suits captured the essence of the modern woman's wardrobe, so much so that Wilson argues that 'the Chanel style was to become the paradigm of the twentieth-century style' (1985: 40).

While some of the age-old sartorial barriers were breaking for women, in menswear the story is a little different. Despite the best efforts of the French designer Jean-Paul Gautier, the skirt remains a potent symbol of 'femininity'. The taboo on men in skirts is so profound that men who dare to go in public wearing one risk ridicule. Thus, while on the one hand one could argue that there was an increasing blurring of the gender boundary in the twentieth century, particularly with the growth of sportswear which tends to promote a 'uni-sex' look, gender differentiation remains a persistent feature of fashion and it looks set to stay that way. While some recent fashions might appear androgynous, such styles have not abolished gender distinctions in clothing.

Indeed androgyny has been a persistent theme in twentieth-century fashion and took on numerous forms over the course of the century. The 1920s 'flapper' represents the first expression of something approximating to an androgynous look. Although for the Duchess of Westminster 'bosoms and hips were definitely *out*. A lovely figure meant a perfectly straight figure and the slightest suggestion of a curve was scorned as *fat*' (Steele 1985: 237), this was, says Steele, something of an exaggeration. The look caused some controversy because it represented a loosening of sexual morality; the woman of the 1920s was worldly wise and supposedly more sexually active than women of the previous generation. The conventions of feminine beauty were also challenged as fashions became 'chic and casual, very young and "semi-masculine", and certainly not traditionally "feminine" and "beautiful"' (1985: 240). Certainly, the emphasis on reed-like slenderness was new after the Edwardian 'matronly' figure and the curves of the 'S' shape. However, while the flapper with her cropped hair and straight dress was considered 'boyish' in her day, the style was more about youth than either boyishness or androgyny (1985: 239).

While androgyny has dipped in and out of fashion, it has merely played at the boundaries of gender which have otherwise been accentuated during the twentieth century. Sport, or at least a 'sporty' look, has continued to exercise a considerable influence over contemporary fashions and has helped to promote androgynous clothing. The American designer Calvin Klein began to market an extremely successful 'uni-sex' look, in clothes and perfume, in the 1990s. The 1950s stands out as the period which promoted a return to old-style notions of 'masculine' and 'feminine'. After the angular contours of the 1940s, when male and female silhouettes were broad shouldered, Dior's 'New Look' of the 1950s promoted a return to a Victorian shape for women, narrow waist and full skirt. The post-war New Look was subject to censure by some as 'wasteful' at a time when material was still scarce; it was also said to signify an ideology of femininity which put women back in the home after their war efforts. However, while the look was overtly 'feminine', the meaning of the New Look was far more complex than this, as Partington (1992) has argued. Partington examines the way in which working-class women appropriated the New Look, adapting it to their own circumstances,

A 1920s 'flapper', whose haircut and loose dress exemplify the new 'boyish', youthful look of the period. Photograph author's own.

and argues that in modifying it, these women inflected the dress with their own meanings.

Menswear and the 'new man'

Partington's insights into the complexity of meanings generated by clothes provide a good starting-point for considering men's fashion. As Edwards (1997) argues, modern men's fashions have been largely neglected; such attention as they have received is generally limited to the question of utility, omitting the nuances of male dress. The theories of Veblen (1953), Flügel (1930) and Laver (1995), discussed above, tend to see the development of modern male dress in terms of the renunciation of decoration in favour of the utility of the sober and constrained suit. However, as Edwards argues, 'the main example of the utility of menswear, namely the suit, is as much a symbol of masculine sexuality in terms of broadening the shoulders and chest and connecting larynx to crotch through collar and tie, as it is a practical (if historically uncomfortable) uniform of respectability' (1997: 3).

The suit, it is said, has the power to convey 'respectability' and the desire to be 'business-like' or 'professional'; but beyond that it has been seen to be devoid of any further meaning. However, these associations by no means exhaust all the possible meanings of the suit in different contexts. Polhemus notes how the 'zoot suit' of the 1940s was the focus of an 'extravagant use of expensive fabric', its 'luxurious accessories' loudly proclaiming 'I've got it made' (1994: 17). He goes on to note that whereas for Flügel (1930) the suit declared the renunciation of decoration, for the emerging black cultural identity in American cities of the 1940s, it became 'a showy extrovert garment' (1994: 18). The meanings of the suit (indeed any garment) are never stable, but subject to constant change and reinvention. When one locates dress in context and considers it as part of the practices of a group, as Polhemus does in *Streetstyle* (1994), rather than merely interpreting it abstractly, then these reinventions, renegotiations become apparent.

However, as argued in chapter 2, there is a tendency to simply 'read' dress at a theoretical distance. In the case of men's dress, the tendency has been to read only utility into men's fashions (as opposed to erotic display, which some theorists see as the only meaning of women's fashions). This stems not from anything essential about the suit but from the prevalent cultural attitude which constructs men as uninterested in the frivolities of fashion and clothes beyond absolute necessity. Hence the study of men's fashion has been stunted by the associations of fashion with effeminacy and the 'persistence of gendered attitudes, gender relations and gendered stereotypes concerning men, masculinity and their place in society' (Edwards 1997: 4). In his analysis of 'men in suits' in the legal profession, Richard Collier (1998) argues for consideration of male corporeality at work, suggesting that different styles of masculinity operate in legal practice but that the '*sexed* specificity of this style has, in contrast to the growing literature on the corporeality of women in the profession, remained largely unexplored' (1998: 32). In other words, men's bodies are taken for granted or rendered invisible, in contrast to the attention paid to female bodies at work and in other public arenas. However, Collier argues that this 'de-sexing' of men has been dependent 'on certain deeply problematic assumptions' and asks, 'does this mean that a courtroom consisting solely of men is without, or beyond the erotic? Such an argument would presume, first, that intra-male relations are asexual...and secondly, that as sexed beings, men's eroticism is confined to the private, affective sphere' (1998: 32). By examining different styles of dress and corporeality at work, Collier argues that the male body at work attempts to distance itself from connotations of the body and eroticism: the suit serves the purpose of desexualizing the male body, 'not in the sense of rendering men in suits beyond erotic attachment (far from it) but rather in terms of erasing the sexed specificity of the individual male body' (1998: 34). In other words, rendering 'invisible' the male body, the suit hides sexed characteristics, but more importantly, 'this body is normative within the public sphere, it has come to represent neutrality and *dis*embodiment' (Thornton in Collier 1998: 34).

The recent focus on the 'new man' concept of the 1980s has 'shown up the lack of previous attention to men's fashions' as well as the inadequacies of theorizing around men's fashions (Edwards 1997: 3). That decade has been seen as a significant moment in the history of men's fashions, representing a break in traditional notions of masculinity and producing, as Frank Mort (1988, 1996) argues, new, more sexualized representations of the male body. Whereas traditional masculinity has tended to locate it in the realm of production (i.e. work), the 'new man' of the 1980s was seen indulging in pleasures of consumption previously associated only with 'femininity'. Sean Nixon (1996) singles out four key sites for the 'circulation' of the 'new man': television advertising, press advertising, menswear shops and magazines for men. He argues that the 'new man' was the focus of marketing, design and retailing, all of which targeted the male consumer and constructed a range of masculinities from products made increasingly available for purchase on the high street. In the 1980s menswear increased significantly with the growth in retail of 'flexible specialization' which allows for greater market differentiation in products. High-street stores such as Next were at the fore of these developments, bringing quality fashion garments with strong design to the high street and 'average' male consumer. The growth and importance of design was also reflected in the rise of style magazines for men such as *Arena* and *GQ* which opened up new, differentiated forms of masculinity. A 'striking feature' of such magazines was 'the sheer volume of visual representations of men' (Nixon 1996: 167).

The analysis of the 'new man' spelled the beginning of serious examination into men and consumption. It also marked the emergence of a more overt eroticization of the male form, particularly in relation to the female gaze (as opposed to the homosexual gaze).

Masculinity, once uncharted and unquestioned, has now become the subject of inquiry, not just by academics, but by the press. Since the 1980s this new, supposedly 'narcissistic' but also 'caring' male has been publicly very visible and seen to be as happy to hold the baby as he was to wear an Armani suit. In newspapers much discussion has focused on the 'reality' of this 'new man': was he merely a media invention or a real 'reconstructed' male? The journalist Polly Toynbee argued in *The Guardian* in 1987 that such a man was a fiction and that 'it does not seem likely that we shall see him in our lifetime' (in Mort 1996: 17). However, asking questions about the veracity or otherwise of representations is fraught with difficulty: it is not always possible to equate representations with reality and it can be very misleading to do so, since the two do not enjoy any 'one to one' correspondence. Moreover, media and cultural theorists have argued that representations have their own 'reality'. Thus, as Mort (1996) argues, this 'new man' was 'certainly not mere chimera'; instead, he suggests that 'the debate over men's changing roles was concretised in a wide variety of settings' with the realm of consumption playing a key role as the place were such debate about masculinity was given an 'extended hearing' (1996: 17). He goes on to examine how, in the 1980s, 'the dynamics of the marketplace occupied a privileged place in shaping young men's wants and needs' (1996: 18).

While these developments in retailing and marketing extended the regime of representations of masculinity, they were not the only sites wherein traditional notions of masculinity were explored and challenged. Since the early 1970s, pop music has provided a forum for the exploration of gender: glam rock bands such as Roxy Music as well as performers such as David Bowie challenged some of the standard conventions of masculine self-presentation. Their exaggerated costumes, elaborate hair and dramatic make-up were the antithesis of conventional sobriety associated with masculinity. Later, in the 1980s, the emergence of new bands associated with the 'New Romantic' movement similarly challenged some of the most potent taboos in male dress. Pop stars such as Boy George wore obvious make-up, nail varnish, hair ribbons and skirts, provocatively playing with conventions, not just of gender, but sexuality too. Whereas heterosexuality has been the standard to which all masculinity has aspired, Boy George brought to the fore from previously underground sexualities a style suggesting both homosexuality and transvestism. The term 'gender-bending' was used at the time to describe the ways in which such taboos concerning (largely male) self-presentation challenged the basic conventions of gender. Oddly enough, however, neither Mort, nor Nixon or Edwards gives any space to popular music in their analyses of masculinity, choosing instead to focus on the 'mainstream' development of the 'new man'. This may have something to do with the fact that these styles had little impact upon mainstream male fashions and the consumption practices of the average 'man in the street'; indeed, these pop stars had more young girls than young men as their principal fans.

Cross-dressing and 'gender-bending'

For all its visibility in the 1970s and 1980s, cross-dressing remains a minority practice. However, in terms of this discussion of the relationship between fashion and gender it is an interesting phenomenon to examine since, in challenging the very terms on which conventions of 'masculinity' and 'femininity' operate, cross-dressing exposes the arbitrary nature of these conventions. Garber (1992) has examined both the 'fact' of cross-dressing in its different contexts (from medieval saints to contemporary pop stars) as well as the recurrent fascination with it in the west. Cross-dressing cuts into debates about sexuality and illustrates the difficulty of separating it from gender. Thus, cross-dressing has been a recurrent theme in lesbian culture; it has also been considered by some to be a sexual perversion, a manifestation of a gender disorder. Cross-dressers may also be confused with transsexuals (who actually believe themselves to be in the body of the opposite sex). However, such classifications are not only problematic, they are often resisted by the very constituency they seek to classify. Given its close association with underground and marginal sexualities, Garber's discussion looks at the way it is bound up with 'homosexuality and gay identity, from "drag" to "voguing" to fashion and stage design, from the boy actors of the English Renaissance stage to Gertrude Stein and Divine' (1992: 4). However, she argues that no account of cross-dressing should restrict itself to the gay and lesbian community since it frequently crosses over into high culture and mainstream popular culture. Cross-dressing was a feature of much Renaissance literature as well as in nineteenth- and early twentieth-century novels: Virginia Woolf's *Orlando* is centred on a cross-gendered character, while Honoré de Balzac's *The Girl with the Golden Eyes* and Théophile Gautier's *Mademoiselle de Maupin* both feature cross-dressing female characters who subsequently masquerade as men to woo female lovers.

Cross-dressing has been a recuring theme in popular culture also: films such as *Some like it Hot, Tootsie* and *Mrs Doubtfire* saw famous male actors, Jack Lemmon, Tony Curtis, Dustin Hoffman and Robin

Williams in drag. For Garber 'one of the most important aspects of cross-dressing is the way in which it offers a challenge to easy notions of binarity, putting into question the categories of "female" and "male", whether they are considered essential or constructed, bio-logical or cultural' (1992: 10). According to Garber, what cross-dressing produces is a crisis in the traditional binary division of male and female, masculine and feminine. Increasingly attention is being paid to the idea of a 'third term', a third sex whose very existence calls into question the stability of the categories of 'male' and 'female'. Thus hermaphrodites can be said to draw attention to the instability of sex and be seen to constitute a third sex. However, all to often, says Garber, cross-dressing is appropriated 'as' one or other of the sexes: it is assumed to be either a male or female phenomenon. However, for Garber, this denies or underestimates the transvestite which she argues produces a third term which '*is not a term*', or even a sex but a 'space of possibility' for the diminution or disappearance of gender (1992: 11). She goes on to note that the third term is always a space of negation – it signals something that *is not* rather than something that *is*, as in the case of the 'Third World' which has no unity beyond the fact of its being *not* the First or the Second World. This negation of the fixed categories of male and female makes cross-dressing so potent: as she puts it, '*transvestism is a space of possibility structuring or confounding culture*; it is the disruptive element that intervenes, not just a category crisis of male and female, but the crisis of category itself' (1992: 17). Gamman and Makinen (1994) are not so confident that cross-dressing is always and neces-sarily transgressive since much depends on the context in which drag is worn. This is echoed by Hotchkiss (1996), who argues that trans-vestism can sometimes confirm traditional order and at other times overturn it or remain an ambiguous trope. Gamman and Makinen are also critical of Garber's failure to make a distinction between cross-dressing and transvestism. The former may be undertaken by individuals for all sorts of social reasons; for example, women in medieval times right through to the early twentieth century cross-dressed in order to experience greater social mobility than that normally allowed for their own sex (Hotchkiss 1996, Wheelwright 1989). Unlike Garber, Gamman and Makinen argue that transvestism is distinct from cross-dressing in that it is linked to sexual pleasure where the transvestite experiences sexual arousal when wearing the clothing of the opposite sex, a pleasure akin to sexual fetishism. Similarly, Woodhouse (1989) argues that there is a difference between the cross-dresser and the transvestite based on the latter's desire to 'pass off' as a woman; cross-dressers, by contrast, aim to draw attention to the artificiality of their appearance. The distinction between the cross-dresser and the transvestite is explored further in chapter 6, as is the topic of sexual fetishism.

Masquerade, gender exaggeration and ambiguity

Cross-dressing reveals the arbitrariness or masquerade of gender: if femininity can be put on at will by men, and masculinity worn in the style of 'butch', or by 'drag kings', then gender is stripped of its naturalness and shown to be a set of culturally regulated styles. Gender is thus dislocated from the body and shown to be performed through style: femininity and masculinity are not the product of female or male bodies and there is no natural connection between female bodies and femininity or male bodies and masculinity. However, if this is the case, it is not just cross-dressers who perform gender and wear drag; we all do, since all dress has only an arbitrary relationship to 'natural' sex. However, what is sex? For Butler (1990, 1993), sex has no essential properties but is the product of our ideas about sexuality and gender which construe to create biological sex. Butler therefore uses the idea of performativity to 'make trouble' by subverting commonly held ideas about sex/gender. She goes on to examine how heterosexuality is the dominant framework, the hegemonic matrix or the 'regulatory framework' for organizing bodies and desires. Thus the sexed body gains its meanings only through the performances of gender which are culturally regulated according to heterosexual ideology. In this respect, Butler's work moves into the territory of cultural theory known as 'queer theory', which examines the way in which sexual desire has been historically and culturally constructed. For queer theorists, language marks out and defines sexuality and how it does so has important implications for gender identity.

Butler's ideas about performativity can be traced back to earlier theorists, although she departs from them in important respects. The psychoanalyst Joan Riviere has been particularly influential in suggesting that gender is performed through dress and body style. Her famous essay 'Womanliness as Masquerade', written in 1929, argues that women working in jobs considered 'masculine' or women with 'masculine ambition' had to hide behind a façade of 'femininity' so as to avoid retribution by men: 'womanliness therefore could be assumed and worn as a mask, both to hide the possession of masculinity and to avert the repercussions expected if she was found to possess it' (1986: 39). These women, often successful,

A transvestite, wearing a basque and women's stockings, draws attention to the artificiality of gender codes. Photograph reproduced with the kind permission of the photographer, Mike Hughes.

professional women, therefore adopted in exaggerated form, the signifiers of 'femininity' and might behave in a flirtatious manner with men they encountered. This exaggerated performance allayed some of their anxieties about their femininity and their desire for masculinity. However, crucially, she suggests that there was no simple distinction between 'real womanliness' and a 'masquerade of femininity': 'the reader may now ask how I define womanliness or where I draw the line between genuine woman and the "masquerade". My suggestion is not however, that there is any such difference; whether radical or superficial, they are the same thing' (Riviere 1986: 39).

The woman who acts in exaggerated feminine fashion is also sometimes referred to as a 'homoeovestite': a 'manly' woman who covers her tracks with a quintessentially feminine performance. The women who might fall into this category include Pamela Anderson, Dolly Parton or even Barbara Cartland, who exaggerate, almost parody, femininity. The difference between Butler's and Riviere's ideas is that whereas Butler challenges the very category of sex, Riviere remains at the level of gender in her analysis, leaving intact the binary male/female. However, despite these differences, they both illustrate the way in which body styles and styles of dress work to construct gender which is cultural rather than natural.

While it would seem that we live in a society where such binaries as 'male' and 'female' are breaking down, in terms of dress (as well as many other aspects of social life) convention still holds to the necessity of making the distinction. Further, clothing still carries a baggage of associations with either 'masculinity' or 'femininity'. For example, when women's fashions move in the direction of suits, angular shapes or coarser fabrics, they are described as 'masculine' or sometimes 'androgynous', both of which point to the importance of gender as a way of making sense of fashion. One might argue that gender is *more* significant today than it used to be. At least as far as elite fashions go, gender differentiation was not as important as class differentiation until sometime in the (early) eighteenth century.

In this chapter I have attempted to describe and analyse the way in which gender is marked out through dress, emphasizing how difficult it is to consider gender as a category separate from class, peer group and occupation etc., since the way in which gender is marked out and constructed varies accordingly. It is also constituted differently according to the specific social context. Thus, codes of gender vary enormously depending on many different factors operating in a given context. The skirt, for example, is the most heavily gender-coded garment, worn almost exclusively by women. It is often explicitly enforced in the dress codes of certain occupations or can be more subtly enforced by social convention, as in the case of certain professional occupations where a skirt is 'preferred'.

In sum, while women enjoy wider freedom in terms of dress today and men, since the 1980s, are able to indulge in previously 'feminine' pleasures such as fashion, contemporary society remains preoccupied with sexual difference, defining particular styles of body and dress for men and women. The boundaries of gender are tangibly still in place, though not totally unbridgeable for a few 'creative' individuals such as Boy George or Jean-Paul Gautier. For the most part, the regime of representations of masculinity and femininity, while broader, are nonetheless resolutely gendered and fashion continues to play on gender, even while it periodically deconstructs it.

6

Fashion, Adornment and Sexuality

If adornment is close to the body, it would seem to go without saying that it is close to sexuality. Modern sexuality is rooted in our (sexed) body, making the things we use to decorate our bodies, potentially at least, sexually charged. Moreover, since our bodies are the location of sexual feelings, it is no surprise to find the properties of adornments, the feel of cloth or the smell of leather, linked to bodily pleasures and eroticized, even fetishized. Steele (1985: 9) goes as far as to argue that 'because clothing is intimately associated with the physical body, at the deepest level all clothing is erotic', as is the 'quest for beauty' which is an inherent feature of fashion. However, it would be misleading to assume that bodily adornments such as clothes, jewellery, tattoos simply *reflect* a pre-sexed and pre-sexual body; in fact, they do much more than this, they *embellish* the body, infuse it with sexuality. The materials commonly used simultaneously cover *and* reveal the body, adding sexual meanings to the body that would otherwise not be there. It is often said that nakedness is uninteresting, not 'sexy', while clothing adds a mystery to the body that makes it all the more provocative. The imagination is an important component in sexuality and clothing which keeps parts of the body hidden can stimulate fantasy and increase sexual desire: indeed, striptease depends upon the mystery of clothes and the imagination of the viewer which are negated once all is revealed. Clothing then is linked to eroticism if we take eroticism to be an 'aspect of inner experience as contrasted with animal sexuality' (Bataille 1986: 29); in other words, if we take it to refer to feelings and passions of the imagination. Animals may have sex but they do not eroticize; only humans with their subjective and imaginative qualities do so. According to Georges Bataille, the decisive factor in the human erotic experience is 'an intangible aspect . . . not an objective quality' of the chosen loved object (1986: 29). If eroticism is imaginative and subjective, this may explain why the erotic objects of others are not always appealing to someone on the 'outside' of the experience (it is not just beauty that is in the eye of the beholder). This is true of all erotic experience: we might find our desires increased by certain items of clothing and we might find our own experience of sex enhanced by the use of clothes. This may explain why nudist camps have little 'erotic' appeal to most: indeed, nudism is not associated with the sexual body but some notion of the 'natural' body. That clothes 'add' sexuality to the body is further evidenced by the fact that nudists will often wear some form of adornment for evening social events as a prelude to a sexual encounter. So, as Steele argues, 'by concealing the body, clothes excite sexual curiosity and create in the viewer the desire to remove them' (1985: 42). Clothes and other bodily adornments are part of the vocabulary with which humans invent themselves, come to understand others and enter into meaningful relationships with them. It would therefore seem inevitable that they are incorporated into the vocabulary of desire and into the imaginative, erotic encounters one has with others. Fetishism provides a particularly extreme case where the object choice, be it a person, article of clothing, piece of fabric or shoe, is transformed in the imagination of the fetishist who endows the object with special powers. However, fetishism exists on a continuum of sexual behaviour; for most people, whether fetishists or not, clothing and adornment play an important feature in erotic life because of their ability to stimulate the imagination.

In this respect, it is not surprising to find fashion obsessed with sex. Fashion, says Steele, is 'a symbolic system linked to the expression of sexuality – both sexual behaviour (including erotic attraction) and gender identity' (1996: 4). Fashion frequently plunders 'underground' sexual subcultures (which as a result are no longer entirely 'underground') and the iconography of sadomasochism and fetishism now reaches the catwalk and the high street. In this respect, Steele argues that 'to understand contemporary fashion, it is crucial to explore fetishism' (1996: 5). Fashion has also drawn inspiration from gay and lesbian subcultures in its exploration of gender and sexual identity. In addition, the paradox of the sexually ambiguous transvestite has reached the attention of the mainstream media and produced a growing awareness of the sexual ambiguity of clothes.

In this chapter, I explore these associations between fashion, adornment and sexuality. I use the term 'adornment' deliberately since it is equally applicable to cosmetics, jewellery such as earrings, ankle chains, naval and nipple rings, tattoos and other bodily embellishments and the role they play in the expression of sexuality. Adornments such as these, while coming in and out of fashion, have in some cases a close relationship to sexual behaviour and practices, and can be linked to an erotic act, a sexual predilection or a sexual identity (homosexuality, transvestism or sadomasochism for example). In this chapter I suggest some of the ways in which clothing and adornment come to play a part in articulating sexual desires, sexual orientation and, indeed, sexual identity. However, as noted in the previous chapter, sexuality is a complex word which is closely interlinked with sex and gender. It is therefore necessary to define this difficult and ambiguous term before examining the ways in which adornment can be linked to the behaviour and practices, ideas and representations of sexuality.

Sexuality, Bodies and Dress

Sexuality is a modern construct. The word did not emerge until the mid- to late nineteenth century, and took some time to gather all its contemporary meanings. Bristow (1997), referring to the *Oxford English Dictionary*, summarizes some of the earliest uses of the word and notes how it developed alongside a growing Victorian preoccupation from the 1860s with classifying sexual types, such as homosexuals and bisexuals, within the context of normative heterosexuality. This Victorian obsession gave birth to sexology as a body of knowledge which seeks to understand sexuality and which started its project by producing typographies of sexual desires considered pathological, such as sadomasochism and nymphomania, as well as homosexuality and bisexuality. The word sexuality is closely related to *sex*, although it too is a difficult word to define since it can refer to an act (as in 'to have sex'), or to a set of anatomical characteristics (as in 'male' or 'female'). However, ironically, while linked to the sex and the reproductive capacities of men and women, sexuality, as a modern construct, is the product of the increasing separation of coitus from reproduction. Sexuality today is more than the sum of sex. It is closely linked to eroticism – to ideas, fantasies, desires, quite independent from the actual sex act or any imperative to reproduce. Thus, as Horrocks notes, sexuality embraces a wide range of human existence which makes it 'not a simple or uniform phenomenon' (1997: 1).

The modern fascination with sexuality also owes much to psychoanalysis: we live in an age still dominated by the theories of Sigmund

Freud, who proposed sex as the core of our identity, the key to a life of happiness and fulfilment. For Freud, babies are born with 'drives' focused around their bodily needs and pleasures. As well as finding pleasure in the satisfaction of basic bodily needs, babies exhibit the drive to be looked at and the drive to look. The libido for looking holds the key to understanding the development of our gendered identities, as well as providing an explanation for the potency of dress in terms of sexual desire. For Freud, boys and girls start out with a desire to look at the body and see the 'hidden' organs. It is this libido for looking that eventually catapults the boy through the Oedipal and castration complexes since it is with looking that one comes to the recognition of sexual difference. Thereafter these drives, the voyeurism and exhibition, acquire a gender: boys develop a desire for looking and girls a desire to be looked at. For Freud, this split comes with the acknowledgement of castration when the boy, metaphorically, if not literally, stares up the skirt of the woman, and recognizes her 'lack'. The shock of this realization can be traumatic for boys who may later come to develop different strategies to cope with this: the adult male may attempt to reduce the potential threat and fear of castration by repressing or compensating for the fact of castration. This might take the form of punishment of woman for her 'lack' and the trauma it produces, or by adding embellishments to the body of the woman. In the first instance, the shock is relieved through obsessive looking, or voyeurism, which fixates on, and interrogates, the body of the woman, often resulting in some kind of humiliation or punishment. In the second instance, it results in an obsessive fixation with a particular female body part, such as the feet, or object associated with it, such as shoes which serve as a penis substitute. Often the fetish object is chosen because of its proximity, temporally or spatially, to one's first sexual memory: shoe fetishism, for example, is sometimes explained by reference to its close association to the experience (real or imagined) of being on the ground looking up a woman's skirt.

Foucault's first volume on the history of sexuality (1979) examines the Freudian legacy and the way in which sex became a topic of considerable debate during the Victorian era. He argues that sexuality was 'put into discourse' through endless prohibitions with the effect of producing sexuality as an important aspect of one's identity. Given its historical contingency, Foucault is critical of the 'commonsense' idea that sexuality is a natural force, transcending time and place. On the contrary, he asserts that sexuality is not a force (which can either be repressed or liberated, as Freudian psychoanalysis and some Marxist philosophers have argued); instead it has no 'essence', no innate or 'natural' qualities, but is the product of systems of power/ knowledge (such as psychoanalysis) which have produced it as important in the process of naming and classifying it. Sexuality, then, is the product of our cultural attitudes towards sex which produce particular practices of sex as well as categories of sexual types. It goes without saying that sexual identity is closely linked to gender identity: the characteristics of gender are often rooted in commonly held notions of the sexuality of men and women. As discussed in chapter 5, these attitudes to gender and sexuality – men's supposed 'assertive' or even 'aggressive' natures and women's supposed 'gentle' and 'passive' natures, stem from what Butler (1990) calls 'compulsory heterosexuality'. Ideas about gender are the product of ideas about (hetero-)sexuality to such an extent that the two are often conflated. Ideas about 'femininity' are closely linked to ideas about feminine sexuality and this can be demonstrated by examining the way in which the two are conflated in debates about women's dress. This chapter examines the example of 'power-dressing' which, as a discourse on the dress of the 'professional' woman, illustrates particularly well the conflation of gender and sexuality. The female body, as this example demonstrates, is a body that is not only marked out as 'feminine' but saturated with 'sexual' meanings too.

The very complex network of associations between sexuality and sexual identity are woven into a whole variety of practices of adornment. Body adornment can be linked to sexual acts, give sexual pleasure, send out sexual signals, mark out sexualized identities. In this way, women's supposed interest in clothes and their desire to look 'sexy' is often naturalized, assumed by some sociologists and psychologists (as discussed in the previous chapter) to be a 'natural' inclination stemming from their desire to attract a suitable partner. Furthermore, men's desire to look at women, their pleasure in the 'props' and accessories of female dress, such as underwear, jewellery and the like, have become so naturalized that voyeurism or the 'male gaze' have become taken for granted as an aspect of male sexual psychology. The supposed 'natural' exhibitionism of women and voyeurism of men have of course been challenged by feminists and indeed, even Freud, who argues that these two distinctive 'drives' – the drive to be looked at and the drive to look – are present in both sexes at an early age; only later are they assigned a gender.

When the sexual pleasures or identities run counter to 'normal' or 'natural' heterosexuality, then the look or style is often deemed 'deviant' or even 'pathological', as in the case of some opinions on clothing fetishisms. Once defined, deviance, especially sexual deviance, often enhances rather than undermines the appeal of something and this may explain, in part, why mainstream fashion frequently plunders 'underground' sexualities such as sadomasochism, fetishism or gay and lesbian identities. Such looks and styles allow the fashion-conscious to 'play' at the boundaries of so-called 'normal' sexuality.

Adornment and Sexual Attraction

Western culture invests much sexual meaning in the female body and as such women are often acutely aware of the potential power of clothes, jewellery and make-up as sexual tropes which can enhance one's sexual appeal. This has nothing to do with any 'natural' feminine identity but the result of cultural associations which tend to see women closer to sex and sexuality than men. However, while the link between clothing and eroticism may seem obvious, it should not be confused with explanations of clothing/adornment based on some crude idea of 'sex appeal' such as Laver's theory of the 'shifting erogenous zone'. As discussed in the previous chapter, Laver's writings on fashion tend to draw on stereotypical ideas of femininity's close relationship to fashion. His idea of the 'shifting erogenous zone' illustrates the way in which women are constantly linked to the idea of seduction through appearance. Fashions for women, Laver (1969) argued, display a concern with seduction (he called it the 'Seduction Principle'). However, as argued in chapter 2, such mono-causal explanations of fashion are too crude to explain the complexity of women's fashions and, indeed, ignore the sometimes overt sexual nature of male clothing at particular periods in history. The motivations behind dress cannot be reduced to a single explanation: at different times we dress for different reasons and on some occasions women may dress for status and men to attract admirers. As Wilson (1985) argues, sex appeal is linked to standards of beauty which are enormously variable. Similarly, Steele's argument (1996) is critical of such a 'sex appeal' theory, which she sees as adopting crude ideas about female sexuality based on old-fashioned sex psychology.

The erotic charge of clothes may also stem from their ability to symbolize the sex organs. Freud interprets dress in terms of sex symbolism, arguing, for example, that fur symbolizes pubic hair, ties and hats the penis, shoes, girdles or veils, the vagina. Adopting a psychoanalytic framework, Flügel (1930) argues that not only could certain items of dress symbolize the sex organs, but so could the entire clothing system, which attempts to reconcile the contradictory desire for modesty and exhibitionism. The appeal of clothes, according to Flügel, comes from the fact that they can simultaneously reveal and conceal the body, enhancing the imagination and stimulating desire. Given that the focus of fashion is the body, it is no surprise to find fashion almost obsessed with sex and sexuality. However, whereas clothing in any culture, western or non-western, traditional or modern, may be linked to private and public erotic ideals, the modern fashion system differs in the way that it *commodifies* the body and sexuality. In other words, the fashion obsession with the sexuality of the body is articulated through particular commodities which are constructed as sexual. Fashion imagery in magazines and in print advertisements play at the boundaries of contemporary mainstream ideas about sexuality.

Power-dressing, Femininity and Sexuality

As argued above, sex and sexuality are closely linked to ideas about gender. This can be illustrated by examining the way in which the female body is produced through the discourse on power-dressing as both a 'feminine' and a 'sexual' body. Power-dressing emerged in the late 1970s in the United States as an explicitly feminine discourse on how to present yourself at work. It addressed the so-called 'career' or 'professional' woman and produced a way of dressing which sought to mark out or gender the female body by rendering it distinctly 'feminine'. The recurring theme of power-dressing is concerned to 'manage' one's sexuality so as to acquire 'authority', respect and power at work. The result is a 'uniform' for work which treads a thin line between 'masculine' dress (i.e. the 'suit') and 'feminine' decoration aimed at 'softening' the tailored lines of the suit. Power-dressing is closely related to the notion of 'dress for success' which had been heralded in the mid-1970s as crucial to the career success of men (Molloy 1980). It became prominent in the early 1980s against the historical backdrop of the women's movement and the increasing visibility of women in previously male-dominated professions. The power-dressing 'uniform' quickly became something of a cliché in the 1980s: tailored skirt suit in navy blue with smart blouse and something 'feminine' around the neck, such as a scarf or ruff. The style was embodied by Mrs Thatcher and many other 'professional' women in the public eye (even Princess Diana became associated with the style on some of her engagements). While power-dressing articulated many of the same concerns as 'dress for success', in particular, the 'commonsense' idea that how you look determines your success at work, it is different from its male counterpart in that it considered a woman's sexuality to be a major obstacle to her career development. Why did concerns emerge at this time about the dress of professional and business women, and why was it considered important for career women to pay particular attention to the potential sexual messages of their dress? Why was this issue unique to women? The answers to these questions lie in the cultural associations in western thought of the female body with sexuality which make female dress more sexually charged than male dress. This style of dressing, linked as it is to a whole discourse on the female body at work, demonstrates the degree to which women's bodies are *sexualized* bodies, and also the way in which gender is conflated with sexuality.

The professional and business workplace has historically been the domain of men and the way in which work is organized has traditionally followed patterns defined by men. Furthermore, the reproductive capacities of the female body led it to become associated with nature, reproduction and sexuality which are especially problematic for working women, since sexuality is deemed inappropriate at work (Gatens 1991, Hearn et al. 1993, McNay 1992, Ortner 1974, Sheppard 1989, 1993). The public realm of work is concerned with the maximization of profit and productivity and these are seen as achievable only through rational control over libidinal drives (Bataille 1986, Burrell and Hearn 1993, Hearn et al. 1993). The ability to do one's job in almost all occupations (except those in the sex industry) require that sexuality be left at home. Women's cultural association with sexuality is therefore potentially undermining for their role, status and authority at work. Feminists such as Hearn et al. (1993), MacKinnon (1979), Pringle (1988, 1993) and Sheppard (1993) have noted that sexuality is often used to undermine women at work. However, it should be noted here that while sexuality can undoubtedly be used *against* women, it can of course, be harnessed *by* women to further their own interests: not only does the prostitute dress to accentuate her body and attract clients, but a saleswoman might decide to dress in a short skirt in order to increase her chances of making more sales with men. In both instances, sexual power might translate into economic power, although how liberating or empowering this is is open to question.

Power-dressing, however, does not attempt to harness sexuality in this way; it is directed at those women in occupations where sexuality is deemed inappropriate. Power-dressing manuals such as Molloy's *Women: Dress for Success* (1980) outline a set of rules which promise the career woman some control over her body and self-presentation

in the face of male-defined notions of female sexuality and the potential objectifying male gaze in the workplace. According to Molloy, the
professional or business woman needs 'authority' if she is to achieve
success in her career. He considers two things as undermining of
'authority': looking too much like a 'secretary' and therefore not
obviously 'professional'; and looking too 'sexy'. The clothing recommended by Molloy diminishes the potential sexuality of the female
body. He advises women not to wear waistcoats for business because
they draw 'attention' to the bust and his advice extends to the sort of
jacket women should wear: it 'should be cut fully enough to cover the
contours of the bust. It should not be pinched in at the waist to
exaggerate the bust' (1980: 50). The jacket is the primary signifier
of 'professional' and is set in sharp contrast to the sweater which, as
well as being associated with secretaries, is also a garment good for
attracting men: 'a cashmere sweater on a woman with even moderate
build is one of the greatest seduction garments in existence' (1980:
77). The popularity of the 'Sweater Girls' of the 1950s (stars like
Lana Turner) testifies to this association. However, while the body of
the career woman must not be deemed too sexual, this requirement
does not mean that women ought to dress like men: on the contrary,
women must maintain their 'femininity' at the same time as resisting
the potential problem of eroticization and objectification. However,
Molloy not only warns career women not to look too sexual, he also
advises against being too 'feminine' at work: wearing 'feminine'
patterns such as floral print, or 'feminine' colours such as salmon
pink are undermining to a woman's 'authority'. He suggests that
scarves are good 'attention seeking devices' at work as they draw
attention to the face and away from the (problematic) breasts. However, while avoiding looking too 'feminine', the aspiring career
woman must also avoid being too 'masculine'. This is one reason
he offers as to why trousers are generally to be avoided in the board-
room and the office. He says that although it can be acceptable in
female-dominated companies, 'you are taking a chance if you have to
deal with men' because apparently men do not like doing business
with women in trousers (1980: 73). A woman in a skirt is therefore
unmistakably 'feminine' and this, according to Molloy, makes her
less threatening to men at work.

    In this way, power-dressing attempts the impossible, negotiating a
veritable tightrope for professional women, balancing the need to
diminish sexuality with the need to maintain femininity in a man's
world of work. The dress advocated as the most appropriate for the
female professional worker is a compromise between the demand to
contain the potential eroticism of the female body and the demand to

look like a woman at the same time. The female business suit sees the body of the woman divided in two: her torso is covered by a fitted jacket which de-emphasizes her breasts, but her femininity is signalled by the wearing of a skirt. By wearing a skirt to the office, the business or professional woman signals her commitment to 'femininity', even though she might be operating in very male-dominated arenas of work. This need for femininity within a man's world is put more plainly by an image consultant I interviewed as part of my research into the dress of professional women (Entwistle 1997b, 2000). She firmly advocates skirted suits for business encounters: 'men', she says, 'like to see a woman's legs'. Thus, while sexuality may be off-limits, the skirt which potentially connotes 'femininity' is not just acceptable, but preferable. However, one might ask whether it is possible to maintain a distinction between the sexuality of the female body and conventions of femininity. Might it be the case that skirts on women are preferred not because they are 'feminine', but because the skirt draws attention to a sexualized area of the female body? Indeed, given the cultural associations of 'feminine' with 'sexual', it could be argued that the two cannot be pulled apart and the dress of women is the outcome of a conflation of the two. The contradictions of power-dressing illustrate the way in which the distinction between sexuality and gender often collapses, particularly where a woman is concerned. It demonstrates how 'woman' is made up, in part, from her associations with sexuality; the two are inextricably linked. The 'rules' or conventions of dressing the female body for work demonstrate how it is still routinely associated with sexuality and how women, as objects of the male gaze, need to 'manage' their bodies to avoid associations with sexuality.

While the term 'power-dressing' has gone out of vogue, the main tenets of this style of dressing have not. Career-minded, professional women still have to manage their dress more carefully than their male colleagues and have not abandoned the skirted suit (Entwistle, 1997a, 1997b, 2000). Professional and business women continue to express concerns about how to present their bodies at work so as not to be read as 'sexual'. This concern with the body gives further evidence of the way in which women have had to become conscious of their bodies and responsible not just for their own sexuality, but for the sexuality of men who might be 'misled' into reading sexuality into their dress. One woman I interviewed suggested that women have to monitor their own dress for the benefit of men who might find it difficult to 'read' women and their bodies. She argues that dressing for work is about not throwing out any kind of sexual signal and I think the workplace is not the right place for that, you know ... but I think in the workplace, particularly with all these cases of sexual harassment, women have to be sensible and sensitive to men and *their response* to the response they might produce ... it is about not sending out the wrong signals be they sexual ... most men would be appreciative of women who don't dress provocatively. (Entwistle 1997a: 246–7)

Her statement here implies that sexual harassment is something that women can have some control over if they dress appropriately and don't throw out a 'sexual signal'. However, given the instability of dress and the potential for any garment to be interpreted as sexual, no style of dressing can ever eliminate the problem of sexual harassment. Indeed, such an attitude is highly problematic, especially when, as in many rape cases, it is invoked to imply that rape is something women invite through their dress (Lees 1999). What this attitude illustrates is the way in which women's bodies are a potential liability at work because of their associations with sexuality. It is hardly surprising to find that the discourse on power-dressing attempts to diminish these associations but at the same time reproduces them in another form.

Fetishism and Adornment

Perhaps the most obvious illustration of the connection between adornment and sexuality is fetishism, where objects themselves become a focus of sexual excitement. While fetishism carries some stigma of 'perversion', it has enjoyed an interesting relationship to fashion since the 1960s or so, when fashion designers began to plunder underground sexual subcultures. At this time the fetish look reached the mainstream through television characters such as Emma Peel in *The Avengers*. The 'kinky' look combined leather, PVC, corsets, stockings and high heels. As Polhemus (1994) notes, many of these garments were created by the designer John Sutcliffe, who ran a small company called Atomage, which made clothes for underground fetish 'enthusiasts'. This world was brought into the public arena and made more readily available by Malcolm McLaren and Vivienne Westwood's shop SEX where overtly 'kinky' clothes were bought by punks in the 1970s.

The term 'fetishism' has three meanings within three different intellectual traditions. It was originally used within anthropology to describe a sacred object, such as a talisman or totem, which was thought to be endowed with special or magical properties by a particular community. It was later taken up by Marx to describe the way in which commodities under capitalism come to have a life of their own, especially when the 'object world is endowed with intrinsic powers, properties, values and meanings' (Slater 1997: 112). Thus, 'commodity fetishism' refers to the way in which commodities come to acquire magic, often in the shape of 'sex appeal'. The third set of meanings, from psychology, sexology and psychoanalysis, is applied to the way in which some objects become associated with sexual feelings to such an extent that the individual needs that object in order to become sexually aroused and/or reach orgasm. As Steele (1996) notes, Alfred Binet and Richard von Krafft-Ebing were the first to use the word in the modern psychological sense. Krafft-Ebing defined fetishism as 'The Association of Lust with the Idea of Certain Portions of the Female Person, or with Certain Articles of Female Attire' (Steele 1996: 11). Krafft-Ebing also coined the terms 'sadism' (after the Marquis de Sade) and 'masochism' (after Leopold von Sacher-Masoch who wrote the classic erotic tale, *Venus in Furs*). In his analysis of fashion and fetishism, Kunzle defines fetishism as 'the individual displacement of private erotic feelings onto a non-genital part of the body, or onto a particular article of clothing by association with a part of the body, or onto an article of clothing in conjunction with its effect on the body' (1982: 1).

A fetish can therefore be a part of the body (legs, breasts or feet, for example) or an article of clothing associated with a particular part of the body (shoes, suspenders or bra); it can also be the combination of the item of clothing with its effect on the body (such as the feeling of constriction when wearing a corset or rubber suit). Any object that adorns the body can lend itself to fetishism – corsets, bras, high heels, as well as materials such as rubber, leather or PVC, whose properties of smell or constriction or shininess make them popular with fetishists. These materials outline the contours of the body and make the body smooth and shiny. Some fetishists enjoy dressing up in their chosen fabric so that their entire bodies are encased and constricted. Sexual pleasure comes from both the feeling of constriction and the sight of one's body as a complete, hermetically sealed object (in symbolic terms, a phallic object).

Fetishisms can of course become fashionable. Sometimes fetishes become so wide as to define the fashion of a particular people or period: as Kunzle notes, 'when fashion (group cultural expression) and fetishism (individual sexual expression) are perfectly harmonised, we may speak of a "cultural" or "national" fetish' (1982: 1); he gives the example of foot binding in China. Steele (1996) notes that western fashions periodically borrow from fetishism: *couture* designers such as Vivienne Westwood, Versace and Thierry

Mugler, as well as high-street stores have all at different times adopted some of the style of fetishism. However, while there is some convergence between fashion and fetishism, we need also to draw a distinction between them. Fashions may 'play' with the idea of fetishism but this playfulness is some distance from the actual experience of fetishism as it is commonly defined within academic literature. While Freud believed that that a certain degree of fetishism is present in 'normal' love, most people are not fetishists in the 'pure' sense of the word as defined by psychologists. Freud argued that we may focus on a part of the body (the legs, buttocks, breasts) as part of our sexual desire in the 'other' but that

> the situation only becomes pathological when the longing for the fetish passes beyond the point of being merely a necessary condition attached to the sexual object and actually take the place of the normal aim, and further when the fetish becomes detached from a particular individual and becomes the sole sexual object. (Gamman and Makinen 1994: 37)

Gamman and Makinen agree with Freud's insistence on 'some degree' of fetishism being present in all of us, but disagree with him on his distinction between 'normal' and 'pathological'. Likewise, Steele warns of taking the term 'pathological' at face value. What Freud, Gamman and Makinen do agree on is the importance of distinguishing between different stages of levels of fetishism and for this they refer to the work of Paul Gebhard as particularly useful, since he is one of few researchers who looks at fetishism in terms of 'stages' or levels. For Gebhard, level one is when there is a preference for a certain type of sex partner, stimulus or activity which is not really fetishism at all but akin to Freud's idea of 'normal' love. Level two is when there is a strong preference for certain kinds of partners and/or activities. Level three is when specific stimuli are necessary for sexual activity and when such objects are needed in order to experience sexual gratification and/or orgasm. Level four is when specific stimuli take the place of the sex partner and is fetishism of the most extreme kind. This is useful when drawing a distinction between fetishism as a sexual predilection and fetishism as fashion style. Fetishism 'proper' involves much more than simply adopting a fetishistic look; it is much more about sexual feelings produced when wearing particular garments. Thus, for Freud, as for most psychoanalysts, fetishism is only 'pathological' when an object becomes detached from the body of the beloved. Gamman and Makinen cite Freud's essay 'Fetishism' (1963), which moves from describing fetishes to giving them a psychoanalytic reading, arguing that they stand in for the 'lost' phallus of the mother. Freud is thus led to the theory that fetishists are more likely to be male, since men are more likely to seek a substitute for the penis and might fetishize the female body in order to allay castration anxieties. This association of men with fetishism is accepted by most psychologists working in the area of sexuality. Stoller (1985), for example, suggests that fetishism is a predominantly male phenomenon, although he describes a small number of women fetishists (such as a woman he encountered who was excited to the point of orgasm when wearing men's clothes). Gamman and Makinen (1994) have challenged this orthodoxy, suggesting that women can be fetishists and frequently do fetishize objects in their adoration of and/or fixation on pop stars, food and clothes. They refer to Freud's argument that

> half of humanity must be classed among the clothes fetishists. All women, that is, are clothes fetishists . . . it is a question again of the repression of the same drive, this time however in the passive form of allowing one to be seen, which is expressed by the clothes, and on account of which clothes are raised to a fetish. (Freud in Gamman and Makinen 1994: 41)

Here Freud is not arguing that women are active fetishists, but that their idealization of clothes is linked to the repression of their desire to be looked at. Gamman and Makinen assert that women's attachment to objects can and does involve active fetishism but their argument depends upon explaining fetishism not in terms of compensation for castration anxiety (as in classic psychoanalytic theory) which would imply that only men can be fetishists. They refer to an alternative view on the origins of fetishism, namely that it can be explained by reference to early memories about separation from the mother, an experience which is as traumatic for girls as for boys. Separation from the mother is sometimes allayed when the child fixes on certain objects associated with her, such as stockings and shoes, which can serve as substitutes in her absence. If this theory of fetishism is adopted, it would seem that women certainly fetishize and Gamman and Makinen offer plenty of examples to support this.

In recent years, images of women in fetishistic clothing have proliferated. A few famous women, such as the English designer Vivienne Westwood and the singer Madonna, have popularized the fetishistic look for women in their exploration of sex and sexuality. The style played an important role within punk subculture; female punks in the 1970s, in their garish make-up, suspenders and stockings, leather and chains, drew inspiration from subversive style to openly flout the conventions of femininity. Madonna's book *Sex*

(1992) explores taboo areas of female sexuality such as sadomasochism, bisexuality and lesbianism and her image around the same
time drew inspiration from such sexual subcultures. As Steele (1996)
notes, fetishism periodically comes in and out of fashion and images
of women in fetishistic clothing have become more commonplace
since the 1960s. She argues that capitalism has played a part in the
rise of fetishistic fashions 'both because fashion itself developed con-
currently with the rise of capitalism and because the fashion industry
has recently stolen a great many items from the fetishistic wardrobe'
(1996: 55). Capitalism has the ability to incorporate much that is
radical and controversial and does so as part of its search for new
markets and continued consumption. In this way, it has brought
previously underground sexual subcultures into the mainstream,
albeit stripping the style of some of its original meaning. Since
capitalism frequently uses sex to sell goods (as noted above, this is
related to commodity fetishism), it is not surprising that goods which
come ready made with sexual meanings are plundered.

However, while it is more acceptable today for women to explore
sexuality openly and while fetishistic clothing is more openly available, there are still few accounts of women as practising fetishists.
There may be exceptions to this: women's enjoyment of underwear
may, for example, provide us with real female fetishists. The controversy surrounding the wearing of the corset in the late nineteenth
century draws attention to the practice of tight-lacing, said by
Kunzle (1982) to be practised among a small group of fetishists
who, he claims, were sexually and socially assertive women. The
corset controversy is an interesting one to examine because of the
questions it raises as to the relationship between clothing, eroticism
and sexuality.

The corset controversy

The corset is a garment that has strong associations with sexuality
and eroticism in both past and present culture: once tied to the
Victorian standard of beauty, it now has links with sadomasochism
in pornographic iconography and enjoyed some popularity as a fashion item in the late 1980s (Steele 1996). More than any other piece of
feminine attire, it has excited considerable controversy: seen as an
instrument of physical oppression and sexual objectification by
Roberts (1977) and Veblen (1953) and by Kunzle (1982) and others
as a garment asserting sexual power, it is now acknowledged as a
stimulant to sexual pleasure for its 'enthusiasts'. There are, therefore,

numerous readings of the corset which Kunzle (1982) and Steele (1985, 1996) are keen to point out. Both recognize the ambivalence of the corset and indeed, all clothing, which expresses two opposing desires: garments cover the body and also enhance and display it. Thus, Kunzle notes that 'the socio-sexual symbolism of tight-lacing and its ritual components reveal its essentially ambivalent purpose to enforce the sexual taboo by objectively oppressing the body, and simultaneously to break that taboo by subjectively enhancing the body' (1982: 2–3).

However, while both Steele and Kunzle agree on the erotic nature of the corset and argue that the established reading of the 'passive' Victorian woman oppressed by her stays needs revising, when it comes to interpreting the evidence on tight-lacing, there is some disagreement. For Kunzle, 'the history of tight-lacing is part of the history of the struggle for sexual expression, male and female' (1982: 2). He goes on to analyse Victorian women (and some men) who were tight-lacing fetishists and did so because they enjoyed the feeling of constriction produced by the corset to the extent that they might become sexually aroused by it. This practice he sees as sexually expressive, even liberatory, especially for women for whom it repres- ented an alternative to the asexual femininity on offer within domin- ant Victorian culture. The enemies of sexual expression for Kunzle were those dress reformers who condemned the corset on moral or health grounds, insisting on an ideology of femininity tied to do- mesticity. He goes on to argue that 'women used their sexuality, and sexualised forms of dress, as women always have, to rise out of a socio-sexual subject position. And they got morally scape-goated for their pains' (1982: 2).

His argument relies on evidence taken from magazines such as the *Englishwoman's Domestic Magazine* (*EDM*) which, between 1867 and 1874, published a series of articles and letters on tight-lacing and became the focus of a debate among tight-lacing fetishists and their detractors. He also draws heavily on personal accounts from diaries and interviews. Such sources suggested that tight-lacers could lace down to waists as tiny as 16, 15, 14 and even 13 inches and pro- claimed the erotic as well as health benefits of such a practice. In addition, tight-lacers frequently spoke of the erotic pleasures of high heels which, together with the tightly laced corset could, says Kunzle, induce pleasurable kinetic sensations of an erotic kind. In addition, the corset itself could play an elaborate role in sexual foreplay:

> the state of being tightly corseted is a form of erotic tension and con- stitutes ipso facto a demand or erotic release, which may be deliberately

PETER ROBINSON'S WORLD-FAMED "CORSET TAILLEUR,"

In Fine Coutille, Black or White	...	...	**8/11**	In Sky, Pink, Cardinal, or Black Satin ... **29/6**
Ditto, First Quality, with extra Busk	...	**17/9**	In Rich Brocades **52/6**

Advertisement for corsets, illustrating the restricted waist, considered beautiful in the late nineteenth century. More than any other single item of clothing, the corset has been singled out for widespread criticism. Reproduced with the kind permission of the Trustees of the Victoria and Albert Museum.

controlled, prolonged and postponed. To the male the corset represents an intricate erotic obstacle, the deft removal of which permitted the development of all kinds of erotic foreplay, and betokened amorous expertise. To the woman, unlacing meant (promise of) sexual release. (Kunzle 1982: 31)

By his own definition of fetishism as the displacement of erotic feelings onto a non-genital part of the body, an article of clothing associated with a particular part of the body, or an article of clothing in conjunction with its effect on the body, tight-lacing fetishism for Kunzle is not the same as corset fetishism. Corset fetishism focuses on the object itself which is associated with certain powers or properties of the loved one, as in the case of the lover who unlaces his beloved. The tight-lace fetishist may not be interested in the corset *per se*, but in the sensations produced by the tightly laced corset and the erotic tension produced when wearing it, as in the case of the woman for whom sexual release comes from being unlaced by her lover, or in the male lover who takes pleasure in the tight effect the corset has on the body of the beloved. There is, therefore, something sadomasochistic about tight-lacing and many of the letters to the *EDM* are sadomasochistic in their celebration of the tension, constriction and pain induced by tight-lacing. Some have a common narrative structure in recounting memories of being forced to wear a tight corset by a strict parent or teacher at a boarding school. As Steele (1996) notes, the letters to the *EDM* focus on three things: extreme body modification as a result of wearing a corset day and night; a sadomasochistic pleasure in domination and humiliation; and cross-dressing – some of the correspondents were male cross-dressers who enjoyed wearing corsets.

Steele (1985, 1996) takes issue with Kunzle's claims for tight-lacing fetishists as sexually and socially liberated individuals, as well as with the evidence on which he bases his argument. However, she first insists on the need to distinguish between ordinary *fashionable* corsetry as practised by most nineteenth-century women, and the minority *fetishistic* practice of tight-lacing: most corset wearing stayed within the realms of ordinary fashion, with only a minority of corset producers reporting greater demands for smaller and smaller corsets. Furthermore, the statistics that Kunzle draws on are inherently unreliable. Those quoted in letters to the *EDM* probably exaggerated the statistics for erotic effect; measuring corsets that still exist today is of little use, as there is no way of knowing how tightly these may have been laced. Concerned philanthropists in the nineteenth century gathered other statistics from lingerie shops which were responsible for measuring women for their corsets. Some corsetiers claimed that the tighter the corset, the smaller it must have been laced. While it is not impossible to imagine some waists as small as 16 inches, Steele suggests that 'such waists are rare' and it is 'time to discard the myth of the 16-inch waist as a touchstone for thinking about the nineteenth-century woman' (1996: 61). She also argues that while there were some habitual tight-lacers, tight-lacing has also to be seen as part of a spectrum of corset wearing. Habitual tight-lacers, or tight-lacing fetishists, she argues, were few and far between and we cannot therefore make generalizations from this small minority. It is impossible to know from the accounts in the *EDM* whether or not there were many female tight-lacing fetishists. While many of the letters to the *EDM* were signed with women's names, this does not mean they were actually written by women since, as Steele (1985) rightly points out, it is a common practice within pornographic literature to attribute sexual tales to a female character. This is not to say that there were no Victorian tight-lacers, as Kunzle claims, but the evidence he provides is inconclusive.

While the corset gradually disappeared from women's fashions in the early twentieth century, it has retained its potency as an erotic garment and still represents one of the most significant fetish objects today. Steele examines corset wearing in the 1990s and quotes from interviews with a number of tight-lacers. One woman, Cathie J., began tight-lacing because of her husband's interest in corsets; she herself does not derive any sexual pleasure from it but does it 'to please [her] husband' (1996: 85). She is, however, careful to distance herself from any association with bondage. Another interviewed woman, Lauren, would seem to be a genuine fetishist, tight-lacing for herself and not a partner, and taking pleasure from how the corset feels on her body and the way it makes her body look. Among male tight-lacers, Fakir Musafar has achieved considerable fame for extreme body modifications and is a corset enthusiast. He argues that corsets are 'very erotic' in that they 'enhance sexual experiences ... all your internal organs and your sexual components are in different positions, with different tensions and so on' which, he says, makes sex while tightly laced with a tightly laced woman especially erotic (Musafar in Steele 1996: 81).

As Musafar's account testifies, the physical properties of clothing and the sensations they produce on the body can become the focus of erotic attention and fetishized. As Steele (1996) notes, fetishes tend to be broadly characterized into 'smellies' and 'feelies'. Rubber and leather are the focus of erotic attention in part because of their smell which for fetishists can be intensely erotic. They are also favoured for their tactile qualities of hardness and smoothness, which enable them to outline the contours of the body as well as constrain the body. Some fetishists like to dress up completely in their preferred fabric and this desire (as with tight-lacers) might mean their fetish is a constraint that borders on the sadomasochistic. However, as Steele notes, this focus on 'hard' fabrics is relatively recent and has come about partly as a result of modern technologies which enable the manufacture of rubber and PVC clothing. In the nineteenth and early twentieth century, 'soft' or 'feminine' fabrics, such as fur, silk, satin and velvet were the focus of erotic attention by fetishists. Leopold von Sacher-Masoch's *Venus in Furs* tells the tale of a dominatrix who always wore furs when she dominated and humiliated her lover. However, while Freud believed fur symbolised pubic hair, and while it has luxurious qualities, fur fetishism is in fact quite rare. In the nineteenth century, silk and satin fetishism were more common among women as well as men. The psychoanalyst Wilheim Stekel (1930) described various fetishisms associated with women and found that in some cases doll fetishism was linked to an adult fetishism for certain fabrics. He summarizes three cases of silk or satin fetishists, one of which was reported in the *Journal de médecine* in 1914 and describes a girl who, growing up in a silk weaver's family, found that caressing silk would send shivers of sexual pleasure through her. Her fetishism led her to steal silk from shops and she was arrested and convicted on a number of occasions; the connection between female fetishism for certain fabrics and kleptomania is also noted by Stekel (1930).

Transvestism

One arena of fetishism which would seem to be almost exclusively male is transvestism, which evidently very often starts from a fetish for women's silky underwear and later progresses to the desire to wear full female dress. The word 'transvestism' can refer simply 'to the act of cross-dressing, when one sex adopts the clothes of the other' (Ackroyd 1979: 10). However, contemporary definitions make it more specific – sexologists and psychologists see it as an act of cross-dressing accompanied by fetishistic obsessions. Ackroyd discussing male dressers draws an important distinction between the transvestite and the transsexual: the former is fetishistic in deriving pleasure from wearing clothes of the opposite sex while the latter moves out of this fetishistic stage to a more 'comprehensive form of feminine "passing" and desire to become the opposite sex' (1979: 14). However, this distinction is not apparent in all the literature: in his account of a 'transvestite', Stekel (1930) describes the case of a woman who exhibits a general distaste for her own sex and a strong desire to have the body of a man as well as dress like one; she experiences no fetishistic pleasure in wearing mens' clothes and, for this reason, it would seem more accurate to describe her as a transsexual than as a transvestite. The distinction between transvestism and transsexualism is important since it would seem that while men can fall into either category, there appear to be very few women who derive sexual pleasure from wearing the clothes of men, making transsexualism more common among women than transvestism. Furthermore, it would be a mistake to assume that the male transvestite shares the transsexual's aspiration to become feminine. As Peter Ackroyd (1979) notes, he may leave clues, unconscious or not, to his masculine identity even when dressed as a woman. Some transvestites feel the need to 'pass' as a woman in public but many are satisfied simply dressing as a woman at home.

While cross-dressing can be found in history among both sexes (as discussed in the previous chapter), the reasons why women cross-dress tend to be social, economic and political rather than fetishistic; there are few accounts of women who cross-dress for sexual pleasure. When cross-dressing is associated with lesbianism, the experience of wearing men's clothes is not likely to be sexual *per se*, but, as argued below, it is worn to signal one's sexual identity as a lesbian, or out of a desire to flout conventions of feminine appearance and articulate a masculine identification. According to Ackroyd (1979), the reason why women do not derive sexual pleasure from men's clothes is because men's clothes are just not erotic. This explanation seems a little simplistic and does not take account of the way in which men's clothes have been eroticized. Historically men's clothing has been erotic, as the codpiece testifies, and in recent years men's underwear has become a centre of erotic attention.

The transvestite is also almost always heterosexual. His fetishistic interest in clothing is sometimes explained by reference to his desire, envy or admiration of women which lead him to dress like one. Some transvestites are open about the fetishistic pleasures of dressing as a woman. However, Ackroyd (1979) notes that other transvestites are less comfortable with this aspect of their dress and choose to play it down. The phenomenon of transvestism has been much discussed within psychological literature and many different theories put forward to explain it. In his analysis, Stoller (1968) explains transvestism by reference to Freud's idea of castration: a man dressed as a woman re-enacts the original childish belief in the phallic woman and subconsciously attempts to resolve or allay fears of castration.

Underwear and eroticism

Underwear is another obvious aspect of dress to be linked with sexuality, although it serves a good many other functions as well.

Underwear as we know it today was not worn before the nineteenth century. As Willet and Cunningham note, 'underclothes have had – and still have – an important "psychological" interest' (1992: 11) and suggest that to consider this dimension we need to look at the meanings of underclothes within their own epoch. This is useful to bear in mind since the development of underwear in the modern sense 'was an important historical stage in the evolving eroticism of dress' (Steele 1996: 116). The first undergarments worn in the medieval period were simple shifts which functioned to protect one's outer clothes from the dirt produced by the body and also to protect the body from contact with stiff, uncomfortable fabrics. In this respect, 'its function was purely utilitarian' rather than erotic (Willet and Cunningham 1992: 21). From the fifteenth century, corsets were worn by the members of the elite and, although at first glance the small waist of the Elizabethan woman might seem to be linked to sexual attraction, the style was more about social status than eroticism.

As Foucault (1979) demonstrates, during the nineteenth century sexuality became the focus of intense interest within a whole range of discourses, a fact which belies the commonsense view of the Victorian era as one of sexual repression. However, while sometimes over-exaggerated, the Victorians did display a 'prudish' attitude towards the body and sexuality which found expression in the layers of clothing worn. Whereas the fashionable woman at the beginning of the nineteenth century had worn little in the way of underwear beneath her diaphanous chemise, by the end of the century the female body was concealed behind a complex combination of camisole, corset, stockings and petticoat. However, once the body became hidden behind more and more layers of stiff clothes, erotic attention transferred 'to its coverings, which became a matter of furtive pre-occupation' and once associated with the hidden parts of the body, underwear began to gather its erotic connotations and become the focus of sexual interest (Willet and Cunningham 1992: 11). This is evidenced by examining attitudes to women in underpants. In the early to mid-Victorian period, the taboo on women in bifurcated garments extended to underpants or pantaloons which, although worn by men, were considered indecent on women, who did not wear them until late in the nineteenth century; modesty called for some coverage when wearing a crinoline cage (which could easily be blown above one's head). However, while, as Steele notes, 'some men complained that the opportunity to glimpse women's genitals had decreased as women adopted underpants, a new voyeurism directed toward the underpants themselves was born' (1996: 120).

The late Victorian and early Edwardian period of the *belle époque* is sometimes singled out as the era when underwear for women became even more elaborate and sexually codified. By the late nineteenth century, the frou-frou rustle of five petticoats had become erotically charged, as had the lacy pantaloons then worn by women. Indeed, the erotic appeal of pantaloons and petticoats was the basis for the popular can-can, in which the kicking legs of the dancers revealed yards of lace (Steele 1996). During this period the eroticization of the secret, hidden layers of the body reached new heights; in addition, new forms of layered erotic device, ranging from nipple piercing to cosmetics, were introduced to enhance the sexuality of the body. Sennett notes how 'the laceration of the breasts, the use of rustling undergarments and some forms of make-up, meant that sensual appeal came through preparations which were hidden by clothing...No one sees those rings unless they see the woman undressed, the petticoats can be heard up close but not seen' (1977: 189). While the 'fashion' for nipple piercing (as for genital piercing) remained underground, gradually towards the end of the century, cosmetics and perfume began to be marketed for women, although the 'respectable' woman had to keep it discreet so as not to be mistaken for a prostitute.

When one considers its proximity to its body, it is not surprising that underwear is the focus of intense erotic interest. It is the last staging-post before the naked body is revealed, an 'intermediate position' between the clothed and naked body which serves to invest a greater erotic charge to the process of undressing (Steele 1996: 116). Underwear therefore plays a crucial role in many different experiences of sexuality. It is important in sexual foreplay and can become the focus of male obsession as a result: it also lends itself to fetishism as the clothing worn closest to the body of the loved one and thus the clothing that intimately evokes the cherished body parts.

As with fetishism, underwear as outerwear has become fashionable in recent years and has associations with fetishism since underwear is one aspect of dress that is commonly singled out and fetishized. Modern underwear has become pared down but the erotic appeal of certain items of underclothing has not diminished and erotic and pornographic material will often draw on the more elaborate aspects of female underwear for its effect. Stockings, suspenders, garters, bras and knickers still play their part in sexual arousal, although there is a considerable difference between women (and their lovers) who take pleasure in gossamer bras, knickers or suspenders and stockings, and fetishists for whom a focus on underwear is obsessive and divorced from the body of the loved one. Some extreme cases of fetishism involve such obsessive interest in underwear that women have had items stolen (Steele 1996). Stockings and suspenders feature heavily in erotic and pornographic literature and have acquired a set of associations which make them almost always erotically charged, even though the vast majority of western women habitually wear pantyhose or tights (this might in part explain some of the appeal of stockings in today's pornography). The eroticism of the stocking comes also from what is revealed and concealed. As Steele (1996) notes, the suspender belt around the waist frames the genital area, while the edge of the stocking draws the eye to the flesh of the upper thighs. The contrast between gossamer fabric and flesh is made more tantalizing when there is a degree of difference in terms of colour: she suggests that black stockings are the most alluring on a white woman, while white or red on a black woman has the same effect of marking the boundary of cloth and skin. These contrasts are sometimes played out in bras: black bras have greater tonal contrast on white skin, red or white on black skin. Now an accepted part of the female wardrobe, the bra is a modern invention. Breasts which had been shaped by the whalebone corset only relatively recently got their own item of clothing, 'somewhere around 1908 more by accident than design' (Hawthorne 1992: 24). As Hawthorne notes, many contemporary fashion designers held claim to having 'invented' it, including the fashion designer Paul Poiret. The film director Howard Hughes, also an industrialist who made a significant contribution to aeronautical engineering, designed Jane Russell's famous bra in *The Outlaws* (1943) and is sometimes considered to be the inventor of the bra as we know it today. As with all clothing, the bra works on the body to transform it: depending on the shape of the cup and the use of bones, the bra can dramatically alter the shape of the breasts which are in turn shaped by fashions of the time. The bra reached its pinnacle (both literally and metaphorically) in the late 1940s and 1950s when, in the wake of Russell's uplifted appearance, conical shaped bras helped to promote the 'sweater girl' look of Hollywood actresses such as Lana Turner. During the 1960s an alternative, flat-chested look became popular; rather than thrust the breasts forward, bras could be purchased that squashed them flat.

What of men's underwear? Willet and Cunningham argue that 'man has never used provocative underclothing; its plain prose has been in singular contrast to the poetical allurements worn by woman' (1992: 16). This statement is not entirely true, since male underwear has been a feature of homosexual interest for much of the twentieth century; white vests, for example, are particularly eroticized in gay iconography. Furthermore, while men's underclothes have not car-

ried the same erotic charge as women's within mainstream heterosexual culture, a relatively recent growth in erotic interest in men's
underwear has paralleled the growth in images of men as sexual
objects. A new 'narcissistic' man whose body became the object of
an erotic gaze emerged in the 1980s. The most famous example was
Calvin Klein's campaign of advertisements in 1982, showing tanned,
muscular men in tight white underpants and boxer shorts (the largest
of these billboards went up in New York's Times Square). While the
erotic appeal of white cotton underpants for men still lingers, the
market has opened up considerably and it is possible to buy male
briefs in a whole variety of fabrics, rubber, leather and PVC. This
would, on the face of it, seem to suggest that a more overt interest in
male bodies and male undergarments is now permitted.

Adornment and sexual identity

Bodies can be adorned not only with cloth, but cosmetics, jewellery,
tattoos, scars and perfume, and these adornments can similarly
become the focus of erotic attention. Tattooing, scarification and
piercing are some of the oldest forms of body adornment and were
originally closely tied to religious rituals and rites of passage in many
different cultures. Within the west, such body modifications as nose
rings, navel rings and tattoos are enjoying a vogue within fashion and
have lost their associations with sacred rituals, though piercing and
tattoos have a longer history. Sennett (1977) notes how in the 1890s
there was a 'passing fashion' for piercing women's nipples. The
practice was, and to some extent still is, isolated to gay, sadomasochistic and fetish subcultures, although it has gained some mainstream acceptance of late. Genital piercing remains a more
marginal practice, although here again, there is now more discussion
of it in the mainstream media than ever before. Part of the appeal of
such piercing for its advocates comes from the pain of piercing itself
which, to sadomasochists, is experienced as sexually pleasurable.
However, once piercings have healed, advocates claim they can exaggerate sexual pleasure, intensifying sexual arousal and orgasm, as well
as facilitating a range of sadomasochistic bondage games. Such
'extreme' fetishistic practices are linked to sexual subcultures, such
as the Pervs, where, as Polhemus argues, 'there is a serious commitment to exploring a new sexuality – one that seeks to replace the
casual, "Your place or mine" promiscuity of the 1960s "sexual
revolution" with an approach that is more relationship-based, and
more ritualistic (even spiritual)' (1994: 105).

Polhemus argues that in recent years, the Pervs have served to redefine and extend 'the meaning of sex itself' (1994: 105). In a world still coming to terms with the effects of AIDS, such exploration of sexuality through adornment has gained increasing visibility and acceptance. On the London club scene, there has been a growing interest in fetishistic practices: the magazine *Skin Two* and special club nights 'Submission' and the 'Torture Garden' have grown considerably over the 1990s, attracting a great deal of attention through the mainstream media. This popularity, says Polhemus, should not surprise us, 'Aids, gender-related issues and a growing awareness of the deficiences of the last "sexual revolution" in the 1960s all point to the need for a new approach to erotic and sexual experience' (1994: 105).

Dress can play an important role in articulating marginal sexualities and otherwise 'secret' desires. Gay men have long used clothing and other forms of bodily adornments to signal to other gay men. The iconography of gay masculinity is littered with sexual codes: ultramasculine styles based around leather and the overt stylization of masculinity through certain uniforms are the two most obvious examples. This theme of dress and the articulation of sexual identity is explored by Rolley (1992) in her examination of clothing within lesbian relationships. She notes how 'familial ties' in general are commonly made visible through dress and uniforms which 'serve both to distinguish wearers from the rest of society and to bind them together into a unified body' (1992: 33). In this respect, 'the lesbian couple who dressed alike emphasised both their special closeness and their difference from the rest of society' (1992: 33). In some cases, this relationship was articulated through similarity, dressing to appear like sisters or twins, but, says Rolley, this serves more to suppress rather than express the physical nature of the relationship. However, when, as in the relationship between Vita Sackville-West and Violet Trefusis, one of the women chooses to dress in a 'masculine' way, 'it served the dual purpose of both sexualising the women's relationship with each other and also excluding any male intruder' (1992: 34). Thus, for the lesbian couple, clothes enable the articulation of the 'masculine lesbian body' and its desires. Masculine clothes also play a role in articulating difference within the lesbian relationship, which replicates the difference found in heterosexual relationships. Dress thus plays a crucial part in articulating sexual identities that would otherwise be invisible. This is the reason why dress and adornment have been so important to gay and lesbian communities. Commonly recognized styles of 'butch' and 'femme' within the lesbian community play on codes that make visible one's sexual orientations: 'how else was a woman recognisable as a lesbian except through her body, her clothes, and the dialogue between the two?' (1992: 38).

In examining the links between adornment and sexuality, this discussion has focused more attention on the 'spectacular' expressions, fetishism and transvestism, which are, perhaps, extreme in their articulation of sexuality, their very marginality seemingly far removed from the realm of 'ordinary' people. However, as Steele (1985) argues, because of its close association to the body, all clothing is in some way related to eroticism or at least has the potential to be erotically charged. It is therefore not just the spectacular and the extreme examples where we find the connections between the body, adornment and eroticism, but the ordinary and everyday aspects of dress which are likely to be related to ideals of beauty at various times. Since dress and adornment often exhibit a strong concern with aesthetics, it is in some way connected with eroticism. Furthermore, as argued above, the more 'mundane' practice of dressing for work, particularly power-dressing, illustrates the extent to which the body and dress, especially for women, is infused with sexual meaning. Clothing and adornment can be linked to expressions of sexuality, from the erotic pleasures they generate on the body to the way in which they can articulate sexual identity and orientation. As discussed at the beginning of this chapter, clothes can 'add' sexual meanings to the body that would otherwise be less apparent. According to the context and the individual, dress and adornment can play an important part in the expression of one's sexuality and the articulation of desire, forming part of the complex ritual of sexual seduction. Individuals can deploy dress strategically for sexual ends and this is no more obvious than the dress of the street-walker or prostitute whose dress and demeanour are heavily sexually coded. However, such codes can be utilized in other forms of sexual encounters just as they can be utilized for commercial sex.

7

The Fashion Industry

Introduction

If, as Leopold (1992: 101) argues, fashion is a 'hybrid' subject, any analysis of fashion has to consider the various agents, institutions and practices which intersect to produce fashion. It is both an industry with particular relations of production and consumption and a discursive arena on such topics as identity, gender and sexuality. Having discussed the latter issues in the preceding chapters, I now turn attention to the fact that fashion is an *industry* of major economic, environmental and cultural significance. Fashion has been significant to the industrial and economic development of a number of countries, such as Britain, where the development of the textile industry set in motion the Industrial Revolution. However, fashion has also played a significant role in global relations between nations. The expansion of capitalism in the eighteenth and nineteenth centuries depended upon the exploitation of resources in developing nations, with devastating effects on their indigenous populations and environment. The extension of 'free-market' capitalism in recent years has meant a continuing search for greater profit by textile and clothing manufacturers, which depends on finding and exploiting the cheapest labour in developing nations, as well as the indigenous immigrant populations at home. The history of the fashion industry is, therefore, a shameful one. Fashion production has fed off the labour of the most vulnerable workers – working-class women and children and new immigrant populations. In the twentieth century, class, gender and race became so interconnected that it is impossible to provide an account of clothing production which does not take account of the ways in which these intersect to make the garment industry one of the poorest in terms of pay and conditions. When taking into account this history, a great disparity opens up between fashion as freedom of expression, playful and fun, and fashion as an oppressive system of production. In this respect, the body of the wearer contrasts strongly with the body of the worker who is almost invariably unable to afford the clothes she makes. In order to maintain an image of glamour, fashion houses have to distance themselves from some very shady, oppressive labour practices. This has to some extent been achieved, with varying levels of success: in recent years, some multi-nationals have been exposed as profiting from the exploitation of female and child labour abroad.

However, as Fine and Leopold (1993) argue, the literature on production tends not to connect with the literature on consumption and vice versa. Within the literature on fashion there is a tendency to privilege either production or consumption and to look to one or the other as the primary agent in determining fashion. This has meant that while economists, historians and sociologists of work and production look at the economic, industrial and technological development of fashion, cultural studies and much cultural sociology focuses attention on fashion as text and discourse. The division is, however, a false one since neither production nor consumption operates independently from each other. Before production can be translated into consumption, income has to be generated, habits formed and products marketed; production is tied closely to consumption, but consumption practices alone do not determine entirely the relations of production. According to Fine and Leopold, 'these chains in the link between production and consumption confirm the problems of defining a single model, either for dependence or consumption upon production' (1993: 72). There are distinct imperatives organizing the production and consumption of different sets of commodities – food, shelter, clothing which leads Fine and Leopold to argue for 'systems of provision approach', which focuses attention on the way in which patterns of production and consumption intersect in any given commodity market. Braham argues something similar when he says that 'it is much more compelling to try to consider fashion in terms of both its cultural and its economic aspects than to deal with one aspect or the other, though it has to be recognised that this approach does not fit well within established disciplinary boundaries' (1997: 133).

In this chapter I examine the literature on fashion as system (more correctly, systems) for the production of clothing, bearing in mind the tendency within the literature to separate production and consumption. I begin with a discussion of the history of textile and clothing production in terms of technological developments and the organization and exploitation of labour and then move on to examine recent research on the contemporary fashion industry which has shown how fashion production continues to be organized along lines of class, race and sexual exploitation. However, production is only one part of the story of fashion and, if it is seen as inextricably linked to consumption, attention needs to be given to the agents who provide the crucial link between the two. As Fine and Leopold argue, the provision of clothes within the fashion industries 'owes as much to the emergence of agents mediating supply and demand (like distribution networks in the clothing industry) as to the development of either set of forces on its own' (1993: 95–6). 'Middlemen' first appeared in the 1880s, supplying fabric to small manufacturers on a contract basis; around the First World War the 'jobber' or stock house in the United States played an important part in defining the shape of women's apparel. Today, many cultural intermediaries play a crucial part in defining fashion – fashion designers, journalists and magazine editors, fashion buyers and retailers, to name but a few. The fashion industry has always been associated with glamour and the work of journalists; photographers and models are therefore important to the process of defining fashion. In a world saturated with images, the image of a fashion house or label has to be carefully manufactured across a number of economic and cultural sites – advertising, marketing, magazines, shop design. The role of these agents therefore needs consideration in a 'systems of provision' approach.

The complex interactions between these various agents and institutions of fashion need to be examined in terms of their temporal and spatial relations to one another. Time is crucial to some markets (womenswear for example) and not to others. Space, in particular, retail space, is relevant not only to the social relations of fashion but to the manufacture of the fashion image of a corporation, so the chapter ends by exploring the nature of the spatial locations of fashion – markets, shops, department stores and shopping centres.

Historical Development of the Fashion Industry

Britain was the first nation to industrialize and textile production, in particular cotton production, was the motor behind this development. Cotton had become fashionable from the eighteenth century as a versatile fabric for household linens and later, as a dress fabric (Wilson 1985). The British cotton industry grew exponentially in the nineteenth century and Britain became a vast consumer of the natural resources of their colonies in the Indian subcontinent, thereby destroying the indigenous market. Chhacchi (1984) argues that British rule led to the destruction of traditional handicrafts and hand-loom production in India, turning one of the oldest textile countries in the world into an importer of textile goods from Britain.

The same industry that squandered resources abroad depended upon the extensive exploitation of labour at home. Images of the dangerous and noisy mills and overcrowded, unhygienic sweatshops have come to stand as one of the defining features of production during the Industrial Revolution in Britain in the nineteenth century. As Howard argues:

> the apparel industry has long been plagued by a noxious creature known as the sweatshop. The word conjures up images of sweltering tenements and dark lofts, of women and children toiling into the night for wages that will barely keep them alive . . . It is the peculiar nature of this industry that such conditions can be found today more or less as they existed a hundred years ago. (1997: 151)

Howard goes on to quote the economist John R. Commons, who in 1901 offered the following definition:

> the term 'sweating' or 'sweating system,' originally denoted a system of subcontract wherein the work is let out to contractors to be done in small shops or homes . . . the system to be contrasted with the sweating system is the 'factory system,' wherein the manufacturer employs his own workmen, under the management of his own foreman or super-intendent, in his own building. (1997: 152)

The reason for the development of this subcontracting chain lies in the 'peculiar nature' of fashion according to Howard. More than most cultural products, clothing, especially for women, is very unpredictable: seasonal changes and movement of fashion mean that the production of clothes for women is particularly risky (as discussed in more detail below). No trader wants to be left with garments they cannot shift and so 'the industry has historically dealt with this unpredictability by pushing risk down through the production chain: from retailer to manufacturer to contractor and subcontractor and ultimately into the worker's home' (Howard 1997: 15).

The result of this 'dog eat dog' approach to subcontracting is poor pay and conditions for those at the very end of the chain, the women

who sew the fabric and put the garments together. The existence of
sweated labour today shows how incomplete the process of industrialization has been within the textile and garment industries. If, as
was thought in the nineteenth century and the early twentieth, technology is progress, one would expect that new inventions for the
spinning of yarn and the cutting or sewing of cloth would have
brought improvements for workers. At the very least, such technology
might speed up the process of making garments. However, compared
with other industries, clothing manufacture is much less mechanized
and technological developments have not eliminated the basic unit of
production, the woman at a sewing machine.

An Imperfect Industry

The history of industrialization within the clothing and textile industry is a history inextricably linked to colonial exploitation abroad as
well as the exploitation of labour at home. Patterns of industrial
relations based on inequality established in the nineteenth century
are reproduced in today's textile and clothing industries. To unpack
the fashion industry, according to Phizacklea (1990) is to unpack the
interconnections between class, gender, race and ethnicity, connections which have deep historical roots. These patterns have their
origins in pre-industrial times: in their analysis of gender relations
in the textile and garment industry, Lown and Chenut argue that
'built into the process of industrial and technological change were
many notions concerning the appropriate gender behaviour of
women workers, and many fears about the implications of any
changes in the familiar patterns of gender roles' (1984: 25). They
examine the structure of textile production prevalent in pre-industrial
Britain under the cottage system (also known as the 'putting out'
system), according to which wool production was organized by the
husband/father in the home: merchants distributed wool to a male in
the household responsible for supervising the spinning, which was
done by women and children. Weaving was a job largely performed
by men and acquired a higher status than spinning. Although some
women were weavers, by the eighteenth century they had been gradually eased out by male weavers who, increasingly insecure about
their position, established guilds to exclude women and children.
With the coming of mechanized means to produce fabric (silk
looms were the first to be mechanized, followed in 1718 by the first
water-powered mill in Derby and later by steam-driven machines),
production was moved out of the home and into the factories. Under

the factory system existing gender roles were reproduced – women and children were employed to operate power looms and men supervised. This division of labour was also a division of pay and status since men were rewarded with higher wages than women who were usually paid on a piece rate (i.e. by the amount of spun yarn produced). Industrialization therefore reproduced unequal gender relations characteristic of pre-industrial times as well as the gendered division between 'skilled' and 'unskilled': tasks associated with men were awarded the higher status of 'skilled' than tasks associated with women. While there is nothing 'natural' about these divisions, ideas about the 'natural' capacities of men and women were employed to legitimate this arrangement. As Elson (1984) argues, myths abound about women in the textile and clothing industry: for example, women are not technically minded; they have 'nimble fingers'; they don't need to earn as much as men since they are dependent upon men. Elson also argues that such myths are still perpetuated in the developing world by governments who sell these ideas about their female workforce in order to attract multinational companies to produce in their countries. She then explores how these myths are underpinned by assumptions about male and female skills. Female skills are seen to 'just happen'; they are 'natural' and therefore without any real art or technique since, as Phizacklea (1990) argues, the acquisition of skill is located in the domestic arena and largely 'hidden' from public view and therefore from recognition. Thus, say Chapkis and Enloe (1984), rather than being 'cheap' women's labour is *cheapened* by cultural attitudes that fail to recognize it or give it adequate status and reward.

New technologies for making clothes which developed over the nineteenth century did not elevate these conditions since technology alone does not produce cultural change. Marx's prediction that the use of the sewing-machine would, with other progress forces, do away with 'the murderous, meaningless caprices of fashion' has not come about (Fine and Leopold 1993: 100). The sewing-machine has remained the primary piece of technology in clothing production in the twentieth century and this dynamic makes clothing production at odds with other forms of mass production, for example the car industry. Instead of large-scale machinery gradually replacing individual workers, the individual worker at an individual machine remains the staple of clothing production, even as the relationship was made increasingly more automatic. While the sewing-machine stimulated factory production and speeded up the time it took to make clothes, 'it also served to reinforce rather than undermine the craft basis of production' (1993: 102). As Fine and Leopold note, by 1882 there were sixty-eight different stitches in use by tailors with greater skill. The sewing-machine may have been designed as a labour-saving device but is also served to heighten what was expected in a dress, so that dressmakers were under pressure to produce more elaborate clothing. However, there was a parallel movement towards the reduction of skill: sewing tasks were broken down as technologies such as the buttonholing machine developed. Thus, say Fine and Leopold, while these inventions speeded up the pace of tailoring tasks, they did not increase the number of garments that could be made up simultaneously. An early exception to this was the introduction in the 1870s of a steam-powered cutting machine, which could cut up to twenty-four layers of cloth at a time.

New technologies are adapted to fit culture rather than bring about change, as some people expect or hope. Existing myths about gender form part of the calculation of companies about what machinery to use and what labour to target. According to Lown and Chenut (1984), in the nineteenth century the textile company Courtaulds deliberately designed machinery that could be operated by young female hands, and sought out female labour in areas were poverty levels were high. They decided on Halstead in Essex because it was a depressed farming area that had suffered greatly not only as a result of industrialization but through the movement of the wool trade to Lancashire. This provided Courtaulds with a ready-made pool of exploitable labour.

Lown and Chenut also examine the similarities and differences between textile production in France, the United States and India. For example, in the United States in the nineteenth century young women from rural communities formed the bulk of textile workers. Relocated from the countryside to factory towns, these girls and young women were expected to send home the vast proportion of their wages. Later in the century immigrant labour from Eastern Europe was exploited. As Howard notes, 'between 1880 and 1900, more than 3 million European immigrants poured into our cities, Jews fleeing the pogroms of Russia, Italians and Slavs and other workers . . . desperate for work at almost any wage' (1997: 152). As a major gateway to the 'New World', New York was fed by this steady stream of immigrants and soon developed as a major centre for garment manufacture. Today this pattern continues with poor immigrant women from South America making up the vast proportion of workers in the garment industry in the United States – each new wave of immigration providing a new group of vulnerable workers whose labour can be exploited.

Gender, Class and Ethnic Relations in the Fashion Industry

As noted earlier, inequality in the textile and clothing industry does not just run along class and gender lines but along the axis of race and ethnicity as well. As Chapkis and Enloe (1984) and Phizacklea (1990) argue, at any particular time the women targeted for recruitment into textile industries tend to be from particular ethnic groupings. Thus racism and ethnocentrism operate globally as western companies legitimize their move to countries in the southern hemisphere by arguing that Asian women are naturally willing to work for longer, naturally more inclined to do repetitive work. Women in developed countries are encouraged to blame other women in the developing world, particularly Latin American and Asian women, for reduction in wages and poor conditions in their own work. As Chapkis and Enloe argue, 'Third world women – so the racist/sexist explanation goes – are "naturally willing" to work for less and "naturally tolerant" of harsher working conditions' (1984: 3).

The link between ethnicity and sexism is complex: according to Enloe (1984), when ethnic groups are organized into a hierarchy, women tend to be pushed into less desirable jobs. This is confirmed by Phizacklea (1990) who examines the interconnections between class, gender, race and ethnicity in the textile and clothing industries across Europe. She describes how the system of subcontracting takes different forms in different countries: in Germany, for example, retailers tend to subcontract to producers in Asian countries whereas in Britain it is generally entrepreneurs at home who co-ordinate the production of short-run clothes. These British firms are predominantly run by ethnic minority men at the end of the 'dog eat dog' subcontracting chain. The chain can mean up to 200 per cent mark up on British goods and paltry sums for the subcontractors and workers, predominantly women. Predominance of ethnic minority men in this industry is an important factor. As traditional jobs decline, many of these men have little option but to pursue an entrepreneurial route but, says Phizacklea (1990), if ethnic men have low status, women are positioned even lower. In fact, she encountered no female entrepreneur in preparing her study.

In such firms the work is sometimes carried out in conditions not unlike the 'sweated' conditions of the nineteenth century – in small and cramped rooms around the East End of London, for example. However, an even 'cheaper' form of production now readily used in Britain and other developed countries is home-working, were the labour is performed in the home and the home-worker pays the fixed costs of fuel, lighting and so on. The status of these women is not helped by their social position *vis-à-vis* immigration legislation in many countries where immigrant women enter as the 'chattel' of their male partner/breadwinner and therefore acquire secondary status in the labour market (Phizacklea 1990). Moreover, fear of racial attack makes home-working safer for such women. In this respect, their status and conditions of existence are tied to other power relations, not least widespread and pervasive racism that is frequently institutionalized. As waves of immigrants are excluded from mainstream job opportunities, they become concentrated in those sectors with poor pay and conditions, largely 'hidden' from view and therefore vulnerable to exploitation.

This naked exploitation of poor working-class women and ethnic minorities has not been met passively: the history of the textile and garment industries is littered with stories of resistance. As Andrew Ross notes, 'because these industries have seen some of the worst labor excesses, they have also been associated with historic victories for labour, and hold a prominent symbolic spot on the landscape of labor iconography' (1997: 11).

For example, Lown and Chenut (1984) note how in 1860 women at Courtaulds went on strike when the company tried to reduce piece rate. Although they were forced back to work after lockout, they were more successful in the following decade when employers, fearful of losing female workers to domestic service, had to improve pay and conditions. Female garment workers were at the fore of industrial action in the United States at the turn of the century when a series of strikes among garment workers left their mark on labour relations. The focus of industrial action was the eradication of the sweatshop which did drop out of view temporarily, although, as Ross notes, it never really disappeared. Perhaps the most famous piece of industrial action in the garment industry is the Triangle Shirtwaist Company walkout of 1909, which sparked widespread strike action among 20,000 shirtwaist makers across the country. This was followed in 1910 by 60,000 cloak makers going on strike. This led to the 'Protocol of Peace', which 'required employers to recognise the union and a union shop, set up a grievance procedure and a Joint Board of Sanitary Control to police health conditions in the shops' (Howard 1997: 153). The optimism of this Protocol was quickly dispelled when 146 workers died six months later in the Triangle Shirtwaist factory. The Protocol led many manufacturers to close down their shops and contract their work out, thereby passing on the liability to monitor working conditions to the subcontractor. As Howard notes, this situation only served to push the sweatshop further to the margins, putting an artificial distance between the manufacturer and the subcontractor which undermined the ability to maintain legal standards in the shops. However, in 1926 a commission was set up in New York to examine the conditions of work in the garment industry, intended to ensure that the manufacturer (or 'jobber') could not escape liability but must share 'joint liability' with the contractor. This did result in a steady rise in pay and conditions, so that by the mid-1960s 'more than half of the 1.2 million workers in the apparel industry were organised and real wages had been rising for decades' (1997: 155).

While it is often thought that such naked exploitation has since been eradicated, the 'basic dynamic has not changed in a hundred years' (Howard 1997: 151). Today, garment workers all over the world are at the mercy of a volatile market which is highly recession sensitive. They are disposable labour, brought in cheaply when there is work and laid off when the market slows down. What has changed to some extent is the location of sweatshops in today's global economy. It is also the case that new relations of exploitation have been built on race and ethnic difference as well as gender. Sweated labour can now be found in developing countries such as those of the Asian subcontinent; they can also be found among the immigrant populations of developed countries in the west. As Ross (1997) notes, the high hopes of the New Deal in the 1960s have been increasingly undermined by political and economic changes since the 1970s as recession, neo-liberalism and *laissez-faire* economics, under the banner of 'free trade', have put increasing pressure on producers in the garment industry to search for ever cheaper labour. Today in the garment industry one finds the most vulnerable and exploited workers whose pay and conditions are the first to go in this global battle. In addition, home-working has returned as a mode of production which keeps costs down and profits up for big corporations. More shocking is the discovery of indentured labour on US soil – in 1995 the contractors El Monte were found to have imported Thai women to work in its Californian factory were they had little freedom and were little more than wage slaves (Su 1997). These relations of exploitation need situating within the context of the clothing industry in general, and women's clothing production in particular.

The Textile and Clothing Industries

Conditions for the production of clothing are heavily dependent upon a wide range of social, political, economic and cultural factors.

Moreover, when we speak of clothing production it is important to note that there are not one, but a number of industries producing clothes, each of them differently organized according to context and whether the industry is orientated towards a mass market or not. As Fine and Leopold (1993) argue, the history of fashion is a history of different 'systems of provision'. Made to measure clothing in the form of bespoke tailoring and *haute couture* still exist alongside mass-produced clothing, which is fragmented into different market segments. Clothing provision has had to meet demands of naturally segmented markets – those for children, men and women – as well as markets of different sizes, with each of these developing different strategies for managing production. Each industry, each subsector, has its own dynamics linking a wide range of agents in the process. According to Fine and Leopold, if one can generalize about the directions taken by the clothing industry in the last 200 years, one can say that it has transformed from consumption of essential items of dress designed to last, to the purchase of multiple garments, bought cheaply and replaced frequently. In this way it has begun to mimic the food industry, where goods are marketed as perishable.

Timing is critical in women's fashion, which emphasizes change and new lines, and this makes turnaround from design to manufacture and distribution very fast. As Fine and Leopold (1993) note, in the 1920s the women's clothing industry was still operating under primitive levels of development compared with other consumer industries like cars and indeed in contrast to men's fashions where production has long been geared towards 'staples' such as suits, jackets, overcoats and the like. This leads Fine and Leopold to ask whether or not the women's clothing industry ever achieved full mass production, and to argue that fashion, as in rapidly changing styles, has come to serve as a compensation for the failure to achieve mass production within women's clothing. As shown above, the story of fashion is largely told as the story of women's clothing and its rapid changing aesthetic. However, according to Fine and Leopold, explanations which see this as emanating from some essential feminine psychological impulse are highly implausible. Instead they argue that the evolution of the fashion system represented an attempt to accommodate the failure to achieve mass production fully. Thus, 'fashion' serves to supply

> the seeming anarchic and rapidly changing proliferation of women's clothes, a feature that distinguishes it not just from other industries but from other branches of the clothing industry as well, served as a substitute for technical innovation, arising not in response to a rise in

incomes or changes in consumer preferences or to the exhaustion of possibilities arising from mass production but rather from the industry's failure ever to fully embrace mass production. (Fine and Leopold 1993: 95)

Leopold (1992) further undermines the arguments (discussed in chapter 5) which link fashion to the essential frivolity or vanity of women, shifting attention away from the psychology of the consumer to the dynamics of the industry. Fashion as transient, fast changing style has become the motor of women's clothing and this explains why clothing production leads to some of the worst labour conditions for workers. Fast turnover of style puts pressure on manufacturers to work quickly and at low cost to reduce the risk of over-production for clothing which, once ready, is no longer 'in' fashion. Producers are therefore more likely to rely on subcontracting which can seek out the most 'flexible' workforce, i.e. the one that can be picked up and laid off at will, with no demand for sickness benefits, maternity leave and the like. In the United States and Britain, successive neo-liberal governments over the years have driven down wage costs, and produced a ready-made pool of such labour at home willing to work for paltry sums.

Demographic factors have also played an important part in the development of mass production in men's clothing: in particular, the movement of populations to the west served to stimulate clothing production for men whose requirements were not for fashionable but for practical clothing. Throughout the eighteenth century Europe exerted an influence over fashions in the United States with merchants importing clothes from London and Paris. However, the growth in settlers in the Midwest swelled the population of rural dwellers. As railways and waterways pushed westwards, this expanding population of male workers needed rugged and protective clothing, their demands spurring technical change in clothing production to increase availability of garments. As a result, tools and materials were adapted from engineering work to clothing production (for example, the use of rivets instead of the hand-sewn seam). Fine and Leopold (1993) argue that the link between new patterns of work and new clothes is shown in the cowboy, who, working in dusty conditions, required strong and protective clothing: a hat to protect his eyes, a bandanna to shield his mouth and so on. Sailors and slaves also required clothing that was hard wearing and tough and these large groups of male workers acted as a stimulus for mass-produced clothes. The spur to industrialization and mass production came from the fact that these early markets were large and uniform while the newly built railroads and waterways also helped to open up new distribution channels for domestic clothing production of mens-wear. The Civil War also aided this process by encouraging the development of the first standardized sizing in men's clothing to aid the production of uniforms. This was a significant development since standard sizing is crucial for the advancement of ready-made clothing.

Women's clothing was hardly affected by such developments: female work did not demand particular kinds of dress and women's culturally acquired skills for sewing meant that many clothes were produced at home. Indeed, the sewing-machine, while stimulating some factory production, also facilitated home dressmaking, spurring the development of commercial patterns made by companies such as Buttericks. Women's factory made clothes did not begin to appear until the beginning of the twentieth century, corresponding to the increasing participation of women in the labour market among other factors. Yet even by the close of the First World War the industrial development of women's clothing continued to lag behind men's 'displaying characteristics increasingly at odds with those conducive to the spread of mass production' (Fine and Leopold 1993: 101).

Fashion as a Cultural Industry

The discussion above suggests that in order to understand fashion it is necessary to go beyond a discussion of pure aesthetics, since what is defined and comes to be recognized as 'fashion' is the product of a chain of activities which are industrial, economic and cultural, as well as aesthetic. As Peter Braham argues:

> what is distinctive about the fashion code is that it must pass through the filter of the fashion industry. Thus the suggested code modifica-tions displayed on the catwalks of Paris stand to be rejected, toned down or embraced not only by a host of publicists, critics, journalists and fashion leaders, but also by garment manufacturers and store buyers. (1997: 134)

At each stage, choices are made by manufacturers, fashion buyers, and retail outlets as to what will sell. Fashion journalists and fashion leaders play their role in the progress of a particular fashion and all these agents point to how a new fashion 'does not merely stand in aesthetic relation to previous fashions, it also has a material relation-ship to the cost and complexity of its design, manufacture and distribution' (Braham 1997: 135). Thus, like Fine and Leopold, Braham argues that fashion is not just culture but industry, not just about consumption but about production. One way to think of fashion is as a *culture industry*. Fashion is the product of a complex set of interactions between various agents set in temporal and spatial relations to one another – between design houses, fabric and clothing manufacturers and retailers and the fashion-buying public. The connections between these agents are so complex that it is sometimes difficult to separate them – some manufacturers have no factories, such as Marks and Spencer in the UK, while some fashion designers are not the producers of the items that bear their name but give a manufacturer the licence to use their name, as is the case with Calvin Klein underwear, for example. If we understand fashion to be a complex culture industry, a whole series of questions open up about the relationship between the production and consumption and the chains of dissemination and distribution that link the two. Who defines what is 'fashion', the designer, the manufacturer, the retailer or the consumer? Who are the key players and what precisely is their role? Where do we need to look to find 'fashion', the design house and catwalk or the street? Does production follow consumer demand or vice versa? Given constraints of time, how does production meet consumer demand for a particular fashion? These questions focus attention on fashion as a socio-economic practice and not as some discrete aesthetic discourse. They also point away from overarching theories of fashion (argued in chapters 2 and 3 as being reductive) to the day-to-day workings of the fashion industry.

Braham (1997) gives a comprehensive overview of the literature on fashion as a culture industry and argues that in order to understand fashion we need to move away from emulation or the 'trickle-down' model which has formed the basis of much discussion of fashion and its dissemination. He summarizes the main debate between the 'trickle-down' model of fashion as proposed by Simmel (discussed in chapters 2 and 3) and looks at more recent reinterpretations of fashion as the outcome of complex socio-economic processes. As Braham notes, Simmel's argument about the diffusion of fashion from elite to majority has formed the basis of much subsequent debate among theorists. In chapters 2 and 3 I argue that this emulation model is too simplistic to be true and that it confuses consequence with intention: wearing of the latest fashion may not, in fact, be an expression of the desire to be like one's 'betters' but some other desire, possibly the desire to be seen as 'modern' and 'in' with the times (Campbell 1989, 1993). However, one can critique Simmel's theory further by examining empirical data on the fashion industry and the operations, decisions and selections that see a style come to be defined as 'fashion'. Emulation is too reductive a model to account for the complex interactions between different bodies in the fashion system who produce a style as fashion. Herbert Blumer has argued that a style becomes fashion not when the elite wear it, but when it corresponds to 'the incipient taste of fashion-consuming public' (in Braham 1997: 139). An elite may influence the direction of taste but they do not control it and attempts made to co-ordinate popular taste can fail. It is true that diffusion of this collective taste may owe much to fashion leaders and innovators who legitimate the taste, but they cannot entirely determine it. The fact that there is something mysterious about this 'incipient taste', but it is difficult to find its origins, does not mean that it is fictitious.

However, despite the difficulty of pinning this taste down, Blumer (1969) proposes some of the elements we need to consider when understanding the formation of fashion. He suggests that fashions are in part the product of selective choices made by designers (who choose what garments to show in their collections) and by journalists and buyers (who select some items as the 'look' for a particular season and not others). Designers are aware that their garments will be filtered through these cultural mediators but can never predict what garments will be picked up by buyers and journalists. Blumer also notes that there is a remarkable similarity between all the buyers and journalists as to what elements they select and this he puts down to the fact that these cultural mediators are so immersed in the world of fashion, and so trained to spot trends, that they usually pick up on the same garments. Indeed, the success of any store buyer depends on the ability to spot the latest trend. The same can be said about the remarkable similarities between the 'ready-to-wear' collections each season in Milan, New York, Paris and London, where one can find similar lines and colours across different design houses. Here again, this can be explained by the fact that, as cultural innovators or mediators, designers occupy the same universe and search for inspiration in the same locations – the high street, popular culture and music as well as 'high' art. Each individual designer and stylist wants to be seen to catch the mood of the time and, in doing so, taps into the same cultural trends. 'Fashion' is therefore the product of interactions between these cultural mediators and their sources of inspiration, as well as the result of the internal dynamics of fashion itself. It can be argued that of all these complex elements, closely interconnected as they clearly are, the most obvious is also the most important, namely the way in which a new, would-be fashion relates to the fashion that is in mode. That is to say, the new fashion seeks –

inevitably – to extend, qualify, comment on or contradict the existing fashion.

While fashion designers, manufacturers and retailers depend upon picking up the latest trends, 'it is altogether more demanding to begin to delineate the precise contents of this communication or to trace its operation' (Braham 1997: 142). We can, however, examine the relationship between the various agents in the process and consider how a style becomes defined as fashion through the processes of selection. This approach, as Braham correctly notes, requires us to move away from a 'trickle-down' model and look at a number of key players in the fashion process and at the crucial connections between production, distribution and retail. Braham considers a number of these key players, in particular, couturiers, retailers and fashion buyers. He also examines a number of recent developments in the production of fashion, most notably the emergence of niche marketing and 'just-in-time' production characteristic of the 'flexible specialization' said to have arisen to cope with market instability. I now examine what Braham has to say about each of these.

As Braham notes, *haute couture* has lost its place at the centre of fashion, no longer dictating the directions of fashion. Paris has been de-centred by a host of developments in the twentieth century, especially the rise of mass production, ready-to-wear collections and the influence of pop music and youth cultures as sources of fashion style, which are now said to 'bubble up' from high street to fashion catwalk (Polhemus 1994). These developments have served to blur the division between high fashion and everyday fashion; the latter hardly lags behind 'high' fashion and in many cases dictates the trends that are only later picked up by *couture*. With new sources of fashion coming up from the street, the orderly dissemination of high fashion from *couture* collections each season is no longer viable. This leads Braham to argue that we now have 'multiple fashions systems': fashion moves up, down and along from various starting-points and in several directions, rather than emanating from a single source or 'trickling down' from the elite to the majority (1997: 145). This decline in the role of the *couture* as the central fashion innovator has not meant that *couture* is irrelevant to contemporary fashion. Indeed, one of the striking features of fashion in recent years is the degree to which *couture* designs have become part of the everyday currency of fashion. Thus, says Braham, just because designers look to the street does not mean to say there is no reason to be interested in high fashion. First, this borrowing from the street may actually enhance the prestige of designers. Second, while Paris may no longer be the centre of fashion, the Parisian *couture* houses have become important as major players in the *prêt-à-porter* collections. Compelling evidence of the influence of designers also lies in the vast economic scope of these fashion houses which are owned by multi-million dollar conglomerates operating on a global scale. As Braham (quoting Davis) acknowledges, the concerns of such multi-national financial backers serve to constrain designers by insisting that some of their designs should be popular and simple enough to be easily translated into mass-produced high-street designs. This economic imperative blurs the line between high fashion and everyday fashion and can be seen in the large number of franchising agreements between fashion houses and manufacturers (of sunglasses, underwear, perfume and cosmetics etc.). For example, the High Fashion Industry Accord, signed in Italy in 1971, shows how important alliances between design houses, fabric and garment manufacturers and financial backers have become. Under this Accord, Italian couturiers receive subsidy if their new lines conform to guidelines agreed with major garment manufacturers who can easily reproduce their designs for mass markets. These examples provide evidence of the degree to which the *couture* designer is now much more part of the everyday world of commodity culture than the exclusive world of elite fashion.

In Britain, the other factor which needs consideration in any discussion of fashion is the art school or college, which plays an influential role in the training of designers. Since the 1960s and the rise of celebrity youth designers such as Mary Quant and later, Vivienne Westwood, British fashion design has become world renowned for its imagination and innovation. This continued in the 1990s with the British 'invasion' of Parisian *couture*: John Galliano first at Givenchy and now at Christian Dior, Alexander McQueen at Givenchy, Stella McCartney at Chloe. According to Angela McRobbie, these designers are examples of a relatively new phenomenon, the designer as *auteur*, a phenomenon fuelled by fashion magazines which play on the idea of the designer as genius. However, they represent the smallest minority of fashion designers, most of whom do not go on to achieve celebrity status but have to carve out work for themselves in an increasingly crowded market. McRobbie (1998: 1) considers the way in which these designers constitute a 'new cultural worker'; in some ways 'prime examples' of 'Thatcher's children' who are 'enterprising' in their ability to sell their skills, either freelancing for corporate chains such as Next or C&A, or as independent designers selling direct to the public through market stalls. With the growth of subcultures, many young designers since the 1960s have found they can service these through small outlets and market stalls, resulting in a rise of 'subcultural entrepreneurialism': this 'self-generated, self-employment demonstrated the existence of a sprawling network of micro-economies initially inside the youth subcultures, and then extending far beyond them' (McRobbie 1998: 8).

The socio-economic context is important for understanding this expansion. Many theorists have commented upon the growth of consumption and the fragmentation of the market into more and more differentiated 'taste markets'. This has served to stimulate the emergence of 'niche marketing' to capitalize on new tastes; an apparently unending growth of symbolic material and images from advertising, marketing and retail design work to weave meanings around commodities to the point where, according to Baudrillard (1983), the thing consumed is the image not the commodity. Such developments, including the increasing globalization of production and consumption, have been characterized under the rubric 'post-Fordism'. In terms of its impact upon fashion, 'the expanded market for images has created the need for a new workforce of image makers and, once again, the cultural intermediaries step in to play this role' (McRobbie 1998: 4).

Fashion retailing

Whether they are intended for corporate design houses or for a market stall, fashion designs have to be sold through some mechanism or another. In this way, retail plays a crucial role in defining fashion and indeed, Braham (1997) argues that large retailers such as Marks and Spencer or Next might exert even more influence on fashion than manufacturers and designers. As Braham notes, in advanced industrial countries the trend is for retailing to be concentrated in major chains: in the UK Marks and Spencer and the Burton group constitute approximately 25 per cent of all clothes sold. Both have had to respond to pressure of market forces for faster turnaround of stock and have to keep pace with the rapidity of fashion change. In the 1980s the trend in retail moved towards 'lifestyle' consumption, which is characterized by small niche markets directed towards an increasingly segmented market of consumers whose identity (age, income bracket, taste etc.) is under constant scrutiny by marketing personnel. The term 'lifestyle' designates a particular approach to marketing, but Shields argues that it can also be used to describe 'affective groupings . . . which emerge through the medium of shared systems of symbolic codes of stylized behaviour, adornment, taste and *habitus*' (1992: 14). 'Lifestyle' marketing has subtly altered the way in which not only fashion, but such commodities as food are produced, distributed, marketed and sold. In the case of Burton, niche marketing led to the creation of distinctly different retail outlets catering for particular market segments: Principles, Top Shop, Top Man and Burton (Nixon 1996). The increasing importance of keeping pace with fashion also led to an emphasis on shorter runs to reduce the risk of over-production and waste. The concern with short runs is also known as 'flexible specialization' (see below). Braham is careful not to assign too much significance to this shift. Given Fine's and Leopold's argument (1993) that mass production, particularly in women's fashion, was never successfully implemented, Braham asks whether the shift towards flexible small batch production is as dramatic as it might at first appear.

However, one feature that does distinguish contemporary fashion is the emergence of 'just-in-time' production, which is supported by the deployment of new computer technologies. 'Just-in-time' production incorporates all the features of 'flexible specialization' – short runs produced quickly through the chain of subcontracting that in the UK draws heavily on the 'flexibility' of home working. However, what characterizes 'just-in-time' production is the use of the latest technologies, particularly communication technologies which collate data on sales between manufacturer and retailer, enabling both to operate with minimal levels of inventory. The goods arrive as and when they are necessary, 'as well as allowing production to be undertaken and completed, as far as is possible, only on the basis of firm orders from retailers' (Braham 1997: 156). This system of provision is most effectively deployed by the Benetton Group, whose production, distribution and retail strategy bring together traditional patterns of production, such as subcontracting, with the latest technologies for the production of clothes, such as advanced dyeing techniques, and the latest in communications technologies for the tracking of sales and the effective distribution of fashion garments 'just-in-time'. However, as Belussi argues in her study of Benetton, technology alone cannot explain the group's success; instead, she focuses her discussion on the 'business milieu in which it occurred' and on the firm strategy employed (in du Gay 1997: 169). In other words, Benetton's success lies in its increasing domination in the market and in the strong links it has forged among the agents involved in the production and distribution systems (suppliers, subcontractors, agents, retailers). It is in the context of this strategy that new technologies are deployed which have contributed to Benetton's latest and most intense development. The Benetton Group, started by Luciano and Guiliana Benetton, is a collection of franchises with each shop paying no royalties to Benetton but adhering to strict policies of shop design and layout. Since the global collection of retail outlets is managed locally, Benetton has little in the way of staff and fixed costs to bear. Further, the effective utilization of subcontractors enables Benetton to keep the costs of production down. With 'low' skilled tasks devolved to manufacturers and to retailers, Benetton concentrates its activities on product development and image management. The investments made by Benetton come in the form of capital investments in new technologies for product innovation (such as the introduction of new dyeing processes), the overall design of garments with an emphasis on 'quality', and the development of information technology that allows the retailers to track customer demand and respond quickly. As Belussi notes, 'patterns of sales and extent of re-orders are regularly fed back from the shops to Benetton, and in this way the time required for the final decision of distribution among subcontractors is markedly reduced' (in du Gay 1997: 174). The close connection to demand enables Benetton to reduce risk: the garments are displayed in the shop and are not stored in warehouses. Overall control of the company's image is carefully maintained by shop design and layout, high-profile marketing and controversial advertising campaigns.

As the above argument shows, 'fashion' or (more precisely, given market segmentation) 'fashions' are the outcome of a range of intersecting practices: market and economic practices, labour relations and practices, technological developments and a range of more 'cultural' practices such as marketing and design. These activities overlap since in some cases, 'producers' as in the Benetton Group, co-ordinate marketing and design. Thus the distinction, traditionally made in fashion literature between production and consumption, is an artificial one that does not shed much light on the crucial relations between the two. Furthermore, as du Gay argues, while we commonly think of 'business' and 'culture' as incompatible concepts, in recent years, companies and business have begun to think and talk about 'culture':

> it has come to be seen as a crucial means of ensuring organizational success because it is held that if you can effectively manage 'meaning' at work, so that people come to conceive of and conduct themselves in such a way as to maximize their involvement in, and hence their contribution to, the organization for which they work, you are more likely to have a profitable, effective and successful firm. (1997: 1)

du Gay uses the term 'cultural economy' to describe the way in which culture and economics intersect in so complex a way that neither sphere dominates or determines the other. Instead, du Gay

argues that 'culture' and 'economics' are 'hybrids', 'mutually consti-
tutive' of one another (1997: 2). On the one hand, no activity is
purely 'economic' since all economic decisions involve cultural ones;
on the other, all 'culture' is 'manufactured' in some way, much of it
mass produced, and therefore the product of economic decision-
making. 'Meaning', says du Gay, 'is produced at "economic" sites
(at work, in shops) and circulated through economic processes and
practices . . . through adverts, marketing materials and the very design
of products) no less than in other domains of existence in modern
societies' (1997: 4). The 'economic' practices he refers to could
equally be described as 'cultural' practices (indeed, advertisements
are often analysed within cultural studies as cultural rather than
economic; see, for example, Williamson 1978). As discussed above,
cultural intermediaries, such as journalists and fashion buyers, mediate between production and consumption. These 'practitioners play
a pivotal role in articulating production with consumption by
attempting to associate goods and services with particular cultural
meanings and to address these values to prospective buyers' (du Gay
1997: 5). By heralding 'brown as the new black', or 'grey as the new
black', as fashion journalists did in the winters of 1997 and 1998
respectively, cultural commentators can help to promote a style,
colour or designer.

From this perspective, we can view a range of practices important
to the production of fashion without making the false distinction
between seeing them as either purely economic or cultural. The
practices I now examine shed further light on the relationship
between economy and culture as they come together in the fashion
experience, namely, retailing locations such as the market, the shop,
the department store and the shopping centre. All these spaces blur
the distinction between the cultural and the economic since shopping
is both an economic activity and a cultural one.

Fashion Locations

Given the argument that fashion is both an economic and cultural
form, the shop (the department store, the shopping centre, the second-
hand market) can be seen as the space which links these practices
very explicitly. The shop is a place where economic exchange is
clearly culturally embedded: shops and markets are spaces of economic activity – buying and selling – that are rooted in a whole series
of other everyday practices and activities. Indeed, one can consume
without purchasing anything, as the term 'window shopping'

suggests; the items consumed are not material goods but the spectacle of the shop itself. There are now many studies of spaces of consumption, ranging from the market, the department store and, more recently, the shopping centre and out-of-town warehouse 'designer villages' (e.g. Shields 1992, Slater 1993, 1997). The spatial organization of these sites is said to be implicated in the constitution of 'modern' and 'postmodern' identities. These spaces are not only prime sites for the consumption of goods and images, they play a crucial role in the articulation of desire, identity and subjectivity in modern, and some would say, postmodern culture. As Foucault (1977) demonstrates in his work on the prison, space is never inert or simply 'there' but active in the constitution of social relations. The layout of a building and the spatial arrangement of streets impact upon the movement of bodies, directing the individual and organizing the flow of the crowd to particular sorts of activities, relations and patterns. In recent years, attention has been focused on aspects of shopping such as shop design and display that direct the gaze of the modern-day *flâneur*. Slater suggests that these spaces of consumption carry an 'enormous ideological load in the modern period and again today: the image of a thriving civil society' (1993: 188–9).

Markets, shops and department stores

Shops occupy an important place within the economic and cultural life of the town and the city. Braudel argues that 'without a market, a town is inconceivable' (in Slater 1993: 191). The market (open air or closed) is the earliest form of shopping space and is a crucial location for the sale of second-hand clothing. Until the early twentieth century when ready-to-wear fashion became available to the vast majority of the population, working-class people wore second-hand clothes purchased at markets in addition to clothes made at home. Clothing was a considerable expense and this put fashion out of reach for most people, although out-of-date fashions could be bought at the second-hand market and 'at least enabled such clothes to be recycled, to outlive their role as fashion goods' (Fine and Leopold 1993: 131). Today, while old-style second-hand markets still exist, they do so alongside department stores, shopping centres and, more recently, out-of-town warehouses and 'designer villages' which stock end-of-line fashions. The pursuit of second-hand clothing became popular once more in the 1960s and 1970s among the young, especially hippies who rejected consumerist lifestyle as wasteful and ecologically damaging. As McRobbie (1994b) notes, there are various interpretations of this style. She cites Hall (1977), for example, who argues that the hippy style indicates an 'identification with the poor' as well as a rejection of middle-class style. However, second-hand style sets itself apart from middle-class values and the greyness of real poverty, a fact which leads some people (the novelist Angela Carter is acknowledged by McRobbie in this respect) to question whether rummaging through jumble sales makes light of those who search in need and not through choice. Whatever the reasons and whatever the interpretations made of second-hand clothing, the second-hand look has continued to be a popular one with many young people. McRobbie argues that most youth subcultures have relied on second-hand clothes for their style and that this style has influenced mainstream fashion and retail to the extent that shops aimed at young people often borrow from the tactics of the market traders when displaying their clothes.

However, modern markets have also borrowed from the tactics of the shop, accepting credit as payment and not simply cash and sometimes fixing prices. Furthermore, the division between streetstyle and mainstream style has become increasingly blurred. McRobbie suggests that there are a number of cross-fertilizations between the two: mainstream fashion, for example, is parasitical on post-punk subcultures and also reworks the already recycled styles of the street markets. Writing about style in the mid-1980s, she suggests that

> the sharpest illustration of these overlaps and cross-fertilizations lies, at present, in the wardrobes of the so-called young professionals, male and female. The new items which now make-up his or her wardrobe were almost, to the last sock or stocking, discovered, restored and worn by the young men and women who worked in, or hung around Camden Market and a whole series of provincial ragmarkets in the late 1970s and early 1980s. (1994b: 138)

McRobbie notes that the female suit announced as the big fashion item of summer 1988 is a reworking of the Chanel suit worn in the early 1960s by such celebrities as Jackie Kennedy, while the tea dresses advertised in the summers of 1987 and 1988 by Next and Laura Ashley are fashioned in the style of 1940s crepe dresses. She goes on to note that 'second-hand style continually emphasises its distance from second-hand clothing' (1994b: 140) and involves the highly selective exercise of taste by the second-hand shopper.

Markets are places of social meeting and interaction, of 'heterogeneous activities' which attract crowds and naturally lend themselves to spectacle (Slater 1993). So too are shopping arcades which brought together a range of activities when they first appeared in the late eighteenth century and early nineteenth. Don Slater, referring to Walter Benjamin's work on arcades, notes how they bring together 'within a single image the idea that a market is, culturally, a gathering place for crowds, offering diverse points of focus for diverse and contingent interests' (1993: 192). Arcades are covered passageways, usually arched and with shops and cafés on one or both sides; in the eighteenth century they occasionally included brothels and other places of urban pleasure. The Palais Royal, built in Paris in 1780, 'contained one such arcade, considered emblematic in showing the roots of modern consumerism in the urban, spectacle-focused crowd' (1993: 193). According to Slater, the arcade brought together three forms of crowd-gathering: 'the pre-modern market, the leisure gatherings of "society", and the city itself' (1993: 193). Arcades thus constituted a space for consumption, part old, part new, which served to promote modern forms of retail and consumption. Unlike the old-style market, where tradespeople sold their wares directly to the public, they separated production from consumption. They therefore stimulated the rise of 'middlemen', such as the shop or stall holder who mediated between producers and consumers. In gathering together a number of merchants, the arcade continued the tradition of the pre-modern market but depersonalized the relations between seller and shopper, for example by relying on fixed prices rather than haggling. The arcade was also a space where the fashionable of 'society' met to promenade. This served to stimulate 'the growth of specific consumer infrastructures, for example the modern shop and the commercialisation of leisure' (1993: 194). A diverse range of social types such as financiers, *flâneurs*, dandies and prostitutes, each pursuing their own interests within the same space, could choose to attend concert halls or vaudeville, meeting rooms or clubs. Such a range of activities were later incorporated into big department stores which at one time housed reading rooms, rest rooms, restaurants and later, hair and beauty salons. As such, arcades were like cities in miniature, simulations of a city within the city itself, not unlike in the modern shopping centre. In recent years, shopping centres have sprung up on the outskirts of cities across the developed world; representative examples include, in Britain, the Arndale Centre in Manchester and, in the US, the Copley Center in Boston. Langman (1992) and Shields (1992) argue that the shopping centre has replaced the Gothic cathedral of feudal times and the factory of the industrial age to become the building/space *par excellence* of contemporary society. However, while seeming a new and 'postmodern' space, as we can see from Slater's discussion (1993), the shopping centre incorporates many aspects of modern as well as pre-modern consumption.

Shops have always enjoyed a special place in the city as spaces of pleasure, desire and fantasy. As Porter notes, 'the eighteenth century brought the emergence of high-class shops, in the City, in Piccadilly and Mayfair' (1990: 199). These shops opened up new pleasures and opportunities for 'respectable' women previously denied the freedom to wander through the city, although their movements were still more restricted than that of their male counterparts (Nava 1992). Shopping could be a pleasurable activity for men too: as the poet Robert Southey wrote in a letter, 'if I were to pass the remainder of my life in London . . . I think the shops would continue to amuse me. Something extraordinary or beautiful is forever to be seen in them' (in Porter 1990: 145–6). Shops were places to marvel at and enjoy: in the 'upmarket' shops of London, goods would be displayed seductively in the window. Shelley noted how 'cunningly' women's fabric was displayed:

> whether they are silks, chintzes or muslins, they hang down in folds behind the fine high windows so that the effect of this or that material, as it would be in the ordinary folds of a woman's dress, can be studied . . . Behind great glass windows absolutely everything one can think of is neatly, attractively displayed, and in such abundance of choice as almost to make one greedy. (in Porter 1990: 144)

Drapery shops led the way in terms of shop-front design but it was the department store, such as the Bon Marché in Paris or Whiteley's in Bayswater, London, which was the 'great Victorian innovation' (Porter 1990: 201). Up until the 1830s, shops had tended to be highly specialist but some shopkeepers, particularly drapers, such as William Whiteley, saw the potential of expanding their product range and clientele (the prices in many such stores were beyond the reach of most people). By including more goods in one space, and by clearly pricing them, the expanding drapery shops of the mid-nineteenth century could afford cheaper prices and enable shoppers to see at a glance the cost of items without the embarrassment of having to ask the price of something. These drapery shops constituted proto-department stores built along the lines of indoor markets that were developed in the 1830s in such cities as Newcastle, where the Grainger market (completed in 1835) housed butchers, greengrocers and fancy goods stalls and 'acted as a magnet to this city redevelopment' (Lancaster 1995: 8). By taking 'the fear out of shopping' through clear pricing, these new stores grew alongside the new lower middle-class household (Porter 1990).

According to Lancaster, 'the origins of the British department store are firmly rooted in the twin processes of industrialisation and urbanisation' (1995: 7), although he acknowledges that such shops have roots which go back further than this. The first department stores in Britain sprang up in the north, for example in Manchester and New-castle. Whiteley's, founded in 1864, was the first such store to open in London, initially as a drapers but expanding rapidly to provide jewellery, furs and other fancy goods. Soon after, large stores such as Dickins and Jones moved to Regent Street and expanded to become a department store in the 1890s, while the Army and Navy stores began business in 1871.

The novelty of these proto-department stores and the later big department stores was their provision of a wide range of goods and services, including restaurants and rest rooms. They were also places in which to to sit around and dream, and this was nowhere more apparent than in Aristide Boucicaut's Bon Marché in Paris, founded in 1852. In style, the Bon Marché borrowed from the international exhibitions: the Great Exhibition in Crystal Palace, London (1851), and later the Exposition Universelle in Paris (1855) and the world fairs of Chicago (1893) and St. Louis (1904). Not only were prices clearly displayed as they had been at the Paris exhibition, but the shop's whole environment was created to be a spectacle, encouraging leisurely browsing. One did not necessarily have to consume anything except the spectacle itself, although one was encouraged to imagine ownership of the goods displayed. The store was built on a grand scale, facilitating a new kind of freedom: 'anyone could enter, browse in departments, wander from floor to floor, without spending a centime. The earliest proto-department stores had been too small and formal to offer such anonymity' (Lancaster 1995: 18). By redu-cing fears about shopping and stimulating desires, the department store became a showcase for an expanding market of goods and commodities to a larger number of people than ever before.

Innovative shop design, window dressing and interior displays facilitated the spectacle of the drapery shop and the department store. While the eighteenth century had 'designed the seductive shop-front' what was lacking until the nineteenth century, says Por-ter, was good lighting. Giant shops like Swan and Edgar's which sprang up in the West End of London had great gas-lit windows that could serve as showcases for commodities (Porter 1990). Thus, new forms of lighting revolutionized modern architecture: as the architectural historian Reyner Baham put it, 'the sheer abundance of light . . . effectively reversed all established visual habits by which buildings were seen' (in Leach 1989: 104). Nowhere was the zest for display more apparent than in the big city department stores of the United States: 'unlike Europeans, who often articulated aesthetic

desires in high art, Americans channeled their desires almost entirely
... into the creation of mass commercial forms' (Leach 1989: 100).
The commercial designers in the US worked to generate 'theatrical
effects' and 'enchantment', 'interpreting and dramatizing commodities and commodity environments in ways that disguised and transformed them into what they were not' (Leach 1989: 100). Not only
did these designers have new forms of lighting at their disposal, they
could exploit new materials and techniques, for example, new ways of
using glass to create etchings, glazes and frosting as well as new kinds
of colour produced by aniline dyes, all with the aim of enticing and
dazzling those who entered. Shop display became increasingly important in the late nineteenth century and it is 'appropriate that the
first significant advocate of display was the greatest of all American
fairy-tale writers, L. Frank Baum, creator of the Land of Oz' (Leach
1989: 107). Baum's philosophy, evident in his fairy-tales and his
interest in merchandizing, celebrated consumption, display and artificial spectacle. As well as writing, dabbling in photography and film
and working in retail and marketing, he founded the first magazine
devoted to display, *Shop Window*, and assembled the first National
Association of Window Trimmers. According to Leach, for Baum
'display was fantasy, childhood, theater, technological play, and selling all rolled into one' (1989: 10). He saw the importance of display
in attracting the attention of passers-by and in stimulating desire for
consumption; in doing so, he 'raised the status of the shop window to
first place among advertising strategies' (1989: 110). What is at stake
in all this is the production of a world of fantasy premised on the
consumption of goods and commodities. Between the late nineteenth
century and the early twentieth, America became the 'Land of
Desire', a place which stimulated the consumption of commodities.
This was a world that emphasized individuality and individual satisfaction, an increasingly secular world of leisure and consumption
which played on hedonism, the libido, dreams and longings. It is no
surprise therefore to find that the 'metaphor of consumption as a
"dreamworld" dominated nineteenth-century discussions of consumption' (Slater 1993: 196).

The emphasis on spectacle is still a feature of large shops and
department stores, especially over Christmas, when goods are extra-
vagantly displayed, often in dreamscapes and fantasy settings. Shop
display has become an important component in retailing practice: the
modern department store as well as many shops are well versed in
strategies for attracting the gaze and directing the feet of consumers
through space and time. In today's shop interiors 'polished wood,
solid-metal finishings, large plate-glass windows, dressing mirrors,

show cards, props, spotlighting and so on' call on shoppers to partake in a spectacle, thus organizing 'ways of looking for consumers' (Nixon 1996: 61). In his analysis of the construction of masculinity in the 1980s, Nixon examines the ways in which retailing practices, such as shop design and interiors, orchestrated the selling of menswear in shops such as Next and Top Man. For Nixon, the design innovations taking place in menswear in the 1980s were shaped 'by their insertion within a set of practices of selling' (1996: 47). In other words, an important part of the selling of new styles for men was their location in particular sites of consumption that were consciously designed. Nixon's account of menswear, unlike other studies that examine fashion by abstracting it and treating it to textual or semiotic analysis, insists that the consumption of a particular fashion is not separate from retail practice; from such things as shop design and layout. These practices are important in the process of marking out particular styles and particular subjectivities associated with them, in this case, the 'new man'. In this respect, Nixon considers the way in which shop design and fashion retailing (along with magazines such as *Arena*) operated in conjunction with each other to produce forms of spectatorship for men in relation to the 'new man' of the 1980s. The same could be said of many contemporary big-name department stores and high-street shops which carefully manufacture the environment of the shop to create the appropriate look. When Ralph Lauren introduced 'Polo' to Selfridges in the mid-1990s in London, the layout was carefully orchestrated by designers from the fashion house to ensure the appropriate image was created for the label.

It is apparent that fashion exists not simply as an abstract force or idea, but is *put into practice* through the actions of individual agents, producers, buyers, magazine editors, journalists, retailers and consumers within the various subsections of the fashion system/s. Fashion has to be translated and made meaningful, a process that cuts across economic and cultural practices to the extent that it is impossible to separate the economic from the cultural since, as du Gay (1997) argues, these do not exist in isolation but mutually constitute each other. However, as Leopold (1992) and Fine and Leopold (1993) argue, this is not recognized in the literature, which tends to focus on either consumption or production, without examining the ways in which they intersect. What is left implicit but unspoken by du Gay and Fine and Leopold is that the body is the prime object of fashion. As argued throughout this book, fashion is an important site for discourses on the body and identity produced across various sites and practices, ranging from designers who design on the body, models who wear and help promote the fashions, to journalists and retailers who interpret the body styles through text and image. The seamstresses who sew the garments cannot be ignored since fashion is produced through the labour (and exploitation) of these individuals. Consumers cannot be left out of the picture since fashions become popular only once they are consumed and worn: in other words, through the active articulation and interpretation of fashion in every-day dress produced at the level of the individual body. Understanding fashion requires understanding the interconnections between these various bodies: the discursive, the textual and the lived body and between the actions of agents who are themselves embodied.

Conclusion

Fashion and dress articulate the body in culture: fashion produces discourses on the body and how to adorn it, dress is the translation of fashion into everyday practice. The fashion magazine, for example, sets out styles of dress and makes such styles meaningful: 'this winter, brown is the new black', for example, as in the winter of 1997. In doing so it often sets out fashion in terms of systems of oppositions, for example:

> Spring is on its way and the mood is fresh and simple. Winter's minimalism has given way to an eclectic combination of the feminine with the sporty. On the one hand, there are clothes that are pretty but wholesome; on the other, is a new utilitarian look. They may seem to sit at opposite ends of the spectrum, but they share an essential simplicity and a relaxed silhouette. (Walker 1999: 107)

The pairing of 'pretty' with 'sporty' and 'utilitarian', and the 'essential simplicity' of these opposing styles, offer the reader a map for making sense of the choices of clothes available at any one time. In setting out choices in this way, fashion magazines not only play a role in promoting certain looks, but in making sense of fashion for potential consumers. The fashion magazine is therefore one example of the way in which 'fashion' – as an abstract idea and aesthetic discourse – and 'fashion' – as the actual clothing made available for purchase each season – connects with everyday dress. The advice offered by fashion journalists and editors plays a part in framing the choices of consumers in their everyday dress. Advice about the 'best buys' on the high street or how to translate *haute couture* styles can now be found everywhere, in newspapers and on television style programmes as well glossy fashion magazines. These texts do not programme consumers to purchase certain things: fashions can and do fail to take off even when they are promoted extensively (stiletto heels promoted by fashion magazines at the end of the 1990s took several seasons of promotion before they could be seen in any significant number to have replaced the large, chunky heels popular on the high street). However, cultural intermediaries, such as journalists, are an important link in the chain of fashion which runs from producer to retailer and consumer.

Thus, 'fashion', as it exists in magazines and other texts, enjoys a complex relationship to everyday 'dress'. Fashion sets the parameters around dress, while dress is the embodiment of fashion, since only when they are worn in sufficient numbers can a style be said to be fashionable. It is impossible to explain exactly why some fashions are successful while others fail, except, as Braham (1997) suggests, by referring to Blumer's idea of 'incipient taste' (1969). A successful fashion captures a 'mood' or emerging 'taste'. If one is to look for ways of connecting fashion and dress, one must trace the connections between producers, distributors and consumers. One obvious place to start is with cultural intermediaries such as journalists and fashion buyers who articulate and promote fashion and in doing so move between producers and consumers.

This book has only touched on the role of such intermediaries, an area for future research. I have aimed here to provide the reader with an overview of the ways in which fashion and dress have been thought and written about. In doing so, I have argued that one needs to examine the way in which fashion, as discourse and practice, articulates the body, making it social and identifiable, and how this making of the body through dress is of considerable importance to the development of modern society. The literature on fashion and dress has generally overlooked the body, choosing instead to abstract fashion from embodiment and the complex social world in which bodies operate. The literature has also tended to draw an artificial divide between the bodies that make fashion and the bodies that wear it, as Leopold forcefully argues. I have tried to suggest that it is important to make connections between production and consumption and link theories of fashion with practices of dress. One way to do this, as discussed in chapter 7, is to examine fashion as a cultural industry and to look at the practices of cultural intermediaries as the link between production and consumption. I have also suggested that the body provides the missing link between the two. Again, I would argue that understanding the body in culture requires understanding

both how the textual body (the body articulated in discourses produced by texts, such as the fashion magazine) relates to the experience of embodiment (the body articulated in everyday life through
experiences and practices of dress). Understanding fashion and dress
requires understanding the relationship between various bodies
within the fashion industry, such as the producers and cultural mediators, and the actions and decisions taken by individuals on and with
their bodies. To study dress as a situated bodily practice is to study
the negotiations that take place between 'fashion' and 'dress'. It
means examining the way in which fashion gets translated into
dress, the way in which the textual body of the fashion magazine is
interpreted and embodied in the practical experience of 'getting
dressed'.

Such a framework suggests the need to explore the way in which a
textual discourse on the body might be translated into an actual
dressed body. To return to the passage quoted at the beginning of
this Conclusion: in order to understand the relationship between
fashion texts/discourses and practices, we need to ask, how did the
utilitarian style promoted by *Marie Claire* in 1999 translate into a
style worn by women? What women picked up this style and why?
What are the demographics of this style: is it worn by women of a
particular age, class, race, ethnicity? How is this style adapted by
women and what factors influence its adaptation? On what occasions
would this style be worn (to work, on holiday, out clubbing?) and on
what occasions would it not be worn (a job interview, a funeral?). Are
there occasions when it might be 'watered down' or mixed with other
styles (perhaps even with the 'pretty' style) and, if so, why? All these
complex negotiations are part and parcel of the everyday experience
of fashion in people's daily dress and yet there is little or no recognition of these in academic studies of fashion. In this book I have
argued for the need to make these connections, between fashion
and dress and between production and consumption, and in laying
out the framework of situated bodily practice, I hope to have suggested what such a study involves and therefore how a sociology of
fashion and dress might proceed.

Bibliography

Ackroyd, P. (1979) *Dressing Up*. London: Thames and Hudson.

Ang, I. (1985) *Watching 'Dallas': Soap Opera and the Melodramatic Imagination*. London: Methuen.

Ash, J. and Wilson, E. (eds) (1992) *Chic Thrills: A Fashion Reader*. London: Pandora Press.

Ash, J. and Wright, L. (eds) (1988) *Components of Dress Design, Manufacturing, and Image-Making in the Fashion Industry*. London: Routledge.

Bailey, R. (1992) 'Clothes Encounters of the Gynaecological Kind: Medical Mandates and Maternity Modes in the US 1859–1990', in R. Barnes and J. B. Eicher (eds), *Dress and Gender: Making and Meaning*. Oxford: Berg.

Bakhtin, M. (1984) *Rabelais and his World*. Indiana: Indiana University Press.

Barnard, M. (1996) *Fashion as Communication*. London: Routledge.

Barnes, R. and Eicher, J. B. (eds) (1992) *Dress and Gender: Making and Meaning*. Oxford: Berg.

Barthes, R. (1985) *The Fashion System*. London: Cape.

Bataille, G. (1986) *Erotism: Death and Sensuality*. San Francisco: City Lights Books.

Baudelaire, C. (1986) 'The Painter of Modern Life', in N. Cameron (trans.), *My Heart Laid Bare and Other Prose Writings*. London: Soho Book Company.

Baudrillard, J. (1981) *For a Critique of the Political Economy of the Sign*. St Louis, MO: Telos.

Baudrillard, J. (1983) *Simulations*. New York: Semiotext(e).

Bauman, Z. (1991) *Modernity and Ambivalence*. Cambridge: Polity Press.

Beck, U. (1992) *Risk Society: Towards a New Modernity*. London: Sage.

Bell, Q. (1976) *On Human Finery*. London: Hogarth Press.

Belsey, A. and Belsey, C. (1990) 'Icons of Divinity: Portraits of Elizabeth I', in L. Gent and N. Llewellyn (eds), *Renaissance Bodies: The Human Figure in English Culture 1540–1660*. London: Reaktion.

Benjamin, W. (1989) *Charles Baudelaire: A Lyric Poet in the Era of High Capitalism*. London: Verso.

Benthall, J. (1976) *The Body Electric: Patterns of Western Industrial Culture*. London: Thames and Hudson.

Bentham, J. (1843) *The Works of Jeremy Bentham*, vol. 4, ed. J. Browring. Edinburgh, London: W. Tait, Simkin Marshall and Co.

Berger, J. (1972) *Ways of Seeing*. Harmondsworth: Penguin.

Berman, M. (1983) *All That is Solid Melts into Air: The Experience of Modernity*. London: Verso.

Berthelot, J. M. (1991) 'Sociological Discourse and the Body', in M. Featherstone, M. Hepworth and B. Turner (eds), *The Body: Social Process and Cultural Theory*. London: Sage.

Blacking, J. (1977) *The Anthropology of the Body*. London: Academic Press.

Blumer, H. (1969) 'Fashion: From Class Differentiation to Collective Selection'. *Sociological Quarterly* 10: 275–91.

Bourdieu, P. (1984) *Distinction: A Social Critique of the Judgement of Taste*. Cambridge, MA: Harvard University Press.

Bourdieu, P. (1989) *Outline of a Theory of Practice*. Cambridge: Cambridge University Press.

Bourdieu, P. (1994) 'Structures, Habitus and Practices', in P. Press (ed.), *The Polity Reader in Social Theory*. Cambridge: Polity Press.

Bradley, C. (1955) *A History of World Costume*. London: Peter Owen.

Braham, P. (1997) 'Fashion: Unpacking a Cultural Production', in P. du Gay (ed.), *Production of Culture, Cultures of Production*. London: Sage.

Brake, M. (1980) *The Sociology of Youth Culture and Youth Subcultures: Sex, Drugs and Rock 'n' Roll?* London: Routledge and Kegan Paul.

Brake, M. (1985) *Comparative Youth Culture*. London: Routledge and Kegan Paul.

Braudel, F. (1981) *The Structures of Everyday Life: The Limits of the Possible*. London: Fontana.

Breward, C. (1994) *The Culture of Fashion*. Manchester: Manchester University Press.

Brewer, J. (1997) *The Pleasures of the Imagination: English Culture in the Eighteenth Century*. London: Harper Collins.

Brewer, J. and Porter, R. (eds) (1993) *Consumption and the World of Goods*. New York: Routledge.

Bristow, J. (1997) *Sexuality*. London: Routledge.

Brooks, R. (1989) 'Sighs and Whispers: A Review of a Bloomingdale Mail Order Catalogue for the Lingerie Department', in McRobbie, A. (ed.), *Zoots Suits and Second-hand Dresses: An Anthology of Fashion and Music*. London: Macmillan Education.

Brooks, R. (1992) 'Fashion Photography, the Double-Page Spread: Helmut Newton, Guy Bourdin and Deborah Turberville', in J. Ash and E. Wilson (eds), *Chic Thrills: A Fashion Reader*. London: Pandora Press.

Bryson, A. (1990) 'The Rhetoric of Status: Gesture, Demeanour and the Image of the Gentleman in Sixteenth- and Seventeenth-Century England', in L. Gent and N. Llewellyn (eds), *Renaissance Bodies: The Human Figure in English Culture 1540–1660*. London: Reaktion Books.

Burrell, G. and Hearn, J. (1993) 'The Sexuality of the Organization', in J. Hearn, D. L. Sheppard, P. Tancred-Sheriff, and G. Burrell (eds), *The Sexuality of Organization*. London: Sage Publications.

Butler, J. (1990) *Gender Trouble. Feminism and the Subversion of Identity*. London: Routledge.

Butler, J. (1993) *Bodies that Matter*. London: Routledge.

Callaway, H. (1992) 'Dressing for Dinner in the Bush: Rituals of Self-Definition and British Imperial Authority', in R. Barnes and J. B. Eicher (eds), *Dress and Gender: Making and Meaning*. Oxford: Berg.

Campbell, C. (1989) *The Romantic Ethic and the Spirit of Modern Consumerism*. Oxford: Basil Blackwell.

Campbell, C. (1993) 'Understanding Traditional and Modern Patterns of Consumption in Eighteenth-Century England: A Character-Action Approach', in J. Brewer and R. Porter (eds), *Consumption and the World of Goods*. New York: Routledge.

Campbell, C. (1997) 'When the Meaning is not a Message: A Critique of the Consumption as Communication Thesis', in M. Nava, A. Blake, I. MacRury and B. Richards (eds), *Buy this Book: Studies in Advertising and Consumption*. London: Routledge.

Cash, T. F. (1985) 'The Impact of Grooming Style on the Evaluation of Women in Management', in M. R. Soloman (ed.), *The Psychology of Fashion*. New York: Lexington Books.

Chapkis, W. and Enloe, C. (eds) (1984) *Of Common Cloth: Women in the Global Textile Industry*. Transnational Institute.

Chhacchi, A. (1984) 'The Case of India', in W. Chapkis and C. Enloe (eds), *Of Common Cloth: Women in the Global Textile Industry*. Transnational Institute.

Clarke, J., Hall, S., Jefferson, T. and Roberts, B. (1992) 'Subcultures, Cultures and Class', in T. Bennett, G. Martin, C. Mercer and J. Woollacott (eds), *Culture, Ideology and Social Process: A Reader*. Milton Keynes: Open University Press.

Colderidge, N. (1989) *The Fashion Conspiracy: A Remarkable Journey through the Empires of Fashion*. London: Mandarin.

Collier, R. (1998) ' "Nutty Professors", "Men in Suits" and "New Entrepreneurs": Corporeality, Subjectivity and Change in the Law School and Legal Practice'. *Social and Legal Studies* 7(1): 27–53.

Cordwell, J. and Schwarz, R. (eds) (1979) *The Fabrics of Culture: An Anthropology of Clothing and Adornment*. The Hague: Mouton.

Cosgrove, S. (1989) 'The Zoot Suit and Style Warfare', in A. McRobbie (eds), *Zoot Suits and Secondhand Dresses*. London: Macmillan.

Coyle, A. (1982) 'Sex, Skill in the Organisation of the Clothing Industry', in J. West (eds), *Work, Women and the Labour Market*. London: Routledge.

Craik, J. (1993) *The Face of Fashion*. London: Routledge.

Crossley, N. (1995a) 'Body Techniques, Agency and Inter-Corporality: On Goffman's Relations in Public'. *Sociology* 129(1): 133–49.

Crossley, N. (1995b) 'Merleau-Ponty, the Elusive Body and Carnal Sociology'. *Body and Society* 1(1): 43–63.

Crossley, N. (1996) 'Body/Subject, Body/Power: Agency, Inscription and Control in Foucault and Merleau-Ponty'. *Body and Society* 2(2): 99–116.

Csordas, T. J. (1993) 'Somatic Modes of Attention'. *Cultural Anthropology* 8(2): 135–56.

Csordas, T. J. (1996) 'Introduction: The Body as Representation and Being-in-the-World', in T. J. Csordas (eds), *Embodiment and Experience: The Existential Ground of Culture and Self*. Cambridge: Cambridge University Press.

Davidoff, L. and Hall, C. (1987) *Family Fortunes: Men and Women of the English Middle Classes*. London: Hutchinson.

Davis, F. (1992) *Fashion, Culture and Identity*. Chicago: Chicago University Press.

de Grazia, V. and Furlough, E. (eds) (1996) *The Sex of Things: Gender and Consumption in Historical Perspective*. London: University of California Press.

de la Haye, A. (1988) *Fashion Sourcebook*. London: Macdonald & Co. (Publishers) Ltd.

Derrida, J. (1976) *Of Grammatology*. Baltimore: Johns Hopkins University Press.

Diamond, I. and Quinby, L. (eds) (1988) *Feminism and Foucault: Reflections on Resistance*. Boston: Northeastern University Press.

Ditcher, E. (1985) 'Why We Dress the Way We Do', in M. R. Soloman (ed.), *The Psychology of Fashion*. New York: Lexington Books.

Douglas, M. (1973) *Natural Symbols*. Harmondsworth: Pelican Books.

Douglas, M. (1979a) 'Do Dogs Laugh?: A Cross-Cultural Approach to Body Symbolism', in M. Douglas (eds), *Implicit Meanings: Essays in Anthropology*. London: Routledge.

Douglas, M. (1979b) *Implicit Meanings: Essays in Anthropology*. London: Routledge.

Douglas, M. (1984) *Purity and Danger: An Analysis of the Concept of Pollution and Taboo*. London: Routledge and Kegan Paul.

du Gay, P. (eds) (1997) *Production of Culture, Cultures of Production*. London: Sage.

Edwards, T. (1997) *Men in the Mirror: Men's Fashions and Consumer Society*. London: Cassell.

Elias, N. (1978) *The History of Manners: The Civilizing Process*, vol. 1. New York: Pantheon.

Elson, D. (1984) 'Nimble Fingers and Other Fables', in W. Chapkis and C. Enloe (eds), *Of Common Cloth: Women in the Global Textile Industry*. Transnational Institute.

Elson, D. and Pearson, R. (1981) 'Nimble Fingers make Cheap Workers: An Analysis of Women's Employment in Third World Export Manufacturing'. *Feminist Review* 7 (Spring).

Emberley, Julia V. (1998) *Venus and Furs: The Cultural Politics of Fur*. London: I. B. Tauris & Co. Ltd.

Enloe, C. (1984) 'Racism at Work', in W. Chapkis and C. Enloe (eds), *Of Common Cloth: Women in the Global Textile Industry*. Transnational Institute.

Entwistle, J. (1997a) *Fashioning the Self: Women, Dress, Power and Situated Bodily Practice in the Workplace*. Ph.D., Goldsmiths' College, University of London.

Entwistle, J. (1997b) 'Power Dressing and the Fashioning of the Career Woman', in M. Nava, I. MacRury, A. Blake, and B. Richards (eds), *Buy this Book: Studies in Advertising and Consumption*. London: Routledge.

Entwistle (1998) 'Sex/Gender', in C. Jenks (ed.), *Core Dichotomies in Sociology*. London: Sage.

Entwistle, J. (2000) 'Fashioning the Career Woman: Power Dressing as a Strategy of Consumption', in M. Talbot and M. Andrews (eds), *All the World and her Husband: Women and Consumption in the Twentieth Century*. London: Cassell.

Entwistle, J. and Wilson, E. (1998) 'The Body Clothed'. *100 Years of Art and Fashion*. London: Hayward Gallery.

Ericksen, M. K. and Joseph, S. M. (1985) 'Achievement Motivation and Clothing Preferences of White Collar Working Women', in M. R. Soloman (ed.), *The Psychology of Fashion*. New York: Lexington Books.

Evans, C. and Thornton, M. (1989) *Women and Fashion: A New Look*. Quartet Books.

Ewen, S. (1976) *Captains of Consciousness: Advertising and the Social Roots of the Consumer Culture*. New York: McGraw-Hill.

Featherstone, M. (1991a) 'The Body in Consumer Society', in M. Featherstone, M. Hepworth and B. Turner (eds), *The Body: Social Process and Cultural Theory*. London: Sage.

Featherstone, M. (1991b) *Consumer Culture and Postmodernism*. London: Sage.

Featherstone, M., Hepworth, M. and Turner, B. (1991) *The Body: Social Process and Cultural Theory*. London: Sage.

Featherstone, M. and Turner, B. (1995) 'Introduction'. *Body and Society* 1(1).

Feher, M., Naddaff, R. and Tazi, N. (1989) *Fragments for a History of the Human Body, Part One*. New York: Zone.

Fine, B. and Leopold, E. (1993) *The World of Consumption*. London: Routledge.

Finkelstein, J. (1991) *The Fashioned Self*. Cambridge: Polity Press.

Flügel, J. C. (1930) *The Psychology of Clothes*. London: Hogarth Press.

Foucault, M. (1976) *The Birth of the Clinic*. London: Tavistock Publications Ltd.

Foucault, M. (1977) *Discipline and Punish*. Harmondsworth: Penguin.

Foucault, M. (1979) *The History of Sexuality*, vol. 1: *Introduction*. Harmondsworth: Penguin.

Foucault, M. (1980) 'Body/Power', in C. Gordon (ed.), *Power/Knowledge: Selected Interviews and Other Writings 1972–77*. New York: Pantheon Books.

Foucault, M. (1985) *The History of Sexuality*, vol. 2: *The Uses of Pleasure*. New York: Vintage Books.

Foucault, M. (1986) *The History of Sexuality*, vol. 3: *The Care of the Self*. Harmondsworth: Penguin.

Foucault, M. (1988) 'Technologies of the Self', in L. Martin, H. Gutman and P. Hutton (eds), *Technologies of the Self: A Seminar with Michel Foucault*. Amherst: University of Massachusetts Press.

Frank, A. W. (1990) 'Bringing Bodies Back In'. *Theory, Culture and Society* 7 (1).

Freeman, C. (1993) 'Designing Women: Corporate Discipline and Barbados's Off-Shore Pink Collar Sector'. *Cultural Anthropology* 8 (2).

Freud, S. (1927/1963) 'Fetishism', in *Sexuality and the Psychology of Love*. New York: Collier Books.

Gaines, J. (1990) 'Introduction: Fabricating the Female Body', in J. Gaines and C. Herzog (eds), *Fabrications: Costume and the Female Body*. London: Routledge.

Gaines, J. and Herzog, C. (eds) (1990) *Fabrications: Costume and the Female Body*. London: Routledge.

Gamman, L. and Makinen, M. (1994) *Female Fetishism: A New Look*. London: Lawrence and Wishart.

Gamman, L. and Marshment, M. (1988) *The Female Gaze: Women as Viewers of Popular Culture*. London: Women's Press.

Garber, M. (1992) *Vested Interests: Cross Dressing and Cultural Anxiety*. Harmondsworth: Penguin.

Gatens, M. (1991) *Feminism and Philosophy: Perspectives on Difference and Equality*. Cambridge: Polity Press.

Giddens, A. (1991) *Modernity and Self-Identity: Self and Society in the Late Modern Age*. Cambridge: Polity Press.

Goffman, E. (1971) *The Presentation of Self in Everyday Life*. London: The Penguin Press.

Goffman, E. (1972) *Relations in Public*. Harmondsworth: Pelican Books.

Goffman, E. (1976) *Gender Advertisements*. London: Macmillan.

Goffman, E. (1979) *Stigma: Notes on the Management of Spoiled Identity*. Harmondsworth: Penguin Books.

Gorsline, D. (1953/1991) *A History of Fashion: A Visual Survey of Costume from Ancient Times*. London: Fitzhouse Books.

Greenblatt, S. (1980) *Renaissance Self-Fashioning: From More to Shakespeare*. Chicago: University of Chicago Press.

Hall, S. (1977) 'The Hippies: An American Movement'. Birmingham: CCCS Stenciled Papers.

Hall, S. and Jefferson, T. (eds) (1977) *Resistances through Rituals*. London: Hutchinson.

Halttunen, K. (1982) *Confidence Men and Painted Women: A Study of Middle-Class Culture in America, 1830–1870*. New Haven and London: Yale University Press.

Haug (eds) (1987) *Female Sexualization*. London: Verso.

Havelock, H. (1928) *Studies in the Psychology of Sex*. Philadelphia: F. A. Davis & Co.

Hawthorne, R. (1992) *Bras: A Private View*. London: Souvenir Press.

Hearn, J., Sheppard, D. L., Tancred-Sheriff, P. and Burrell, G. (eds) (1993) *The Sexuality of the Organization*. London: Sage Publications.

Hebdige, D. (1979) *Subculture: The Meaning of Style*. London: Methuen.

Hollander, A. (1993) *Seeing through Clothes*. Berkeley: University of California Press.

Hollander, A. (1994) *Sex and Suits: The Evolution of Modern Dress*. New York: Alfred A. Knopf.

Hoodfar, H. (1991) 'Return to the Veil: Personal Strategy and Public Participation in Egypt', in N. Radcliffe and M. T. Sinclair (eds), *Working Women: International Perspectives on Labour and Gender Ideology*. London: Routledge.

Horrocks, R. (1997) *An Introduction to the Study of Sexuality*. London: Macmillan.

Hotchkiss, V. R. (1996) *Clothes Make the Man: Female Cross Dressing in Medieval Europe*. London: Garland.

Howard, A. (1997) 'Labor, History, and Sweatshops in the New Global Economy', in A. Ross (ed.), *No Sweat: Fashion, Free Trade and the Rights of Garment Workers*. London: Verso.

Hudson, D. (1974) *Munby: Man of Two Worlds*. London: Abacus.

Jenkins, R. (1992) *Pierre Bourdieu*. London: Routledge.

Jones, J. (1996) '*Coquettes* and *Grisettes*: Women Buying and Selling in Ancien Régime Paris', in V. de Grazia and E. Furlough (eds), *The Sex of Things: Gender and Consumption in Historical Perspective*. London: University of California Press Ltd.

Kohler, C. (1963) *A History of Costume*. New York: Dover Publications Inc.

Kuchta, D. (1996) 'The Making of the Self-Made Man: Class, Clothing, and English Masculinity', in V. de Grazia and E. Furlough (eds), *The Sex of Things: Gender and Consumption in Historical Perspective*. London: University of California Press Ltd.

Kuhn, A. (1988) 'The Body and Cinema: Some Problems for Feminism', in S. Sheridan (ed.), *Grafts: Feminist Cultural Criticism*. London: Verso.

Kunzle, D. (1982) *Fashion and Fetishism: A Social History of the Corset, Tight-Lacing and other Forms of Body-Sculpture in the West*. Totowa, NJ: Rowan and Littlefield.

Lancaster, B. (1995) *The Department Store: A Social History*. London: Leicester University Press.

Langman, L. (1992) 'Neon Cages: Shopping for Subjectivity', in R. Shields (ed.), *Lifestyle Shopping: The Subject of Consumption*. London: Routledge.

Laquer, T. and Bourgois, L. (1992) *Corporal Politics*. Cambridge, MA: MIT List, Visual Arts Centre.

Laquer, T. and Gallagher, C. (1987) *The Making of the Modern Body: Sexuality, Society and the 19th Century*. London: University of California Press.

Laver, J. (1950) *Dress: How and Why Fashions in Men's and Women's Clothes have Changed during the Past Two Hundred Years*. London: John Murray.

Laver, J. (1968) *Dandies*. London: Weidenfeld and Nicolson.

Laver, J. (1969) *Modesty in Dress*. Boston: Houghton Mifflin Co.

Laver, J. (1969/1995) *A Concise History of Costume*. London: Thames and Hudson.

Leach, W. (1989) 'Strategies of Display and the Production of Desire', in S. Bronner, (ed.), *Consuming Visions: Accumulation and Display of Goods in America, 1880–1920*. Ontario: Penguin Books, Canada.

Lees, S. (1999) 'When in Rome'. *The Guardian*, 16 February, 6–7.

Leopold, E. (1992) 'The Manufacture of the Fashion System', in J. Ash and E. Wilson (eds), *Chic Thrills*. London: Pandora.

Lewis, R. (1996) *Gendering Orientalism: Race, Femininity and Representation*. London: Routledge.

Lewis, R. and Rolley, K. (1997) '(Ad)Dressing the Dyke: Lesbian Looks and Lesbian Looking', in M. Nava, A. Blake, I. MacRury, and B. Richards (eds), *Buy this Book: Studies in Advertising and Consumption*. London: Routledge.

Lown, J. and Chenut, H. (1984) 'The Patriarchal Tread: a History of Exploitation', in W. Chapkis and C. Enloe (eds), *Of Common Cloth: Women in the Global Textile Industry*. Transnational Institute.

Luck, K. (1992) 'Trouble in Eden, Trouble with Eve: Women, Trousers and Utopian Socialism in Nineteenth Century America', in J. Ash and E. Wilson (eds), *Chic Thrills: A Fashion Reader*. London: Pandora.

Lurie, A. (1981) *The Language of Clothes*. New York: Random House.

MacKinnon, C. A. (1979) *Sexual Harassment of Working Women*. New Haven: Yale University Press.

Mauss, M. (1973) 'Techniques of the Body'. *Economy and Society* 2(1): 70–89.

McCracken, G. D. (1985) *The Trickle-Down Theory Rehabilitated*. New York: Lexington Books.

McDowell, C. (1992) *Dressed to Kill: Sex, Power and Clothes*. London: Hutchinson.

McKendrick, N., Brewer, J. and Plumb, J. H. (1983) *The Birth of a Consumer Society: The Commercialization of the Eighteenth-Century*. London: Hutchinson.

McNay, L. (1992) *Foucault and Feminism: Power, Gender and the Self*. Cambridge: Polity Press.

McNay, L. (1999) 'Gender, Habitus and the Field: Pierre Bourdieu and the Limits of Reflexivity'. *Theory, Culture and Society* 16(1): 95–117.

McRobbie, A. (1981) 'Settling Accounts with Subculture', in T. Bennett, G. Martin, C. Mercer and J. Wollacott (eds), *Culture, Ideology and Social Process*. London: B. T. Batsford Ltd.

McRobbie, A. (eds) (1989) *Zoot Suits and Second-hand Dresses: An Anthology of Fashion and Music*. London: Macmillan.

McRobbie, A. (1991) *Feminism and Youth Culture: From 'Jackie' to 'Just Seventeen'*. London: Macmillan.

McRobbie, A. (1994a) *Post-Modernism and Popular Culture*. London: Routledge.

McRobbie, A. (1994b) 'Second-hand Dresses and the Role of the Ragmarket', in A. McRobbie (ed.), *Post-Modernism and Popular Culture*. London: Routledge.

McRobbie, A. (1998) *British Fashion Design: Rag Trade or Image Industry?* London: Routledge.

Mead, M. (1935) *Sex and Temperament in Three Primitive Societies*. New York: William Morrow.

Merleau-Ponty, M. (1976) *The Primacy of Perception*. Evanston and Chicago: Northwestern University Press.

Merleau-Ponty, M. (1981) *The Phenomenology of Perception*. London: Routledge and Kegan Paul.

Miller, D. (1987) *Material Culture and Mass Consumption*. Oxford: Basil Blackwell.

Modleski, T. (1982) *Loving with a Vengeance: Mass Produced Fantasies for Women*. Hamden, CT: Shoe String Press.

Molloy, J. T. (1980) *Women: Dress for Success*. New York: Peter H. Wyden.

Moore, H. L. (1994) *A Passion for Difference*. Cambridge: Polity Press.

Moore, H.L. (1994) *A Passion for Difference*. Cambridge: Polity Press.

Mort, F. (1988) 'Boy's own', in R. Chapman and J. Rutherford (eds), *Male Order: Unwrapping Masculinity*. London: Lawrence and Wishart.

Mort, F. (1996) *Cultures of Consumption: Masculinities and Social Space in Late Twentieth-Century Britain*. London: Routledge.

Mulvey, L. (1975) 'Visual Pleasure and Narrative Cinema'. *Screen* 16(3).

Nava, M. (1992) *Changing Cultures: Feminism, Youth and Consumerism*. London: Sage.

Newton, S. M. (1974) *Health, Art and Reason: Dress Reformers of the 19th Century*. London: John Murray Ltd.

Nixon, S. (1992) 'Have you got the Look? Masculinities and Shopping Spectacle', in R. Shields (ed.), *Lifestyle Shopping: The Subject of Consumption*. London: Routledge.

Nixon, S. (1996) *Hard Looks: Masculinities, Spectatorship and Contemporary Consumption*. London: UCL Press.

Oakley, A. (1976) *Sex, Gender and Society*. London: Temple Smith.

Ortner, S. (1974) 'Is Female to Male as Nature is to Culture?', in M. Rosaldo and L. Lamphere (eds), *Women, Culture and Society*. Stanford: Stanford University Press.

Ortner, S. B. (1996) *Making Gender: The Politics and Erotics of Culture*. Boston: Beacon Press.

Partington, A. (1992) 'Popular Fashion and Working-Class Affluence', in J. Ash and E. Wilson (eds), *Chic Thrills: A Fashion Reader*. London: Pandora.

Perniola, M. (1990) 'Between Clothing and Nudity', in M. Feher (eds), *Fragments of a History of the Human Body*. New York: MIT Press.

Phizacklea, A. (1990) *Unpacking the Fashion Industry: Gender, Racism and Class in Production*. London: Routledge.

Polhemus, T. (1988) *Bodystyles*. Luton: Lennard.

Polhemus, T. (1994) *Streetstyle*. London: Thames and Hudson.

Polhemus, T. and Proctor, L. (1978) *Fashion and Anti-Fashion: An Anthology of Clothing and Adornment*. London: Cox and Wyman.

Porter, R. (1990) *English Society in the Eighteenth Century*. London: Penguin.

Pringle, R. (1988) *Secretaries Talk: Sexuality, Power and Work*. London: Verso.

Pringle, R. (1993) 'Bureaucracy, Rationality, Sexuality: The Case of Secretaries', in J. Hearn, D. L. Sheppard, P. Tancred-Sheriff and G. Burrell (eds), *The Sexuality of the Organization*. London: Sage.

Radway, J. (1987) *Reading the Romance: Women, Patriarchy and Popular Literature*. London: Verso.

Ramazanoglu, C. (ed.) (1993) *Up against Foucault: Explorations of some Tensions between Foucault and Feminism*. London: Routledge.

Ribeiro, A. (1983) *A Visual History of Costume: The Eighteenth Century*. London: B. T. Batsford.

Ribeiro, A. (1992) 'Utopian Dress', in J. Ash and E. Wilson (eds), *Chic Thrills: A Fashion Reader*. London: Pandora.

Richardson, J. and Kroeber, A. L. (1973) 'Three Centuries of Women's Dress: A Quantitative Analysis', in G. Willis and D. Midgley (eds), *Fashion Marketing*. London: Allen and Unwin.

Riviere, J. (1929/1986) 'Womanliness as a Masquerade', in V. Burgin, J. Donald and C. Kaplan (eds), *Formations of Fantasy*. London: Methuen.

Roach, M. E. and Eicher, J. B. (eds) (1965) *Dress, Adornment and Social Order*. New York: John Wiley and Sons.

Roberts, H. (1977) 'The Exquisite Slave: The Role of Clothes in the Making of the Victorian Woman'. *Signs* 2(3): 554–69.

Rolley, K. (1992) 'Love, Desire and the Pursuit of the Whole: Dress and the Lesbian Couple', in J. Ash and E. Wilson (eds), *Chic Thrills: A Fashion Reader*. London: Pandora.

Ross, A. (ed.) (1997) *No Sweat: Fashion, Free Trade and the Rights of Garment Workers*. London: Verso.

Rouse, E. (1989) *Understanding Fashion*. London: BSP Professional Books.

Said, E. (1985) *Orientalism*. Harmondsworth: Penguin.

Schulze, L. (1990) 'On the Muscle', in J. Gaines and C. Herzog (eds), *Fabrications: Costume and the Female Body*. London: Routledge.

Sekora, J. (1977) *Luxury: the Concept in Western Thought, Eden to Smollet*. Baltimore: Johns Hopkins University Press.

Sennett, R. (1977) *The Fall of Public Man*. Cambridge: Cambridge University Press.

Sennett, R. (1994) *Flesh and Stone: The Body and the City in Western Civilization*. London: Faber and Faber.

Sheppard, D. L. (1989) 'Organisations, Power and Sexuality: The Image and Self-Image of Women Managers', in J. Hearn (ed.), *The Sexuality of the Organization*. London: Sage.

Sheppard, D. L. (1993) 'Women Managers' Perceptions of Gender and Organizational Life', in A. Mills, J. and P. Tancred (ed.), *Gendering Organizational Analysis*. London: Sage.

Shields, R. (ed.) (1992) *Lifestyle Shopping: The Subject of Consumption*. London: Routledge.

Shilling, C. (1993) *The Body and Social Theory*. London: Sage.

Silverman, K. (1986) 'Fragments of a Fashionable Discourse', in T. Modleski (ed.), *Studies in Entertainment: Critical Approaches to Mass Culture*. Bloomington: Indiana University Press.

Simmel, G. (1950) *The Sociology of Georg Simmel*. London: Collier Macmillan.

Simmel, G. (1904/1971) 'Fashion', in D. Levine, (ed.), *On Individuality and Social Forms*. London: University of Chicago Press.

Slater, D. R. (1993) 'Going Shopping: Markets, Crowds and Consumption', in C. Jenks (ed.), *Cultural Reproduction*. London: Routledge.

Slater, D. R. (1997) *Consumer Culture and Modernity*. Cambridge: Polity Press.

Smith, A. (1776/1986) *The Wealth of Nations*. London: Penguin.

Soloman, M. R. (ed.) (1985) *The Psychology of Fashion*. New York: Lexington Books.

St Martin, L. and Gavey, N. (1996) 'Women Body Building: Feminist Resistance and/or Femininity's Recuperation'. *Body and Society* 2(4): 45–57.

Steele, V. (1985) *Fashion and Eroticism: Ideals of Feminine Beauty from the Victorian Age to the Jazz Age*. Oxford: Oxford University Press.

Steele, V. (1988) *Paris Fashion: A Cultural History*. Oxford: Oxford University Press.

Steele, V. (1996) *Fetish: Fashion, Sex and Power*. Oxford: Oxford University Press.

Steele, V. and Kidwell, C. B. (eds) (1989) *Men and Women: Dressing the Part*. Washington: Smithsonian Institute Press.

Stekel, W. (1930) *Sexual Aberrations: The Phenomenon of Fetishism in Relations*. New York: Liveright Publishing Corporation.

Stoller, R. J. (1968) *Sex and Gender: On the Development of Masculinity and Femininity*. London: Hogarth Press Institute of Psychoanalysis.

Stoller, R. (1985) *Observing the Erotic Imagination*. New Haven: Yale University Press.

Su, J. (1997) 'El Monte Thai Government Workers: Slave Sweatshops', in A. Ross (ed.), *No Sweat: Fashion, Free Trade and the Rights of Garment Workers*. London: Verso.

Sydie, R. A. (1987) *Natural Women, Cultured Men*. London: Methuen.

Synnott, A. (1993) *The Body Social: Symbolism, Self and Society*. London: Routledge.

Tarrant, N. (1994) *The Development of Costume*. London: Routledge.

Taylor, L. and Wilson, E. (1989) *Through the Looking Glass*. London: BBC Books.

Thornton, S. (1995) *Club Cultures: Music, Media and Subcultural Capital*. Cambridge: Polity Press.

Triggs, T. (1992) 'Framing Masculinity: Herb Ritts, Bruce Weber and the Body Perfect', in J. Ash and E. Wilson (eds), *Chic Thrills: A Fashion Reader*. London: Pandora.

Tseëlon, E. (1992a) 'Fashion and the Signification of Social Order'. *Semiotica* 91(1/2): 1–14.

Tseëlon, E. (1992b) 'Is the Presented Self Sincere? Goffman, Impression Management and the Postmodern Self'. *Theory, Culture and Society* 9(2).

Tseëlon, E. (1997) *The Masque of Femininity*. London: Sage.

Turner, B. (1985) *The Body and Society: Explorations in Social Theory*. Oxford: Basil Blackwell.

Turner, B. (1991) 'Recent Developments in the Theory of the Body', in M. Featherstone, M. Hepworth and B. Turner (eds), *The Body: Social Process and Cultural Theory*. London: Sage.

Turner, T. (1996) 'Bodies and Anti-Bodies: Flesh and Fetish in Contemporary Social Theory', in T. Csordas (ed.), *Embodiment and Experience: The Existential Ground of Culture and Self*. Cambridge: Cambridge University Press.

Veblen, T. (1899/1953) *The Theory of the Leisure Class: An Economic Study of Institutions*. New York: Mentor.

Vickery, A. (1993) 'Women and the World of Goods: A Lancashire Consumer and her Possessions, 1751–81', in J. Brewer and R. Porter (eds), *Consumption and the World of Goods*. London: Routledge.

Walker, E. (1999) 'Catwalk Special'. *Marie Claire*, February, 107–15.

Weatherill, L. (1993) 'The Meaning of Consumer Behaviour in Late Seventeenth- and Early Eighteenth-Century England', in J. Brewer and R. Porter (eds), *Consumption and the World of Goods*. 206–27. New York: Routledge.

Weatherill, L. (1996) *Consumer Behaviour and Material Culture in Britain 1660–1760*. London: Routledge.

Weiner, B. and Schnieder, J. (eds) (1991) *Cloth and the Human Experience*. London: Smithsonian Institute Press.

Wheelwright, J. (1989) *Amazons and Military Maids: Women who Dressed as Men in the Pursuit of Life, Liberty and Happiness*. London: Pandora.

Willet, C. and Cunningham, P. (1992) *The History of Underclothes*. New York: Dover Publications.

Williamson, J. (1978) *Decoding Advertisements: Ideology and Meaning in Advertising*. London: Marion Boyars.

Willis, G. and Midgley, D. (eds) (1973) *Fashion Marketing: An Anthology of Viewpoints and Perspectives*. London: Allen and Unwin Ltd.

Willis, P. (1975) 'The Expressive Style of a Motor-Bike Culture', in J. Benthall and T. Polhemus (eds), *The Body as a Medium of Expression*. London: Allen Lane.

Willis, P. (1978) *Profane Culture*. London: Routledge and Kegan Paul.

Wilson, E. (1985) *Adorned in Dreams: Fashion and Modernity*. London: Virago.

Wilson, E. (1991) *The Sphinx in the City*. London: Virago.

Wilson, E. (1992) 'The Postmodern Body', in J. Ash and E. Wilson (eds), *Chic Thrills: A Fashion Reader*. London: Pandora.

Wolf, N. (1991) *The Beauty Myth*. London: Vintage.

Woodhouse, A. (1989) *Fantastic Women: Sex, Gender and Transvestism.* London: Macmillan.

Wright, L. (1992) 'Out-grown Clothes for Grown-up People: Constructing a Theory of Fashion', in J. Ash and E. Wilson (eds), *Chic Thrills: A Fashion Reader.* London: Pandora

Yarwood, D. (1992) *Fashion in the Western World 1500–1900.* London: B. T. Datnford Ltd.

Young, I. M. (1995) 'Women Recovering our Clothes', in S. Benstock and S. Ferriss (eds), *On Fashion.* New Brunswick: Rutgers University Press.

Index